MW01639895

Tacitean Visual Narrative

Also available from Bloomsbury

Tacitus, Rhiannon Ash
Tacitus: Annals I, edited by Norma Miller
War as Spectacle, edited by Anastasia Bakogianni and Valerie M. Hope

Tacitean Visual Narrative

Philip Waddell

BLOOMSBURY ACADEMIC
LONDON • NEW YORK • OXFORD • NEW DELHI • SYDNEY

BLOOMSBURY ACADEMIC
Bloomsbury Publishing Plc
50 Bedford Square, London, WC1B 3DP, UK
1385 Broadway, New York, NY 10018, USA

BLOOMSBURY, BLOOMSBURY ACADEMIC and the Diana logo are trademarks of Bloomsbury Publishing Plc

First published in Great Britain 2020

Cover design: Terry Woodley
Cover image © Gemma Claudia, 1st century AD. Kunsthistorisches Museum, Vienna, Austria. Leemage/Getty.

A catalogue record for this book is available from the British Library.

A catalog record for this book is available from the Library of Congress.

ISBN: HB: 978-1-3500-9700-1
ePDF: 978-1-3500-9701-8
eBook: 978-1-3500-9702-5

Typeset by RefineCatch Limited, Bungay, Suffolk

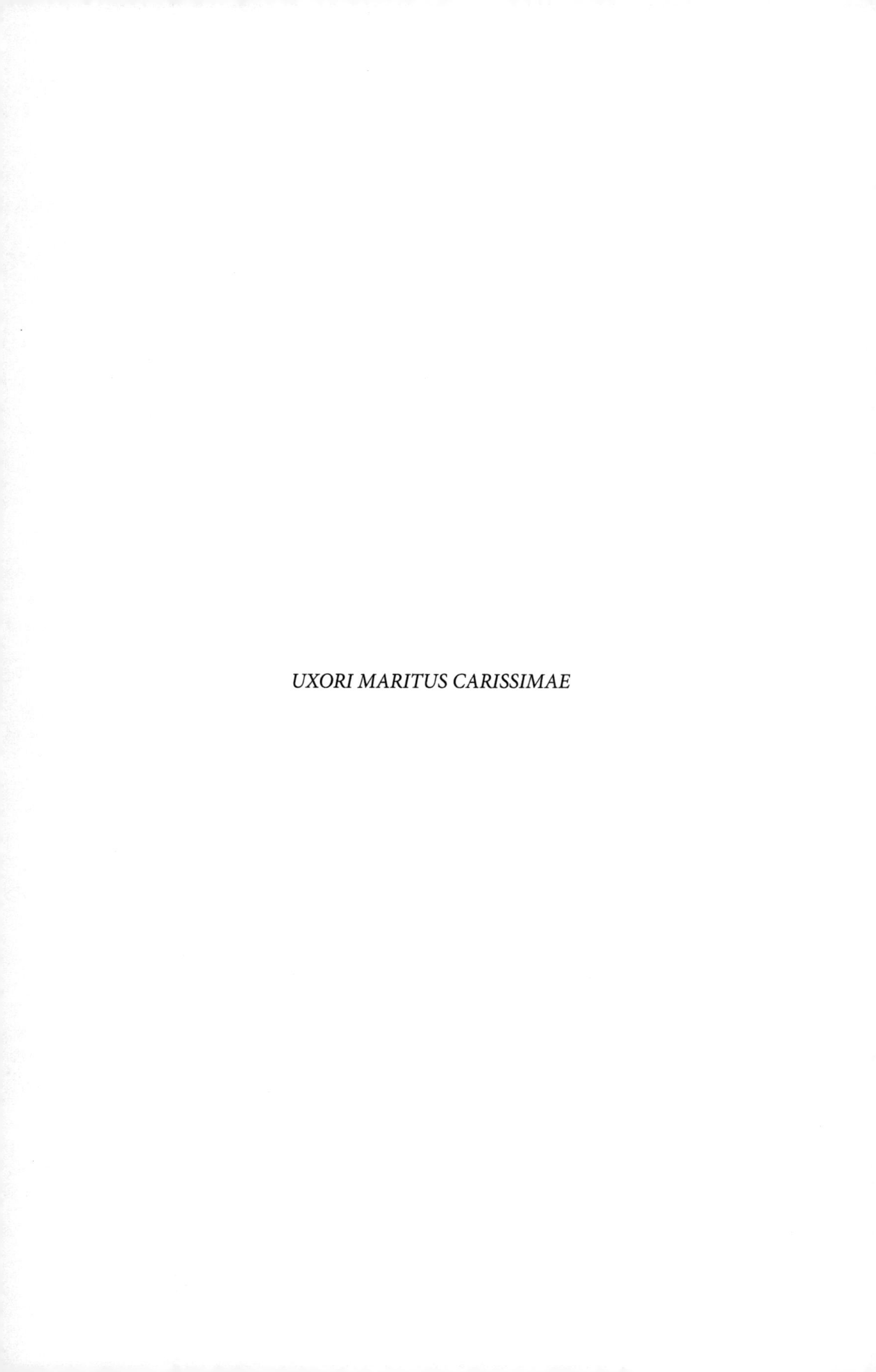

UXORI MARITUS CARISSIMAE

Contents

Figures

Acknowledgments

As this monograph arose from my dissertation, I would like to begin by thanking my doctoral committee at the University of Missouri for their diligence and care not only in editing the dissertation, but also for providing help throughout all of its stages of completion: Ray Marks, David Schenker, Jim McGlew, Larry Okamura, and, most especially, Dennis Trout, without whose constant advice, support, and patience, this project would not have been possible. I am also grateful to the University of Geneva for their cordiality in allowing me access to their library during much of the research stage of this project, as well as to my department at the University of Arizona and the supportive faculty I am lucky to work among. I thank Monica Cyrino, of the University of New Mexico, who provided guidance and input throughout this process, and Anna Cooper and Barbara Selznick, from the University of Arizona School of Theater, Film, and Television, who were kind enough to assist me in navigating the vast corpus of film scholarship. I also thank Cynthia Damon for her kind permission to use her recent Penguin translation of the *Annales*. I am further grateful to the anonymous reviewers and the editors at Bloomsbury, Alice Wright, Lily Mac Mahon, and Georgina Leighton, for their patience, expertise, and assistance during the publication progress.

Introduction[1]

Narrative is the essence of history. . . . Narrative records and explains what happened—imagination compels it to be seen and shared.

Ronald Syme[2]

Classics and Film

The dialogue between film and the world of classical antiquity has expanded rapidly since Jon Solomon's *The Ancient World in Cinema* was first published in 1978. This rich area of research, once a niche outside the mainstream of Classics, has not only gained wider acceptance among classical scholars, but has in recent years deepened in both scope and breadth to embrace a wide range of viewpoints, and opened new avenues of discussion within the larger field of receptions studies. Comparisons and juxtapositions of such seemingly disparate and distanced narratives as classical text and film have great value not only in terms of sparking interest in the classical world and relating the foreign cultures of ancient Greece and Rome to our students and colleagues, but also in challenging classicists to better understand their own subject matter through analogy.

Scholarship on film and the classical world has tended in one of two major directions. The first investigates the reception, screening, and re-working of ancient stories or themes into modern adaptations. Solomon began the discussion along these lines, tracing the cinematic presentation of ancient stories. Solomon's work, organized around broad genres, each assigned to a Greek muse, did much to turn the study of classics in film—even including camp films such as *Jason and the Argonauts* (Chaffey, 1963)—into texts worthy of scholarly attention. The study of filmic representations of the ancient world has gained ever-widening acceptance, propelled by the works of such scholars as Maria Wyke and Monica Cyrino.

The subject of ancient Rome, especially Roman history, on screen is the focus of Maria Wyke's (1997) *Projecting the Past: Ancient Rome, Cinema and History*. In this work, Wyke continues Solomon's genre-based framework of studying classics in film, focusing specifically on historical-based cinema. Wyke, however, uses film not only as a discussion of reception in and of itself, but also as a way of parsing notions of history and historiography. This work is thus a metapoetic analysis of ancient history, not only as it is received, but how it is studied and conceptualized. *Projecting the Past* thus opens the possibility that classical studies can benefit from engaging with film in terms of advancing textual and theoretical scholarship and understanding.

Monica Cyrino has contributed greatly, and in many regards, to the study of classical receptions in film. Her monograph *Big Screen Rome* (2005), continues Solomon's work, focusing on films that present Rome and Romans as sources of spectacle. Cyrino examines nine films dealing with Rome in temporal order from *Quo Vadis* (LeRoy, 1951) to *Gladiator* (Scott, 2000). This work devotes a chapter to each film, and explores the intricacies of the film's basis in classical texts, production issues, and the major themes at work. In addition, Cyrino has spread the interest in classical visual reception to the small screen, editing two volumes on HBO's *Rome* and co-editing a volume on STARZ *Spartacus*,[3] as well as through the editing of the University of Edinburgh Press's *Screening Antiquity*, promoting a broader and more nuanced understanding of the complex interplay between classical antiquity and the screen.

The goal of this kind of receptions studies is two-fold: the examination of antiquity as most people, including students and non-specialists, may have encountered it; and the variety of ways that these representations are markers for the times and culture(s) within which they were created. Thus, the depiction of Roman legionaries in film has been employed to invoke Nazis or Soviets as opposed to a persecuted Judeo-Christian minority.[4] These receptions of classical narratives are complicated by the fact that they were often based on nineteenth-century historical or biblical novels that were themselves receptions, instead of direct engagement with classical source material. The scholarship of classics receptions generally, and of filmic receptions more specifically, enables us to learn not only about antiquity, but also about ourselves through our retelling and refashioning of ancient themes and morals.

The second major direction of classical receptions studies in film examines how ancient stories, characters, and broader themes can play out in seemingly unrelated films. Suggestive of the growing interest in Classics for receptions studies in recent years, two journals have devoted entire issues to showcasing new scholarship along these lines. The first of these was Martin Winkler's *Classics and Cinema*, comprising a full issue of *Bucknell Review*.[5] The articles in this volume signal the potential breadth of films suited to classical receptions studies, with offerings in which the "Amazonian" characters of *Conan the Barbarian* (Milius, 1982), *Red Sonja* (Fleischer, 1985), *The Terminator* (Cameron, 1984), and *Alien* (Scott, 1979) are examined in terms of the classical notions of martial women;[6] *Chinatown* (Polanski, 1974) is viewed in terms of Sophoclean tragedy;[7] and James Baron's "*9 to 5* as Aristophanic Comedy."[8] This trend continued in 2008, with a special volume of *Arethusa* (41.1), edited by Kirsten Day, entitled *Celluloid Classics: New Perspectives on Classical Antiquity in Modern Cinema*.[9] This volume contains a comparison of *Minority Report* (Spielberg, 2002) to Sophocles' *Oedipus Tyrannos*,[10] and a discussion of the reception of the Pygmalion myth of the man-made woman through *Vertigo* (Hitchcock, 1958), *Pretty Woman* (Marshall, 1990), *The Stepford Wives* (Forbes, 1975), and *Blade Runner* (Scott, 1982).[11] In the last five years, two monographs have addressed different aspects of classical receptions in modern film: Kirsten Day's (2016) *Cowboy Classics: The Roots of the American Western in the Epic Tradition* and Mark Padilla's (2016) *Classical Myth in Four Films of Alfred Hitchcock*. This aspect of classical receptions scholarship focuses on the classical influence as it pervades modern culture, often indirectly or without modern authorial intent. Investigations along these lines broaden the discussion of classical receptions beyond the direct portrayal of classical or ancient subjects in modern culture, and thus provide insight into the ways in which Classics continues to shape seemingly unrelated media.

In this book, I hope to continue and expand this ongoing dialogue between classical antiquity and film by reversing the lens we are using. Rather than using classical antiquity to study film and its reception therein, as Solomon, Wyke, and Cyrino have done, or exploring the use of classical themes in film, as in the works of Winkler and Day, I use the terminology of film studies to help us better understand rhetorical and visual nuance in ancient literature. The techniques used to create effective cinematic narrative closely parallel the devices employed by Tacitus throughout his historiography, and these corollaries can provide an additional layer of understanding as we read the *Annales*. Naturally, I am not the first scholar to have noted the strong parallels between ancient authors and filmmakers. In her introduction to *Cowboy Classics*, Kirsten Day notes the inherent cinematic quality of certain classical texts and suggests that reversing the lens, using filmic techniques to better illustrate and help discuss these ancient literary works, offers another methodology for classical receptions studies.[12]

The purpose of this book is to provide readers new to Tacitus, or new to thinking about the literature of Tacitean narrative, with an introduction to his visual historiography. This necessitates an introductory discussion of the several fields of interdisciplinary study that, through complementing methodologies, enable us to make this inquiry: visual historiography, narratology, narrative in Roman art, and classical Hollywood film.[13] The premise of my argument, then, is to provide a systematic analysis of the rhetorical effects present in the *Annales*, using the double lenses of ancient visual narrative and modern film, in order to augment and expand the narratological investigation of Tacitus. Rather than arguing against current narrative theories, I hope to build upon them and join in the ongoing discussion of the visual in ancient historiography. The book will be structured in two parts: Lens and Voice, and Transition and Connection. The first part, which comprises three chapters, deals with the techniques keyed to sensory interpretation. These include focalization, alignment, and the use of close-ups, all of which manipulate the reader's perception of truth by coloring the delivery of information. The second part, containing two chapters, focuses on motion and the devices Tacitus uses to alter narrative timing, bridge meaning across disparate events and characters, and forge connections through apposition. In each chapter, I will examine Tacitus' work in light of contemporary Roman art and illustrative parallels in classical Hollywood cinema in order to help elucidate and understand the complex narrative techniques at play within the *Annales*.

Roman Visuality

The Romans' Visual World

Tacitus lived and wrote in a highly visual world, full of monuments and visual texts of all varieties, many of them having to do with Roman identity and history, and Romans were culturally trained to interact and respond to their visual surroundings.[14] It is important to keep in mind that the narrative devices I will discuss in the following sections all have their parallels in ancient art contemporary with the writing of the *Annales*. That these analogous devices and effects existed at the time Tacitus was writing is highly suggestive of a level of awareness of visual narrative in the Roman world, and lends credence to the belief that Tacitus' audience would have been able to interpret the subtle levels of visuality in his historical works.

In Roman static art, especially narrative art, one of the vital questions that we must pose to understand what is being depicted is that of the gaze,[15] which is a multi-dimensional question that asks "who views" or "who watches" in the context of a given image. All art, generally speaking, is designed to be viewed, and thus to draw the gaze of the viewer. A viewer interacts with a given image, and in so doing converts the external objective image into his or her own subjective experience. When people view, they also interpret. The art a viewer experiences creates internal meaning, and in that subjective retelling the viewer creates a narrative in relation to the image.

In addition to the external viewer, some images also contain one or more internal viewers, which results in a complex gaze that raises additional questions for the external viewer. A still-life painting of a single flower leaves only a narrow margin of speculation; we, the viewer, are watching. There is no one else present to be watching, and no other individual is suggested from the image. Some images, however, are more complex. Take for example the well-known painting *American Gothic* (Grant Wood, 1930), in which a stalwart-looking man and woman stand before an Iowa farmhouse. The man, located on the right-hand side of the painting (as we view it), is holding a pitchfork, while the woman stands slightly behind him on the left. The man looks directly out of the painting and to the right, while the woman watches the man. Her gaze appears critical, condescending, frustrated, or sarcastic. There are many interpretations of the piece, but all of them turn on the way in which we understand the gaze of the woman, the internal viewer.

In this book we will consider a number of Roman works which exhibit similar *tableaux* and challenge audience engagement. As scholars, we must question what each image asks of its potential viewers. The visual techniques used by Roman artists to alter and manipulate the gaze through focalization were also employed by Tacitus in order to color his narrative at the level of the story. Tacitus is not alone in his visuality, and recent work has been done to parse out both the complex language of Roman static art and the relationships between image and text, the latter with specific attention to the historiography of Livy.

Feldherr's Visual Historiography

The concept that Roman authors, and specifically the Roman historians, used visual language and imagery to forge a subtext of meaning in their works has been convincingly discussed by Andrew Feldherr regarding the historiography of Livy. Feldherr's *Spectacle and Society in Livy's History* has provided a set of useful tools for investigating and understanding how visual imagery both constructs and drives Livy's narrative.[16] The visual components of Livy's historiography, especially his descriptions, *tableaux*, and spectacles all manipulate the gaze of the reader, leaving a vivid echo and forming a *monumentum* of Rome's historical past. Livy, according to Feldherr, wrote in the context of Roman visual culture, where great battles and deeds were celebrated and remembered through narrative monuments in the form of victory temples.[17] Throughout the Roman Republic, it was customary for a general, in the course of an important battle, to request the help of one of the gods. In return for aid on the battlefield, a general would promise to dedicate a temple to the designated god upon his triumph over the foe. The founding and dedication of such a temple would, of course, have the added benefit of preserving that general's name and achievement for posterity. The senate usually confirmed the general's request, and many of these temples were constructed along the route for Roman triumphal processions. Thus, each temple became part of a larger, ongoing story of Roman victory with each successive general taking his place in history in a physical, visual, and monumental way.[18]

According to Feldherr, Livy wanted his history to be a part of this story, and wanted successive generations to read it in conjunction with, and as a component of, this physical memorialization already in progress. Victory monuments told their stories in a series of pictures, where Romans were shown in battle and conquering their enemies in faraway places. In keeping with this tradition, Livy illustrated his histories with beautiful *tableaux*, descriptive passages full of lifelike imagery. He also selected specifically visual terminology and language, suggesting that his readers view his history.[19]

Livy's descriptive *tableaux* are perhaps the most striking and compelling aspects of his history, bringing the past to life for his readers. They are also a helpful illustration of two important ancient concepts, *enargeia* and ekphrasis. *Enargeia* exists when an author writes a descriptive passage so compellingly that it feels as though the action is happening right before the reader's eyes.[20] In ekphrasis, the author describes a subject, usually a single physical object, in extreme detail and endows it with more characteristics than would be realistically possible. Tacitus' use of both *enargeia* and ekphrasis has been recently discussed by Elizabeth Keitel, who describes the narrative effect of both visual techniques in stressing the central historical and morally didactic themes of senatorial misconduct, the devastation of society, and the contested control of memory.[21] Ancient Greek and Roman readers prized authors who successfully employed *enargeia*, as realistic and compelling writing was seen as evidence of a skilled rhetor or speaker.

By presenting his history as a visual work, Feldherr shows that Livy also meant his readers to experience the events of his text as though they themselves were present at them, thus allowing the reader to learn from the examples of the past. The mechanism for this audience participation is the inherent interplay of the gaze. The external viewer experiences the art in a subjective way, as the image (whether received visually or textually) becomes real before the eyes of the observer (through *enargeia* and ekphrasis). In terms of literature, the more vivid and life-like the description, the greater the potential level of audience participation. Thus, as noted by Feldherr, Livy uses *enargeia* to forge a monument that stimulates a visual reaction in his audience,[22] and invites his readers to become active spectators of the events of history.

These engaging visual narrative moments were also designed to benefit Livy's readers in successive generations, as the most vivid portions of his history are also didactic *exempla*. These examples of virtuous behavior were provided to inspire readers to lead upright lives and undertake brave deeds (or, by contrast, offered as examples of bad actions to avoid), and were an important component of not only Livy's work but of Roman literature more generally. By writing his *exempla* in visual terminology, Livy was able to draw his readers into the greatest moments of history and, by witnessing these great deeds first-hand, Livy hoped to inspire future Roman virtue (*praef.* 10). The fact that so many of our extant sources mention techniques of vivid writing, and the kinds of impressions they create, suggests that a Roman audience was aware of the impact of these scenes.

In addition to his work with Livy, Feldherr also notes the visuality of Tacitus, and nods to this fact in his epilogue, where he notes the differences in political climate during which both men were writing, especially the difficulties Tacitus would have faced writing under the emperors. Tacitus served as a senator under the tyrannical Domitian, and saw the slaughter of Roman senators, the reinstatement of the *maiestas* (treason) trials, and the employment of the *delatores*, groups of paid informants seeking to expose traitors to the emperor (*Agr.* 2, 24). As Feldherr notes, Tacitus' account does not, and thematically cannot, contain the same kinds of *exempla* that are found in Livy—it is not peopled by great men and inspiring times (4.32–33), and indeed the only recognizable "heroes" are the individuals or small groups who bravely fought against the state.[23]

Notwithstanding the differences in political climate, and the resulting change of *exempla* from hortatory to cautionary tales, Feldherr points out the highly visual and descriptive nature of Tacitus' work, seeing in it a stylistic parallel to Livy's technique and methods.[24] Feldherr's observations are excellent and accurate; Tacitus did not have the same freedom of political expression, nor a similar choice of laudatory subject matter, in composing his history. As I will show through the course of this book, however, Tacitus mobilized visual language to convey his meaning in a very real, visceral, and image-driven manner. Tacitus is not attempting to inspire his readers to emulate his characters, but rather to learn from them lessons about survival in a dangerous age.

Visual Historiography

The historiography of Tacitus has long been noted for its vividness and dramatic presentation of events. Beginning in the early twentieth century, scholars explored Tacitus' use of images in his creation of vivid *tableaux*.[25] Tacitus' ability to depict crowds and battles was seen as analogous to huge panoramic canvases. In the late 1950s, Syme wrote in answer to the growing question, posed by scholars such as Walker,[26] concerning Tacitus' validity as a reliable historian. Answering in the affirmative, Syme described Tacitus' rhetorical and dramatic techniques in detail, including mirroring, foreshadowing, scene changes, as well as the use of omens, obituaries, portraits, and spectator commentary.[27] Syme pointed out that Tacitus was a master of hidden knowledge, and accepted the necessity of what Cicero might call *inventio* (elaboration) in Roman historiography, if employed to achieve the proper effect.[28] Syme noted that all of this might seem to place Tacitus much closer to prose fiction and drama than to history,[29] but he was quick to defend the basic truthfulness of Tacitus' works.[30] Rather than taking critiques of Tacitus' rhetorical style as damning to his credibility as an historian, Syme argued that these techniques were vital to Tacitus' presentation of the principate, and showcased Tacitus' literary skill as well as his command of the historical material. Syme's work had a profound effect on later Tacitean scholarship that focused on Tacitus' literary artistry as a method of conveying historical truth.

Examining Tacitus' rhetorical techniques, and building on the scholarship of Syme, Goodyear argued that Tacitus' style, rather than belonging to the static visual arts or to drama, should be described as "pictorial-dramatic."[31] This style, Goodyear pointed out, was not used solely to describe events of great historical importance, but was deployed whenever Tacitus could rhetorically do so. Furthermore, Goodyear saw possibilities for future research along the lines of Tacitus' visuality: "More modern analogies can also be illuminating. For instance, the constant variation of tempo in Tacitus' narrative and the way close-up changes to panorama and vice versa strongly suggests the technique of the cinema."[32] Goodyear's suggestion of visual, especially cinematic, language as a way to understand Tacitean historiography has broadened the possibilities of scholarship to include evidence and theories not formerly associated with historiography. The way is opened to consider Tacitus from a more than purely textual stance.

Anthony Woodman, in his *Rhetoric in Classical Historiography: Four Studies*, stresses the literary nature of ancient historiography, in many ways building upon Syme's and Goodyear's view that the writing of history was not incompatible with literary artistry in antiquity. Woodman stresses the goal of verisimilitude (plausibility) in ancient historiography, in addition to the deployment of *enargeia* as a tool for achieving the reader's belief.[33] Woodman concludes this volume with a brief epilogue, noting that ancient historiography should be viewed as a form of literature, rather than as modern academic history.[34] At the end of this epilogue, Woodman notes that the aims and methods of film are surprisingly analogous to those of the ancient historians.[35] Visual media are widely regarded as true due to film's ability to self-authenticate, wherein the audience believes because they see.[36] Tacitus' *Annales*, filled with the directed gaze, rhetoric, and drama, must have had much the same effect on its audience.

Mellor is even more explicit in his discussions of Tacitean visuality. In his *Tacitus*, he discusses the visual and pictorial effects of Tacitus' works, including comments made by such figures as Racine and Napoleon, who both regarded Tacitus as a visual artist.[37] Mellor notes that Tacitus' use of the visual is not often explicit, as opposed to, for example, Suetonius' biographical portraits. Tacitus' visuality is instead concerned with the description of scenes, rather than the outward appearance of characters, giving the narrative a covert ability to access the view of the audience. Mellor moves beyond Racine's view that Tacitus was antiquity's greatest painter, noting that Tacitean visuality is not static, but flowing and cinematic.[38] Later in his *Tacitus*, Mellor notes how often darkness or sudden light is used to visual effect in the *Annales*,[39] and provides a wealth of examples of Tacitus' literary devices, both rhetorical and visual, which the historian employs in his writings.

In his *Tacitus' Annals*, Mellor enlarges on his discussion of Tacitean visuality.[40] Here, Mellor describes Tacitus' literary context as one pervaded by the visual arts, which were often, in turn, influenced by specific literary works.[41] In this context of art-informed literature, Tacitus uses the visual language of sculpture and fresco to give depth and meaning to his historiography. Mellor, however, notes that Tacitean visuality is not at the surface level. Indeed, Tacitus' ability to bring characters to life in a vibrant way seems to be belied by the lack of physical descriptions of people or places that the reader finds in Suetonius, Livy, or Caesar. Rather, according to Mellor, Tacitus engages the reader psychologically during his *tableaux*, and paints pictures not for the eye, but for the mind. Mellor notes that Tacitus "conjures up pictures; he does not describe."[42] Mellor notes that Tacitus' visuality tends to be based more on mood and action, rather than directly visual ideas of color.[43] In his discussion of Tacitus' description of the mutinies in *Annales* book 1, Mellor points out that the effects of Tacitus' insistence on motion and ambience are best understood through the metaphor of film:

> [Tacitus' description of the mutinies] is not a static painting, but a cinematic drama into which individual scenes and characters are brilliantly interwoven: menacing darkness sets the mood. Amid the grand movements, gestures, and emotions of the crowds of angry soldiers, Tacitus, like a director of grand historical films (e.g., D. W. Griffith, Sergei Eisenstein, David Lean), shifts his focus from the sweeping panorama of a faceless mob to glimpses of individual faces and brief close-ups until the camera's restless eye settles on particularly telling images.[44]

In this statement, Mellor notes that the feel of Tacitus' narrative is one of darkness, without color descriptors or adjectives. Again, Tacitus' visuality is not that of Vergil or Livy, where the full range of color and description is available, but is based on lighting, motion, and framing. Tacitus directs the reader's gaze toward exactly those people and situations that create the correct impressions in the reader's mind. Thus, Tacitus' reader must forge meaning from the selection of vignettes and *tableaux* that the historian presents.[45] In Mellor's example, Tacitus narrates the events of the mutinous legions by artfully selecting what portions of the panorama to focus on, and what unsettling images to end with. Mellor points out the fundamental necessity of understanding Tacitean visual narrative through ideas most readily available in film.

Narratology

The complexities of Tacitus' cinematics, while vivid and exciting, are often hard to parse for a modern reader. Tacitus' writing style is compressed and biting, often relating complex interactions in a few sentences, and changing narrative voice within the space of a few words. Although the text strikes us at an emotional level, we often are unsure why or how. To illustrate and understand Tacitus' visuality, it is necessary to break narrative into its constituent parts, so that we no longer have only the final textual level to deal with. Rather, we can understand how Tacitus shapes our engagement at all narrative levels through the theory of narratology.

On a basic level, a literary text often contains a set of characters, a series of recounted events, character motivations and plot, and one or more thematic arcs. These large building blocks are a helpful beginning, but in order to engage in a more informative and nuanced discussion, additional tools are required. Thus, narratology provides a standardized set of terminology and definitions which enable a reader to parse the mechanics of a given work, and to gain a deeper appreciation for the structure and construction of a given story.[46] The theory of narratology was developed in order to enable scholars to discuss, with a high level of accuracy and precision, the levels, voices, and manipulations at play within narrative texts.

Based in the ideas of *mimesis* and *diegesis* found in the rhetorical work of Aristotle and Plato, narratology began to coalesce in the 1960s and 1970s as the result of the combination and contribution of several discrete endeavors that were all interested in narrative, including semiotics, structuralism, linguistics, and anthropology.[47] In the 1980s, Mieke Bal advanced a unified theory of narratology, building on the work of Roland Barthes, Gérard Genette, Gerald Prince, and, in her discussions of film, David Bordwell.[48] I follow Bal's theory of narrative, which focuses especially on narrative at the level of story—the level at which the reader of Tacitus' *Annales* undergoes the most manipulation. Narratology is a broad discipline which cannot be fully covered in this introductory section, but this overview is provided for the benefit of readers unfamiliar with these concepts to help them better understand the arguments made concerning the levels of Tacitean narrative.

At base, narratology is concerned with understanding the interplay between key elements in the formation of narrative, a form of storytelling. Every narrative occurs simultaneously on three levels: text, story, and fabula.[49] The most basic level of narrative is the fabula. While I have described it as basic, it does not exist before the story or text. Rather, it is a "memory trace that remains after the reading is completed."[50] Simply put, the fabula consists of a series of events that are accomplished by actors within a space and time. Time in the fabula follows normal temporal order, with events occurring one after another in succession. Agency at the level of the fabula lies with the actors, who (attempt to) achieve ends through action. The question that is answered by discussions of fabula is: "Who acts?"

The next level of narrative, moving from basic to complex, is story. In a story, the events of a fabula are colored, described, and given specificity. The fabula's actors, through description and characterization, become characters. Space becomes described and specified to create the story's place, and time can function out of sequence, which can take the form of anachrony (events told out of sequential order, in the manner of flashback and flashforward) or achrony (wherein time seems not to exist). The description and specification at the level of story imply a viewer, called the focalizor, where point of view and the gaze are centered. The question at the level of story is: "Who sees?"

The highest level of narrative, the text, is the point where the story is put into its final form, whether visual, auditory, or literary. For all genres that contain narrative, including written narratives, static paintings, films, sculpture, etc., I follow Bal in applying the term "text" with the understanding that all of these narratives contain stories that must be "read" in order to create meaning in the reader/viewer/audience.[51] For the text to have its final form, it must, either perceptibly or not, be rendered from the narrator to the reader. This transfer of story involves sensory communication, which can be described as speech. The narrator is the answer of the textual question "Who speaks?" and speaks through the text, which includes the medium of the narrative: words on a page, paint on a canvas, or filmic image on a screen.

The narrator, the most revealing participant of any narrative act, cannot be identified with the author/creator of the work.[52] Instead, the author selects a narrative stand-in, employing a voice that is unique to the work and may have no relation at all to the actual author.[53] The point of making this distinction is that the narrative levels and voices can be retained as separate registers of subjectivity within the telling of the story. As readers of historiographical texts, it is even more important to realize that subjectivity is not added to the text as "icing" on the "cake" of historical objective fact, but is always present.[54] From the selections of episodes (fabula), to the coloring and visuality of those events (story), to the words used in conveying all of this (text), subjectivity is inextricable from historiography. It is important to note, as I have when discussing fabula, that these three levels are not ordered in the point of creation nor at the incidence of reading.[55] Readers must first encounter the text, which must then be engaged and processed. Readers are both active in creating meaning through their reading experiences, and manipulated by the coloring and visuality of the story as they engage the narrative text.

Much of the benefit of discussing a text using narratology consists in the tools it provides to engage with multiple layers of speaking and seeing enclosed within narrative text. There is the possibility of multiple narrators within a single work, who may or may not be explicitly perceived (using the narrative pronoun "I" or not).[56] These narrators may be external, and not participate in the events they relate, or they may be internal—involved as characters.[57] Further, these multiple narrators can be nested, with a primary narrator telling stories narrated by other characters.[58] In the *Annales*, Tacitus often quotes the speech, either direct or indirect, of other narrator/speakers. Several focalizors can also be present in narrative, with many of the same distinctions that narrators have: internal/ external, perceived/non-perceived, nested or alternating.[59] These multiple, sometimes nested or engaged, speakers and viewers can all operate within a single narrative, encoding voice and point of view into what were once assumed to be objective statements. These complexities can be fruitfully and revealingly discussed using the tools of narratology, especially when narrative theory is wedded to more traditional areas of classical scholarship.

The applicability of narratology to the study of non-fictional texts, such as historiography, has been acknowledged in the scholarship of Gerald Prince and Mieke Bal, who stress the universal nature of narrative regardless of medium or genre.[60] In neither author, however is there a discussion of the complications, if any, which arise when historiographical texts are analyzed. Unlike works of fiction, historiography is based entirely in the realm of reality, describing actors, places, and times that actually existed, and relies on historical material, rather than the imagination and creation of the author. The question of narratology in historiography was directly addressed by Dorrit Cohn, who argued that historiography is narrative and so can be fruitfully explored through narratological theory, based on the centrality of plot in historical writing.[61]

Although Cohn proposed that there is overlap between historical and fictional narrative, she also argued that historiography is a special class of narrative, in need of additional theoretical tools and delineation from fiction.[62] Since history, unlike fiction, is based on historical material and documentary evidence, Cohn posited an additional narratological level: reference.[63] At this level the historian must "emplot" the historical data into a sensical narrative, choosing a beginning and an end for the historical work and selecting which historical elements must be included in the story.[64] The referential level underlies fabula and, unlike other levels of discourse in narratology, comes before the others in time. Cohn understands the referential level to be one of authorial interpretation and meaning-making in advance of the normal narratological process, at the end of which the reader interprets and makes meaning of the narrative text.[65] The addition of the referential layer is useful and certainly adds to our conception of the unique work of historians, especially in the insistence on the historians' necessary choice of elements from the historical source material.

For Cohn, however, historiography is differentiated from fictional narrative through narrative markers and its narratological limitations. Cohn points out that history, unlike the novel, includes a "perigraphic apparatus" consisting of commentary, footnotes, and endnotes that mediate the emplotment of the narrative from the historical material to the text which has no analogue in the novel.[66] The further narrative limitations on historiography deal with time and focalization. According to Cohn, historical texts are much more bounded in time and cannot "play" with time as novels do, purely for aesthetic reasons, but must be motivated by argumentation based on the source material.[67] Cohn's third delineation of historiography is its inability to enter the thoughts or mind of a historical character without the "must have thought" language of inference.[68] For Cohn, this limitation is a hard line, separating forever the narratives of historiography and the fictional novel: "This category [focalization], however, designates only what historical discourse cannot be and do: it cannot present past events through the eyes of a historical figure present on the scene, but only through the eyes of the forever backward-looking historian-narrator."[69]

For Cohn, the inability of the historical narrative to focalize through anyone but the author of the work makes historiography narratively defective, compared with the novel that may be focalized at multiple levels and through several focalizors.[70] Cohn's last signpost, distinguishing fiction from historiography, is the relationship between authors and narrators—a key concept in narratology. For Cohn, while this distinction must be upheld for all fictional works, even works in which the narrator is more difficult to describe, it is meaningless for historiography. Cohn alleges that history has a "stable uni-vocal origin, that its narrator is identical to a real person: the author named on its title page."[71] Cohn here argues for the collapse, in the case of historical narratives only, of the narrator into the author of the work: the historian. Cohn's additional layer of historical narrative, reference, is a useful analytical tool, and adds precision to the ways in which we can describe history's unique features. The delineating signposts of historical narrative, however, do not map well onto ancient historiography, possibly because Cohn has a limited notion of the variety and narrative breadth of historiographical texts. The limitations of Cohn's signposting model of historiography have been noted by Irene de Jong, who, following Bal, has done much to bring narratology into the theoretical mainstream of Classics.[72]

De Jong, in line with Genette, Bal, and Cohn, notes the benefits of narratological analysis of historiography, accepting Cohn's fourth narrative layer, which de Jong terms "material."[73] In terms of Cohn's several signposts of historiography, de Jong argues that, while these distinctions might assist in analyzing modern historiography, they do not appear to hold true for the ancient historians, noting that in classical antiquity, historiography was considered a literary pursuit akin to poetry. As de Jong points out, ancient historians had no qualms about representing the thoughts, feelings, and dreams of their characters, and do so often.[74] In answer to Cohn's assertion that historians cannot play with time, de Jong points out Herodotus' complex temporal structure of nested backshadowing and anachrony throughout his *Histories*, as opposed to the stable forward-moving narrative that Cohn has described.[75] Cohn's equation of the historical narrator with the historian/author is regarded as naïve by de Jong, who argues that the historians, even if their names survive with their texts, had many strategies of self-presentation in their construction of historical authority.[76] As is shown by de Jong, ancient historiography has much more in common narratologically with works of fiction than with the modern historical works characterized by Cohn. In this monograph, I follow Bal's theory with de Jong's correctives on Cohn. With de Jong, I see no need or benefit in a separate historical narratology, and accordingly I do not see the need to treat ancient historiography as a distinct "defective" sub-category of narrative. There is ample reason to analyze narrative in ancient historiography using the framework initially outlined by Bal, taking into account Cohn's material narrative layer.

Toward an Understanding of Visual Narrative

Narratology provides a theoretical framework and a set of tools for discussing narrative texts, including ancient historiography. This toolset has several difficulties for classical scholars to whom it is unfamiliar. The first of these is the reluctance of many classical scholars to engage in (at times) opaque and heavy-going theoretical scholarship.[77] There is a language to be learned when reading narratology that can certainly be daunting, especially in the shorthanded equation format. As an example, according to structuralist narratological notation a sentence from Couperus's *Of Old People* is represented as:

EN(p) [EF1 [CF2 (Ottilie)] – Steyn (p)]

indicating that a perceptible external narrator (EN(p)) narrates and focalizes (EF1) with a nested focalizor, the character Ottilie (CF2 (Ottilie)) the perceptible sound of Ottilie's husband Steyn (Steyn (p)).[78] While this description is exact and compact, it takes getting used to and can be alienating for a newcomer to theory. Moreover, this language conveys none of the emotional reactions that the reader of the original passage experiences, nor is it equipped to discuss how these emotions color the reader's creation of meaning from the narrative.

Throughout his narrative, Tacitus generates emotions in the reader through the sub-textual coloring of the narrative, which is extremely difficult to parse at the textual level. Tacitus uses the rhetorical devices of temporality, focalization, and omission to manipulate his narrative at the level of the story. To understand Tacitean historiography, we must consider the visual narrative created within the story and its emotional and psychological impacts on the reader. In addition to narratology, we need a further set of complementary tools to help us understand and analyze this subjective coloring of the story which is an integral part of visual narrative.

The benefit in discussing narratology through a visual text is evident in an example put forth by Bal, who describes how narratology can aid in the analysis of film. Bal illustrates the levels of text and story through their subjects (narrator and focalizor, respectively) in a discussion of *Schindler's List* (Spielberg, 1993).[79] In the film, Bal notes, Schindler is an unquestioning Nazi, until he is forced to see the Jews as individuals, rather than a collective. The change in viewing—that is, in how Schindler sees—is made clear through the visual narrative device of making a single little girl's jacket red against the backdrop of a (largely) black-and-white film. We, the audience, see through the newfound change in Schindler's vision, and focalization, as he puts a face to the Holocaust. In seeing Schindler seeing this girl, we are watching narrative. When, later in the film, Schindler sees a pile of bodies of victims, the little girl's coat is again shown in red. In both scenes, Schindler's gaze follows her. Thus, the film twins Schindler's path from evil to good along the same lines as the girl's from life to death. Bal identifies the change in viewing to match Schindler's as focalization, and the intertwining of the dual transition of Schindler and the girl to the level of narrative.[80] Film, being a visual text, gives a useful cipher for the layers of impact possible in visual narrative regardless of the form of the text.

Bal discusses visual narrative in two ways: static visual description within text and inherently cinematic text.[81] In the first category, Bal discusses the visual effects of Proust come to life through the metaphor of photography and static visual art in his *À la recherche du temps perdu*.[82] In the passage discussed, the narrator/protagonist visits his grandmother, who, unbeknownst to him, will die soon. The narrator/protagonist not only describes what he sees, but questions his own identity as a disembodied watcher. The focalizor questions his status as a viewer, and renders the flat and still image of his grandmother figuratively into a photograph. Here Bal draws a parallel between ekphrasis and the psychological and metaphorical effect of seeing through the focalization of a character. Following and building upon this example, Bal notes the cinematic visuality inherent in the novels of Ian McEwan.[83] In her analysis of a passage from McEwan's *Enduring Love*, Bal notes that:

> On all levels, also, the novel is concerned with the visuality as the motor of story-telling. While there is only one narrator uttering this sentence, it is easy to imagine the scene, the backdrop, the cast of characters. The CN (Joe)[84] is, it seems, writing the film script already ... The description zooms in on the date and name of the wine ... The interruption of the peaceful, pastoral scene suggests a cinematic shot/reverse shot: "We turned to look across the field and saw *the* danger." The spectator sees the two figures, sees them turn, then sees what they see ... As the description was waiting to be interrupted, so this novel was waiting to be put into film. The story of this novel is not a film script but it is such a strongly visual and sensory vision of the events that the film director must have been unable to resist.[85]

The visuality of the narrative here propels the novel, for Bal, into an entirely visual and cinematic register, which she analyzes through narratological theory and the specific terminology of film. Bal indicates that visual narrative may be addressed in this manner, but does not discuss the application of these techniques in great detail. She notes that one of the key benefits that narratology can provide in the context of visual narrative is the enrichment of scholarly analysis of literary texts,[86] which is precisely the focus of this monograph.

Visual Methodology

The final area of study which this book draws upon for foundational support is that of narrative film. For a modern audience, film is the most readily available comparative media for visual narrative. Although nineteenth- and some twentieth-century scholarship urges the stage-play as an appropriate parallel (and indeed, in some cases, the stage provides an excellent source of illustration), highly complex authors like Tacitus employ a number of techniques and devices which cannot be represented in the theater. Plays, for example, cannot demonstrate authorial alignment, engage in quick-cutting, and have only limited capabilities for the use of focalization. The effects created through these methods, therefore, cannot be discussed using the parallel of the stage-play, and we must seek a more appropriate medium.

One benefit to the use of film as a comparative is its permanency. Unlike plays, which may vary widely in interpretation (due to directorial cutting, personal interpretation, staging changes, etc.), a movie remains exactly the same each time it is watched. Thus, it provides an excellent, and static, example of the technique illustrated, and grants all students and scholars (wherever and whenever located) a consistent performance. Naturally, there are some films that have been released in different versions, such as a director's cut or edited re-release, but generally speaking, it is possible for two people anywhere in the world to experience an identical viewing. Thus, film furnishes us with a mechanism not only excellent for viewing visual narrative techniques, but also one that is consistent and relatively permanent.

Film is an incredibly rich and diverse world, covering the productions of numerous countries and more than a century's worth of techniques and advancements. Naturally, there is a great degree of variation in how visual narratives may be crafted, filmed, acted, and edited, and opinions as to who/what the author of a film is.[87] Given the breadth and evolution of cinematic techniques, attempting to speak of film generally is far too broad, and does not provide us with a helpful framework.[88] It is necessary to locate a particular group of films which closely parallel our subject, and which tend to employ the same kinds of techniques and methods that we wish to consider. Tacitus uses an array of visual devices, but he does so sparingly, and only when their effects can be mobilized for significant results. Thus, films that employ a large percentage of montages or special effects would not be appropriate, and instead films that focus more on characters, interpersonal motivations, and the interplay of motive and method—that is, films that strive for the illusion of realism in their stylization—are a closer fit.

Film Paradigm: The Classical Hollywood Film

Fortuitously, there is one well-defined and well-studied group of films which provides an excellent fit for our comparison, those which David Bordwell defines as "classical Hollywood cinema."[89] Generally, films made following the tradition of 1917–1960 Hollywood have similar narrative styles and film languages, in part due to economic considerations and those of censorship.[90] They are referred to as "classical" because certain aspects of their style of filmmaking have remained popular even to the modern day, and "Hollywood" because the form was initially developed in the studios of Hollywood, California.[91] There are a number of key elements common to the films of classical Hollywood cinema, which I will here outline.[92]

For Bordwell, the classical Hollywood cinema can be defined by a shared set of stylistic rules that govern its films. These include: the importance of narrative as the guiding concept for film, often following Aristotelean ideas of unity in time, space, and theme;[93] the presentation should have verisimilitude if not absolute truth; the film's rhetorical means of storytelling should be hidden through continuity effects and "'invisible' storytelling"; and the film should be easily comprehensible, and accessible through emotion which should transcend societal divisions.[94] This stylistic base as the study for classical Hollywood cinema is, admittedly, only one of the possible ways of discussing film in general, or for categorizing the films of this period. Other methodologies, including the examination of film based on audience(s) reception(s), as well as economic and societal norms or constraints on the studio system would be fruitful methodologies for gaining a fuller understanding of the stressors from without and within Hollywood.[95] As Kristin Thompson has noted, even after the 1960 terminus Hollywood films still generally follow these guidelines, especially in terms of narrative style.[96]

The key component of classical Hollywood cinema is that the action is derived from or motivated by human agency, and is often desire-based and goal-oriented.[97] Natural disasters or social problems may feature in these films, but it is the characters and their personal or psychological motivations that drive the narrative. These characters often meet opposition, either from situations, forces, or other characters. These films also generally adhere to fixed ideas of causality, space, and time.[98] Through causally linked narration, we see that, generally, these characters achieve their goals. Further, the narrative style of these films is, in the main, objective—the camera remains detached from any one person's perspective and thus is aloof and authoritative.[99] This objectivity is not absolute, however. There are moments, many of which we will be examining in the coming chapters, when subjective techniques are employed. These include moments when we, the viewers, seem to join the action of the film, through point-of-view filming or eyeline-matching. In addition, in classical Hollywood cinema the narration remains generally unrestricted, meaning that the camera is able to show us things that the characters do not see.[100] Finally, these films provide a strong sense of closure for the audience, leaving few (if any) unanswered questions at the end of the picture.

The benefits of using Bordwell's definition of classical Hollywood cinema are many. First, Bordwell is very clear concerning the divergences possible within the general aesthetic of classical Hollywood, wherein the majority of filming is in medium-distance, with special framing and editing work kept in reserve for dramatic moments.[101] Further, in opposition to the "illusionist model," wherein the viewer of film is a passive receptacle of image and narrative in all but the most artistic films, Bordwell posits an active reading, envisioning a spectator with previous experiences with viewing cinema, spectatorship, specific genre cues, and real life, all of which are constantly in play as the spectator reads and reacts to film.[102] Bordwell provides a useful framework for understanding the broad cinematic practices of the early-mid twentieth century. Throughout this work, I will consider and discuss, as appropriate, the works of other film scholars, but will look to Bordwell's definitions and concepts to construct a comprehensive system for the discussion of visual narrative.

How Classical Hollywood Cinema Applies to Tacitus

Tacitus was not free to write, as though he were an author of fiction, whatever and however he chose. Rather, he was writing within the literary tradition of ancient historiography. That this tradition allowed for individual stylistic expression need hardly be pointed out, when Herodotus, Livy, and Velleius Paterculus could all be counted among the ancient historiographers. The bounds of that tradition adhere very closely to Bordwell's discussions of narrative-driven cinema, in that a set of pre-existing expectations concerning the scope and nature of the final product defined the space in which the author was able to construct and develop his narrative.

All of these works function as part of a central framework of chronological narrative within a given space and time, usually framed at the beginning of the historical work. Further, these works, to the extent possible for their subject matter, retain Aristotelean unity of narrative. While Tacitus may refer to events of the Roman Republic, he is bounded by his own subject matter and generally moves from the beginning to the end of his narratives in roughly year-by-year progression. Tacitus also takes as read that the events of the Julio-Claudian emperors occurred as a direct result of human intention, rather than gross accident. Indeed, the moralizing force of the *Annales* would collapse if humans were no longer objects of praise and blame. In terms of historicity and verisimilitude, however modern scholarship places Tacitus within that continuum, it can certainly be said that truthfulness and/or its appearance was of paramount importance to the historian and his readers.

In order to suggest more than he could explicitly tell, Tacitus, as chapters 4 and 5 will show, was extremely successful in achieving "invisible storytelling" through scene juxtaposition and temporal movement interwoven into the main narrative. From an initial impression, the majority of Tacitean narrative and description would be characterized as authoritative and objective—in that events, places, and people are described from an external and safe distance in time, and only on exceptional occasions are these elements viewed subjectively. Narrative subjectivity, though rare when examining the *Annales* as a whole, is an outstanding feature, and will be discussed in much greater depth in chapters 1–3. The use of an authoritative style enables Tacitus to retain a detached narrative voice, and he can frequently show the reader events, thoughts, and motivations, of which the characters in the narrative are unaware. As to the potential parallel between Tacitus and classical Hollywood cinema's method of ending a work, as the conclusion of the *Annales* is lost, we can only speculate about Tacitus' ability to tie up all of the loose ends of the narrative. Moreover, as historical narrative does not come to a set ending point, since human endeavor continues after the action of the story, the historian has much more to choose and narrate in crafting the finish of historiography. In regard to all of these stylistic norms, Tacitus is remarkably in agreement with the salient narrative elements of classical Hollywood cinema.

For the creation of meaning, Bordwell's discussion of viewer matches very closely the ideal Tacitean reader, who must think through and during Tacitus' narrative, helping the historian to create the image of Julio-Claudian history. The likelihood that Tacitus' ancient readers interpreted his work visually is suggested by the nature of Roman culture, wherein people were keyed to observe and interpret visual cues—spanning all forms of thought and communication.[103] An illustration is found in our evidence for a memorization technique, commonly employed by those who needed to remember lengthy or complex speeches.[104] In this mnemonic device, the person imagines physical objects "standing in" for the various concepts that need to be recalled. These objects, according to the theory, are then mentally placed in various locations along the person's accustomed route. In order to remember these ideas, the person will mentally "walk" this route, recalling the objects placed there and the concepts which they represent. This technique for memorization, coupled with the extensive artistic record from the ancient world, suggests that Romans were extremely visual people, and that they were accustomed to visualizing their thoughts.

It is perhaps unsurprising that a vivid work such as Tacitus' *Annales* would come alive for such an audience, able to visually represent the techniques encoded in his words. The internal impression of the text would function in much the same way as modern film. It is true that we have parallel examples available to us in Roman static art, as there are numerous instances of engaged gaze and complex visual dynamics in, for example, Pompeiian fresco and Roman sculptural art, but we are now at a great remove both from Tacitus and the art of his day. Thus, a modern visual medium that speaks through similar devices can help to bridge this gap between Tacitus' world and our own.

Since its development, film has captivated audiences through its immediacy and the intuitive nature of its language. People from different linguistic backgrounds, with no shared cultural referents, can still understand the films of another country or culture.[105] There is, therefore, something universal and essentially human about visual narrative. By removing linguistic restraints, we are brought to a more deeply human place. Since the middle of the twentieth century, film has dominated popular culture, and has surpassed literature and theater in terms of modern popular canon. In fact, in order to remain *au courante*, previous forms of visual media (e.g., novels, comic books, musicals, and even the works of Shakespeare) have been adapted for the screen, to the point where many people have only experienced this material through film. Film is the most appropriate way to illustrate the techniques of Tacitus primarily because a number of his devices are not easy to discuss or express in terms of traditional narrative theory. Film is able to illustrate the various and diverse methods of Tacitus, and its language provides us with the best and most effective way to discuss the visuality of his works.

Therefore, this book is created with the hope that, through the combined studies of narratology, film studies, art history, and historiography, the modern reader may gain a better understanding and appreciation of the depth and intricacy of Tacitus.

Part One

Lens and Voice

1

Focalizing Empire

In writing his history of the Julio-Claudian emperors Tacitus brings to bear a number of rhetorical and narrative techniques, enabling him to bring his reader into the moment and to experience events in a visual, personal, and at points, authorial manner. In order to achieve these effects, Tacitus controls the gaze of his audience, ensuring that proper attention is paid to subtle references and coloring the way in which readers interpret character motivations and important events. While remaining true to the events of history, Tacitus is able to mobilize sentiment and temporal connection in order to give weight to rumor and suggest multiple, complex layers of hidden meaning.

One of the most visible ways in which Tacitus manipulates reader interpretation is through the use of focalization. Focalization is a major component of what is generally referred to, in both film narrative and traditional narratology, as "point of view." It is useful for my discussion of Tacitean historiography to divide this broader concept of "point of view" into two primary categories: focalization and alignment.[1] This divide is necessary, as the term "point of view" inherently contains two distinct narrative questions, those of "who sees" and "who speaks."[2] In employing the terms focalization and alignment, it is much easier to discuss these two aspects of viewpoint separately and clearly: focalization is concerned with "who sees," while alignment concerns an alteration in narrative voice, complicating the question of "who speaks."

For the modern reader, the concept of focalization is readily understandable in the context of film studies. The narrator of a film rarely changes, but the angle from which the camera shoots (and the subject matter it is thus able to capture), does so often throughout the film. It is common for the camera to adopt the perspective of a character, and thus convey to the viewer what that individual is seeing. This is an authorial action, as the selection of camera position dictates the direction of the narrative.[3] The filmic viewpoint created by the camera can move from a general depiction of a scene, which allows the audience to construct filmic space within which an action occurs, to that of a specific character. Thus, with little to no prior signaling, film can change its focalization from a point outside the story to within a particular character's vision, and back again.

In literary texts, focalization occurs when the narrative voice of the work assumes the perspective, opinions, and interpretation of events of a particular character.[4] This switch may last for an extended period, or may be limited to the choice of a single word. It is important to note that the *authorial voice* makes this change. Focalization is not concerned with moments in narrative, either filmic or literary, in which a character is speaking on his or her own behalf. When an author employs the technique of focalization, there must be a character who is the recipient of this attention—the focalizer. By changing the authorial voice to reflect the perspective or view of the focalizer, the reader is brought into closer sympathy with that character. Additionally, in telling the story from the perspective of the character, the author is able to direct the gaze of the reader or viewer, showing the audience the exact scenes, images, or impressions that the author desires to portray, and can do so from the ideal angle.[5]

Narrators focalize in order to tell a portion of a story from a particular character's perspective, allowing the reader to see this character's thoughts, intentions, emotions, and reactions. In most accounts, this technique is limited in duration and occurs during an excursus or, in some cases, in a moment of heightened drama. Where it would benefit the narrative in some way, such as increasing suspense or either aiding or intentionally obscuring a reveal, an author may choose to show a particular scene from a character's point of view rather than relate the account from an unengaged perspective. Focalization can also provide reader or viewer with insider access to the focalizer character's impressions, feelings, actions, or motivations.[6] This technique may be used to great effect for either protagonists or villains, depending on the type of story being told and the kinds of effects desired by the narrator.[7] When the reader's view is focalized through a villain, he or she can see what plans that character is putting into place and can force a strange alliance between reader and villain, analogous to that generally assumed to exist between the reader and the protagonist.[8] When the villain is powerful or intelligent, the reader may be forced into a helpless and passive perspective, able only to watch as the protagonist is overcome or destroyed by the villain's plans.

Film critic John Fawell notes that the effect of rendering the audience powerless serves to deepen the audience's involvement in the narrative: a fact no less true for Sophocles than for Hitchcock.[9] In failing to assist the protagonist, the viewer becomes a party to evil.[10] The powerless audience, through its inability to intercede, is implicitly culpable. This concept, which Tacitus mobilizes throughout the *Annales*, brings his reader into the nightmare world of the Caesars, and imbues his history with a true sense of these times.

Focalization and Visual Control

Tacitus' use of focalization also capitalizes on the reader's natural voyeuristic pleasure in being privy to information which is unknown to characters in the narrative. Through shared knowledge, the reader has an uneasy alliance with the focalizer who, in Tacitus, is usually a villain. The tension in the narrative is further exacerbated by the element of impending danger and suspense that this situation creates. The reader knows what the villain is going to attempt to do, and in some way hopes that these plans are carried out.[11] There is, in this type of narrative, a somewhat unsavory connection between villain and audience.

Added to this atmosphere of tension is the audience's anxiety as to whether or not the protagonist will be able foil the villain's plan. The narrator adds suspense by controlling knowledge: by showing the protagonist's obstacles and the villain's machinations, the audience is left with a sense of immediacy and fear. The reader has more information, but is powerless to assist,[12] reinforcing the uncomfortable association. The more charismatic the malefactor or, in some cases, the more uninteresting the protagonist, the stronger the bond forged between reader and villain. Tacitus exploits this natural tendency, focalizing through villains (and their victims) in order to achieve these feeling of suspense and unease.

The Third Man

The creation of suspense through focalization is well-demonstrated in film. In Carol Reed's *The Third Man* (1949), we follow a hack American western novelist, Holly Martins (Joseph Cotton), as he tries to find out what has happened to his friend, Harry Lime (Orson Welles) in post-war Vienna.[13] After tracking down leads from the false report of the accident that supposedly killed Lime, the two friends meet at the Prater amusement park at the foot of the Riesenrad, one of the earliest Ferris-wheels. The viewer, along with Holly, has discovered that Harry was heavily involved in the black-market sales of cut-dosed penicillin.

When Holly and Harry finally meet, Harry suggests they talk in the closed compartment of the Riesenrad. Harry explains his amoral stance by noting that "Holly, you and I aren't heroes." Holly, still grappling with Harry's callousness, asks whether Lime has ever seen his victims. Lime, as he moves to unlock the

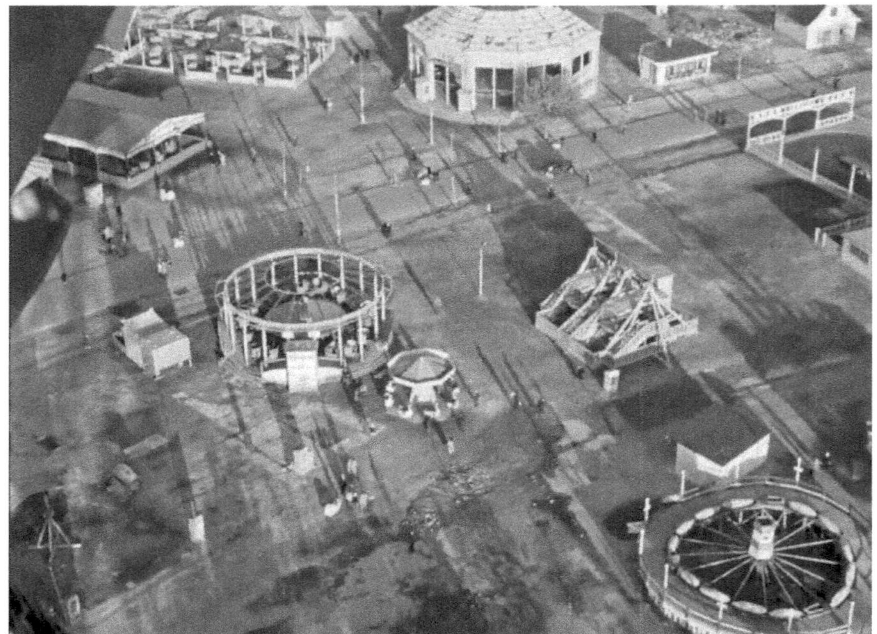

Figure 1.1 *The Third Man*, directed by Carol Reed © London Film Productions 1949.

door of the car near the top of the wheel, says "You know, I never feel comfortable in these sort of things. Victims? Don't be melodramatic." Lime then opens the door of the car, and invites Holly to "look down there."

At this point in the film, the filming changes from the third person medium shot showing both Holly and Harry, to a view of the amusement park. Invited by Harry, Holly, and we as viewers, look down at the amusement park filled with tiny people. Harry then, in voice-over, comments on what Holly and we are seeing: "Would you feel any pity if one of those . . . dots stopped moving forever?" Harry's pregnant pause on the word "dots," taken with the change in perspective high in the air show a use of focalization. We, along with Holly, briefly see the world as Harry sees it, complete with Harry's thoughts.

The illusion doesn't last long, as the shot changes to Harry, in profile, as he continues, "If I offered you £20,000 for every dot that stopped would you really, old man, tell me to keep my money or would you . . . calculate how many dots you could afford to spare? Free of income tax, old man, free of income tax. Only way you can save money nowadays." After this speech, the filming returns to the shot-reverse-shot normal for conversations that allows the viewer to watch whomever is speaking.

The effect of this change in perspective on the viewer is instant and visceral. For a moment, Holly and we have looked at life through Harry Lime's warped and amoral view, where people are all "suckers," and life should be lived even at the expense of others. Tellingly, Holly's information in *The Third Man* all comes through visual means; viewing pictures of Harry's victims and, later, visiting their hospital ward. Changed by these sights, Holly must ask Harry whether he has seen them. Harry evades the question by bringing the viewer into his own point-of-view. It is through this focalization that Harry is at his most seductive and dangerous, when, we imagine, Holly might waver and support his onetime friend.

The use of focalization in *The Third Man* allows us, along with Holly, to be briefly tempted by Harry's selfish and destructive ideas. This shared view, through focalization, involves the viewer in Harry's guilt and eventual downfall. Although Holly helps the police chase and eventually kill Harry, we as viewers can't forget that we, for a time at least, shared Harry's view.

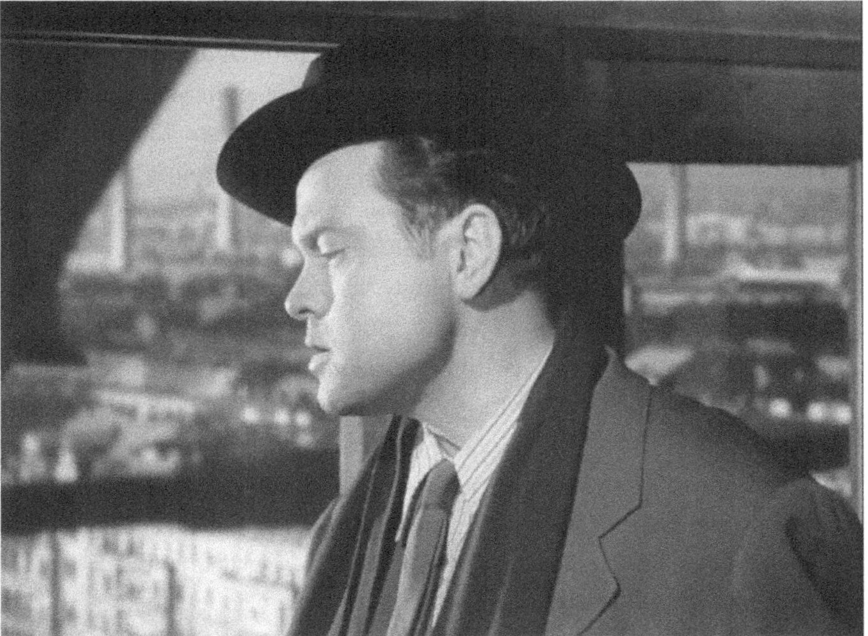

Figure 1.2 *The Third Man*, directed by Carol Reed © London Film Productions 1949.

Pompeian Ariadne

This use of focalization in the visual arts is also found in the works of ancient Rome. A parallel example of this type of focalization in Roman material culture is the set-piece of the Ariadne story.[14] In the myth, Theseus, after escaping from the Labyrinth with the help of Minos' daughter Ariadne, abandons her on Naxos either, depending on the tradition, of his own free will or at the urging of Dionysus. Ariadne, then, is usually shown on the beach, watching unhappily as her lover's boat sails away.[15] In some images she is shown alone, but in others she is joined in her sorrow by Eros, other mourners, or additional spectators. In certain instances, the image of her sorrow is paired with that of her coming joy, as her future lover Dionysus is shown either in anticipation or in the process of discovering her alone on the shore. There were a number of extant depictions of this myth left to us in Pompeii, however, due to deterioration of the pictures many are only available now via nineteenth-century sketches or renditions. One example, preserved in a line drawing by Discannio, was found in the Casa delle Fortuna (Pompeii IX.7.20), and is shown at Fig. 1.3.

In this image, Ariadne is shown mourning, semi-nude, on the beach as Theseus' ship sails away in the distance. The story of Ariadne would have been well known to a Roman audience, and seeing the image of her sorrow would naturally elicit pathos.[16] As we (the external viewers) stand beside her, we see the boat out at sea and feel a modicum of her loss and pain. In this way, positioned as an additional viewer to the scene, we share her view of the situation, and are thus drawn into the image sharing her point of view. We see Theseus' ship as though we too are Ariadne, and thus our gaze is focalized through her.

This image has a second component, however, which adds another layer of complexity. On the left-hand side of the painting is the god Dionysus. In the myth, Dionysus is so overcome by Ariadne's beauty that he marries her. And so, in this image, Ariadne's sad fate is offset by her coming joy. Ariadne, in addition to her projection of sorrow, is also shown in a sexualized manner. Her well-executed form is bare to the waist and invites the male gaze. She is thus depicted as both vulnerable and available. As the viewer appreciates her beauty, however, the imposing figure of Dionysus stands ready to claim the object of his affection. We become spectators at a second remove, watching his discovery and appreciation of the lonely woman on the shore. In seeing Ariadne as a sexual representation, we are focalizing through Dionysus, seeing her as she would appear to him. And, by realizing that we are watching him as he gazes upon her, we become additionally aware of the complex language of competing looks going on within the image.

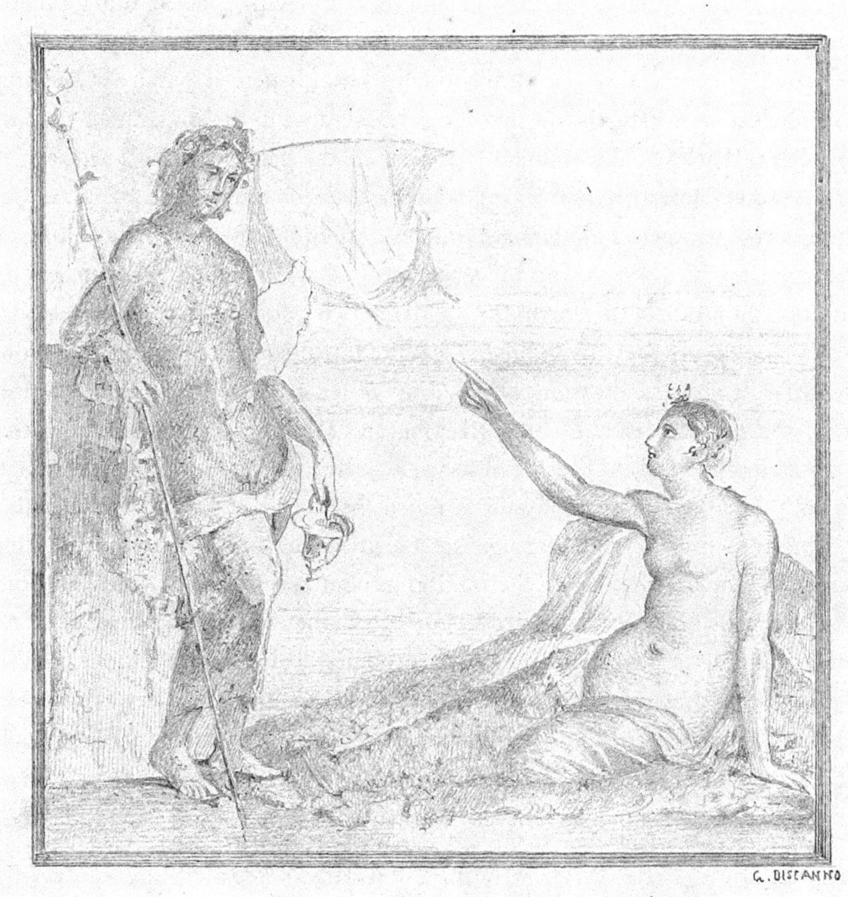

Figure 1.3 Line drawing by Discannio of a now-lost fresco of Ariadne originally found in the Casa delle Fortuna (Pompeii IX.7.20).

Elsner notes that the addition of a secondary figure can offer the external viewer a way in which to understand the gaze, and provide context as to how a scene should be read. In this instance, Dionysus' view instructs us to see Ariadne not only as a mourning victim. Ariadne's grief and beauty become a form of spectacle, with both an internal and external audience.

Finally, there is the ambiguous gesture. It is an unfortunate consequence of the deterioration of the original that, from the sketch, it is now impossible to tell whether Ariadne is pointing toward the ship of Theseus, and thus at the sorrows of the past, or at her new lover Dionysus. Given the nature of other Ariadne paintings that we have extant from the period, I would conjecture that her hand is raised to draw attention to the ship and the cause of her present unhappiness. The images that contain Dionysus often depict him behind Ariadne, or at an angle where he would not be visible to her. Thus, I believe it is more in keeping with the extant artistic record that she is responding to the ship, rather than to the deity. That said, the ambiguity present in the gesture as we now have it preserved is interesting, as it leaves open the question as to which character we, the external viewer, should be harmonizing with in interpreting the meaning of the painting. That we can no longer be sure of the intended gazes makes us additionally aware of the possibilities and different potential readings. Moreover, we cannot be sure that this ambiguity was not intended in the original rendition.

Regardless of the meaning of Ariadne's raised hand, we view this painting from the point of view of both Ariadne and Dionysus, as well as from the distanced remove of the outside observer. In effect, we are drawn into the image as both Ariadne and as Dionysus, in much the same way we are brought into sympathy with two characters on screen. It is the same interplay that film directors employ when using the traditional shot-reverse-shot of conversation, wherein at each line we focus on the correct character. At the beginning of our understanding of the myth, we focalize through Ariadne. As we understand the image, we are drawn into the sexualized gaze of Dionysus. Then, as we recognize his authoritative stance and remember his place in the myth, we step back and leave him to discover and protect her. This moment, when we realize that we have focalized (and, in this case, potentially transgressed a boundary of propriety), is much like the moment in which Holly steps back, horrified at having shared the views of Harry Lime.

This chapter will examine Tacitus' use of focalization, and discuss its impact on the reader. In these moments, the reader experiences the *Annales* on a visceral and highly personal sub-narrative level. By changing how a reader views the material, Tacitus is able to shape and guide the internal, subjective impressions created in the mind, thus providing the reader with a richer, if often more disturbing, impression of the early empire.

Tiberius

Since focalization naturally channels the direction of the reader's gaze through a character in the narrative (the focalizer), it is perhaps unsurprising that Tacitus uses this technique to great effect with regard to Tiberius, Sejanus, and Agrippina the Younger. Making his readers share the perspective of a villain places them within the action, and forces viewers to experience unpleasant or uncomfortable deeds both visually and viscerally.

Asinius Gallus

Tacitus brings focalization into the narrative early in the Tiberian books. By the time Tiberius assumes the principate, the senate had grown accustomed to Augustus' rule.[17] The sudden change, from the known proclivities of Augustus to those of the less-than-popular Tiberius, was an occasion for uncertainty in the senate. Tiberius was aware of his precarious position, and did not wish to seem too eager to inherit the purple, but his reticence appeared cagey or disingenuous to the senate, adding to their sense of distrust. Shortly after making the laudable statement that he would only take that part of the government the senate left him, Tiberius was asked by Asinius Gallus which part of government he had in mind (1.12.1–2). In addition to containing a thinly veiled barb at Tiberius' ambition, this witty response demanded clarification on the exact point that Tiberius had attempted to avoid: what position Tiberius would occupy under the supposedly restored Republic. Thanks to Augustus' grant of *tribunicia potestas*, Tiberius was already *princeps* with regard to military function, but he had qualms about fully accepting his adopted father's place.[18]

According to Tacitus, Tiberius hated to be understood too clearly for fear that his intentions would be manifest (*Tiberioque etiam in rebus quas non occuleret, seu natura sive adsuetudine, suspensa semper et obscura verba.* 1.11.2). In order to make these sentiments clear to us, his readers, Tacitus breaks from the omniscient voice of the historian and, through focalization, gives a clear account of what Tiberius was thinking. The narrative, which had up to this point been moving briskly (with years, and then weeks, quickly summarized in single sentences), suddenly slows and focuses in on this one moment. Much like the visual narratives of Livy's *tableaux*, Tacitus brings to life the characters in this exchange, focusing on what was said and how it was received. The *Annales* slows to the speed of conversation, recording characters' direct speech.[19] Then, with the hammer fall of Gallus' question, the narrative grinds to a halt. The reader is made to feel the difficulty and awkwardness of the moment, focalizing through Tiberius as the emperor struggles to find a suitable answer.

> perculsus improvisa interrogatione paulum reticuit; dein collecto animo respondit nequaquam decorum pudori suo legere aliquid aut evitare ex eo, cui in universum excusari mallet.
>
> 1.12.2

> Upset by the unexpected query, Tiberius fell briefly silent. Then, collecting his wits, he responded. *It does not suit my sense of decency to choose—or avoid—some of what I would rather be entirely excused from.*

Tacitus portrays Tiberius as totally unready for this sudden and probing question. Tiberius is struck (*perculsus*) so thoroughly by the unexpected (*improvisa*) question that he is forced to stop the flow of his speech and be silent (*reticuit*) in order to get his thoughts in order (*collecto animo*) before giving his answer: that he would rather be excused entirely. Tacitus implies that Tiberius' considered answer is patently untrue, since the emperor was forced to formulate an acceptable answer in accordance with his prior and unbelieved sentiments (*plus in oratione tali dignitatis quam fidei erat*, 1.11.2). The reader understands and, to a point, agrees with Tiberius' resentment at Gallus' interruption of the narrative flow.

After Tiberius' strained answer, Tacitus shifts the focalization from Tiberius to Gallus. Much like modern filming where the camera tracks the flow of conversation, here Tacitus directs our view from Tiberius to Gallus. We remain suspended in this digression; the narrative is made vivid and suddenly visual by the pause in narrative flow, a moment pulled from the timeline and expanded in order to demand specific attention.[20]

> rursum Gallus (etenim vultu offensionem coniectaverat) non idcirco interrogatum ait, ut divideret quae separari nequirent, sed ut sua confessione argueretur unum esse rei publicae corpus atque unius animo regendum.
>
> 1.12.3

> In return, Gallus, inferring offence from Tiberius' expression, said: *My question did not mean to divide what cannot be split, but to show by your own confession that the body of the state is one and must be ruled by one man's mind.*

Tacitus, ever the director, shows the reader the cue that would be missing from a mere dialogue: Gallus' reception of Tiberius' gaze. Gallus inferred from Tiberius' expression (*vultu*) that he had offended his emperor, and Tiberius, through his look, has told Gallus all that he needed to know. Tacitus' ancient audience (aristocratic and senatorial Roman readers) would have recognized only too well the danger that a misplaced comment or a displeased look could mean. Tacitus did not need to elaborate further in order to convey the implicit threat or Gallus' natural fear.[21]

After this brief look through Gallus' eyes, Tacitus summarizes the key points of what must have been a long speech of apology.[22] Tacitus then breaks in on his own narrative with the outcome of this scene, employing a temporal elision to reveal information which would only be known later; Gallus' placatory speech had not softened Tiberius' anger (*nec ideo iram eius lenivit*, 1.12.4). Then, to explain Tiberius' continued suspicion of Gallus, Tacitus again resumes the Tiberian-focalized narrative, unpacking the reasons for Tiberius' deep-seated hatred (*pridem invisus*). First, Gallus (like his father, Pollio) was renowned for his outspoken opinions. His father was a supporter of Antony in the Civil Wars, and thus serves as a reminder of the family's anti-Augustan politics. Furthermore, Gallus was married to Vipsania, Tiberius' former wife, which Tiberius likely took as a personal insult (*pridem invisus, tamquam ducta in matrimoniam Vipsania, M. Agrippae filia, quae quondam Tiberii uxor fuerat*, 1.12.4). Finally, Tiberius was predisposed to mistrust Gallus due to a letter he had previously received from Augustus, in which the elderly emperor listed, for the benefit of his soon-to-be successor, the names of individuals who would desire and/or be capable of *imperium* (1.13.2). Among those mentioned was Gallus. The reader, focalizing through Tiberius, becomes additionally suspicious of Gallus' targeted comment.

Tacitus closes this discussion by outlining the fates of those mentioned in the letter and in the preceding passage; with only one exception, all were later trapped by charges instigated by Tiberius (*omnesque praeter Lepidum variis mox criminibus struente Tiberio circumventi sunt*, 1.13.3). Tacitus implies that the reality of these senators' disloyalty was immaterial, suggesting that danger lurks not in reality but in perception under Tiberius. These focalized glances into Tiberius' personality show his character as suspicious and unforgiving. Thus, Tiberius' paranoia affects historical events, and sets the tone for the latter portion of the *Annales*.

Agrippina at the Bridge

Later in the Tiberian narrative, Tacitus again uses focalization to color the deepening suspicions between Tiberius and his adopted son, Germanicus.[23] These moments occur on the margins of what is predominately a discussion of the German wars. Each time Tiberius does appear, however, Tacitus goes to great lengths to contrast his foreboding presence with the positive, open-countenanced portrayal of Germanicus.

As the divide between the two historical figures reaches a crisis point, Tacitus brings Tiberius back to the center of the narrative through the use of focalization. This key moment occurs during Agrippina the Elder's much-discussed scene at the Rhine bridges (1.69.1–2). Agrippina, Germanicus' wife, had for some time been exhibiting dangerous (and, for a Roman *matrona*, unseemly) behaviors, taking over military duties and rousing the troops to bolster her husband's popular support.[24] At this point, Tacitus changes dramatically from his own authorial voice, discussing the historicity of Agrippina's conduct at the Rhine bridges, to a narrative voice colored by Tiberian focalization.[25] The reader again has a view, this time a fairly lengthy and penetrating one, into Tiberius' mind.

> id Tiberii animum altius penetravit: non enim simplices eas curas, nec adversus externos <studia> militum quaeri. nihil relictum imperatoribus, ubi femina manipulos intervisat, signa adeat, largitionem temptet, tamquam parum ambitiose filium ducis gregali habitu circumferat Caesaremque Caligulam appellari velit. potiorem iam apud exercitus Agrippinam quam legatos, quam duces; compressam a muliere seditionem, cui nomen principis obsistere non quiverit.
>
> 1.69.2–5

> This made its way deep into Tiberius' consciousness. *These attentions are not ingenuous, nor is the soldiers' favour sought for opposing foreigners. Nothing is left for commanders when a woman inspects troops, approaches standards, tests largesse. As if there wasn't enough favour-seeking in showing off the general's son in military garb, and wanting a Caesar to be called "Little Boot." Agrippina now has more power among the armies than do legates and generals. A mutiny that the Emperor's name could not stop—suppressed by a woman!*

The reader is once again witness to the almost physical impact of speech on Tiberius. Much as Gallus' question "struck" him (*perculsus*), the news of Agrippina's action "pierced deeply" (*altius penetravit*) into his mind. Before any thoughts are discussed, in each of these instances Tacitus gives the reader a measure of the impact experienced by Tiberius. Tacitus then transfers to Tiberius as focalizer in indirect discourse, omitting the verb of thinking which governs the entire passage. This omission makes the transition between historical narrative and Tiberian focalization nearly seamless, as the reader suddenly sees through Tiberius' eyes.[26] Tacitus uses anaphora throughout this rant in order to make the passage resemble the stream-of-consciousness of Tiberius' febrile and agitated mind. The lack of connectives in this passage draws attention to the change in authorial voice and the character-focalized perceptions.

Further, many of Tiberius' thoughts in this passage are incomplete, leaving numerous gaps in reasoning that must be filled in and/or connected by the reader.[27] Agrippina seems to be convincing the soldiery not to oppose a foreign enemy (*nec adversus externos*), but, it is implied, a domestic one: Tiberius. Agrippina is more influential with the soldiers than legates, than leaders (*quam legatos, quam duces*), perhaps even more than the *princeps*. Thus, Tiberius is shown unable to admit his fears, even to himself, but leaving the reader in no doubt as to their implications.

Agrippina's presence seems to be more able to quell a mutiny than the name of the princeps (*nomen principis*). This suggests to the reader that, perhaps, this is the real reason why Tiberius did not himself travel to the German frontier to assist Germanicus, and that the emperor may have feared rejection by the soldiers (*quod aliud subsidium si imperatorem sprevissent*, 1.47.2). These inferences imply that Tiberius felt personally threatened by Agrippina's campaigning. This fear, so eloquently displayed with Tiberius as focalizer, makes understandable to the reader the distrust which Tiberius feels for Germanicus at this point in the narrative.

In abandoning his usual (and expected) authoritative voice as historian, and taking on the mantle of Tiberius' thoughts, language, and stylistics, Tacitus places the reader in an uncomfortable and vulnerable position. Stripped of the dependable narrator, the reader has no one to trust but the impressions of a paranoid Tiberius. Even though these passages are very brief, their impact is enhanced by the pacing of these scenes; set out from the normal flow of the *Annales* and shown, like an embedded play or *tableaux*, in real time. Thus, Tacitus makes use of focalization to demonstrate to the reader the gnawingly persistent fears that haunt Tiberius' principate.

After showcasing Tiberius' fears, bringing them to life for the reader through the use of focalized language and gaze, Tacitus takes the discussion to a further remove by showing the source of these doubts and suspicions. It seems that Tiberius is not alone in reading the reactions of those around him and constructing his fears, but is instead aided (and fueled) in this regard by his ambitious and far-from-altruistic minister, Sejanus. Indeed, Tacitus tells us that Sejanus consistently raises his concerns, bringing them to the forefront of Tiberius' thoughts (*accendebat haec onerabatque Seianus, peritia morum Tiberii odia in longum iaciens, quae reconderet auctaque promeret*. 1.69.5). Thus, we are provided with a glimpse into Sejanus' plans and motivations, as he controls Tiberius via fear. Up to this point in the *Annales*, Tiberius' infamous minister has only been mentioned once, and he will not appear as a major character until the beginning of book 4. Here, in the first book, however, his machinations against the Julii are already on display. Tacitus informs us that Tiberius' worries were known to Sejanus, just as they are to the reader, and that Sejanus put them to his own uses. Thus, the question of focalization becomes additionally complex, and additionally interesting. Are the thoughts expressed at 1.69.3–4 the fears of Tiberius alone, or, if not, to what extent are we seeing a projection of the inner mind of the as-yet unfamiliar character of Sejanus? Through the use of Tiberius as focalizer, we see that Sejanus' insinuations have become active fears. As a result, the reader becomes uncertain about the reliability of Tiberius' version of reality. Tacitus throws the authorship of Tiberius' paranoiac fears into question to highlight how suspicion drives the emperor's actions.

Choosing a Successor

As the *Annales* progress, Tiberius is increasingly confronted with the problem of succession. After the fall of Sejanus and the subsequent reign of terror, the emperor has few candidates for the inheritance. Tacitus illustrates Tiberius' mental calculations amid his hesitation to name a successor, focalizing through the old emperor's eyes.

> gnarum hoc principi, eoque dubitavit de tradenda re publica, primum inter nepotes, quorum Druso genitus sanguine et caritate propior, sed nondum pubertatem ingressus, Germanici filio robur iuventae, vulgi studia, eaque apud avum odii causa. etiam de Claudio agitanti, quod is composita aetate, bonarum artium cupiens erat, imminuta mens eius obstitit. sin extra domum successor quaereretur, ne memoria Augusti, ne nomen Caesarum in ludibria et contumelias verterent, metuebat: quippe illi non perinde curae gratia praesentium quam in posteros ambitio.
>
> 6.46.1–2

> Tiberius knew this, was therefore undecided about consigning the state. Between his grandsons, first. Drusus' offspring, by blood and affection nearer, had not yet entered maturity. Germanicus' son had manhood's vigour, the crowd's support—the very things that produced hatred in his grandfather. Tiberius even considered Claudius: age settled, desirous of virtue's attainments; impaired mind an obstacle. A successor chosen from outside the household? *Augustus' memory and the Caesars' name will be exposed to derision and insult*, he feared. Tiberius' concern was not contemporary goodwill but rather seeking posterity's favour.

In this passage, the reader can see Tiberius weighing up the relative merits of his potential successors. Beginning with his close relations, Tiberius broadens his search ever outward until he considers the prospect of passing the state outside of the imperial family. First considered is Gemellus, Tiberius' favorite, who had not achieved sufficient age. Then Caligula, whose popularity Tiberius holds against him. Claudius, although possessing good qualities, is discounted because of his mental handicap. Tiberius then ponders a successor outside the imperial family, but dreads that he would thereby besmirch the family name.

Again, the narrative has shifted from a bird's-eye, or third-person, view to Tiberius as focalizer. The reader should note that Tacitus does not confirm or deny any of Tiberius' opinions about his potential successors; Tacitus simply offers insight into Tiberius' thoughts. The question of truth does not enter, as the question is decided based on Tiberius' perceptions of reality, rather than reality itself. Tacitus ends with an epigram stating that Tiberius had little thought for the present, but rather a longing for the esteem of future generations. Here again, the reader sees Tiberius as paranoid and concerned about popularity, not in the present, but in history.[28]

Tacitus, through the use of focalization, makes the reader a party to and complicit in Tiberius' anger, suspicion, and guilt. Like the audience of *The Third Man*, Tacitus' reader is forced to consider the opinions and perspective of the villain, and to see how the world looks through his eyes. After repeated focalization, the reader has been trained to think Tiberius' thoughts, and, in a way, bears a sort of emotional onus for them. What began as reasonable suspicion in the case of Gallus becomes paranoid fear in the case of Agrippina, and ends with dread at the judgment of posterity. Throughout the first six books, Tacitus has shown his reader how it feels to be Tiberius, living under a pall of fear while casting long, terrible shadows of doubt across the empire.

Sejanus

Tacitus also employs the technique of focalization with great effect to Tiberius' often scheming minister, L. Aelius Seianus. Sejanus, although in a position of power throughout Tiberius' rule, does not actually appear as a regular character in the narrative until the beginning of the fourth book of the *Annales* (4.1.1).[29] After an extremely Sallustian biography, Tacitus wastes little time expanding the character of Sejanus through both insinuation and focalization.[30] The latter technique is especially effective, as it enables Tacitus to avoid direct statements of agency. Sejanus is not explicitly shown as the author of many deeds, but his involvement is suggested, and throughout his character is described in a pervasively unsettling tone.[31] Often, Tacitus forces the reader to infer the relationships between Sejanus, his agents, and the effects of his plans. In order to make these links explicit Tacitus often focalizes through Sejanus, giving the reader insider access to the true intentions of Tiberius' minister before the deeds are committed. As we saw in the case of Tiberius, focalizing through a villain has the effect of building suspense in the narrative. The reader knows what Sejanus intends, but the protagonists do not. The reader can only look on, at the same time dreading and also anticipating the fulfillment of those plans. Thus, focalization not only serves to enhance reader engagement with an otherwise shadowy character who spends little time in the spotlight, but also involves the reader in the formulation of his schemes.

Plotting against Drusus

At the beginning of book 4, Tacitus informs us that Sejanus intends to gain control of the imperial family. He plans to do so by maneuvering Tiberius, a skill in which he has already demonstrated prowess, and by removing all potentially problematic characters from his path. Sejanus, at this point in the narrative, has already succeeded in making himself sole Praetorian Prefect and in combining the city's praetorian camps into one location, thus consolidating his power (4.2.1–2). Additionally, Tacitus details Sejanus' methods for garnering a support base, including ingratiating himself with the members of the guard, personally selecting the officers, and rewarding sympathetic senators with offices and provinces. Tiberius, completely taken in by Sejanus' personality, has allowed his minister to reach out long arms into the realm of imperial influence.

> facili Tiberio atque ita prono, ut socium laborum non modo in sermonibus, sed apud patres et populum celebraret colique per theatra et fora effigies eius interque principia legionum sineret.
>
> 4.2.3
>
> Tiberius was amenable and so well-disposed as to honour him—*partner of my labours!*—not just in conversation but before senators and populace, and to permit offerings to Sejanus' statues in theatres and public squares and at legionary headquarters.

Tacitus has summarized the position of Sejanus very quickly; only a few paragraphs after his introductory biography, Sejanus' power is spelled out in detail. Tiberius is described as being duped by his minister (*facili Tiberio . . . prono*), and Sejanus' likeness is coupled with the emperor in politically and, to an extent, religiously charged contexts. Tacitus' choice of *coli* suggests the offerings made to Roman deities; thus, as Tiberius is celebrated, so too is Sejanus.

After this description of Sejanus, including a run-down of his *modus operandi*, Tacitus moves from the discussion of honors granted to Sejanus to Sejanus' own thoughts.[32] Using a thematic shift to connect scenes, Tacitus moves from his own voice to a focalized narrator, and the scenes are linked through Sejanus.[33] Thus, just as with Tiberius, Sejanus' thoughts can intrude on the narrative with no more warning than the mention of his name.

> ceterum plena Caesarum domus, iuvenis filius, nepotes adulti moram cupitis adferebant; et quia vi tot simul corripere intutum, dolus intervalla scelerum poscebat. placuit tamen occultior via et a Druso incipere, in quem recenti ira ferebatur.
>
> 4.3.1–2
>
> But his house was full of Caesars: adult son and grown grandsons hindered Sejanus' desires. Since destroying numbers simultaneously was unsafe, Sejanus' plot required intervals between crimes. He decided, however, on an approach still more secret, beginning with Drusus, against whom he was moved by fresh anger.

As we have seen in the Tiberius examples, Tacitus here turns the narrative flow from the action of history to the thoughts of a character.[34] In this instance, Tacitus seamlessly weaves Sejanus' focalization into the narrative. The lack of a clear introduction, such as "Sejanus thought . . .," complicates the narrative by undermining reader expectation; it would be easy for a reader moving quickly through the material to overlook the shift, and even a careful reader may find it difficult to determine the identity of the focalizer. The first sentence, in which Tacitus states that the imperial house was well stocked with heirs (*ceterum plena Caesarum domus*), could be Tacitus' factual statement proceeding from his *auctoritas* as historian, recording a blessing for Tiberius or an obstacle for Sejanus. After the reader progresses a few words further into the Latin, this thought is revealed to be focalized through Sejanus as he contemplates the necessary intervals between the murders of his rivals (*dolus . . . poscebat*). The reader is, therefore, left questioning how much of what has gone before was told through Sejanus, as opposed to having been related by the impartial historian.[35] This ambiguity gives the scene an unsettling and disturbing quality, which Tacitus creates through historiographical technique. By creating meaning in this way, the reader is left to experience the awkward feelings of the senators of this time period; expecting to receive the words of an appropriate authority (Tiberius, Tacitus), it is Sejanus they find themselves listening to. In this way, Tacitus is able to deliver a visceral, deeply unsettling message, which has much greater impact and effect than a mere factual listing of the malfeasance of Sejanus the minister.

After Sejanus has achieved the complete trust of Tiberius, his next stumbling block is the size of the imperial family, and thus the sheer number of heirs which must be put out of the way before he can assume power. In this scene, there is the dark and ominous question, almost humorous in its exposition, of how Sejanus should go about killing so many Caesars. Tacitus allows the reader not only to see his intentions, that is, the deaths of Tiberius' heirs, but also to see Sejanus' preferred methodology. Rather than violence, which would be hazardous with so many potential victims (*quia vi tot simul corripere intutum*), he plans to use trickery (*dolus*). Even better, to Sejanus' mind, is the rather involved plot (*placuit tamen occultior via*) against the younger Drusus.

As discussed in the introductory section for this chapter, when a reader's or viewer's gaze is directed through a villainous focalizer, an uncomfortable relationship is created. Unable to warn other characters, or to consider the situation from a different perspective, the audience is forced into the role of passive accomplice. With Sejanus as focalizer, the reader contemplates the problem of how one would, in fact, kill so many people in such a way as not to arouse suspicion. Through the use of focalization, Tacitus shows the reader the mind of Sejanus, stressing his qualities as a scheming, behind-the-scenes villain.

Destroying the House of Germanicus

Later in the fourth book, Tacitus again shows Sejanus' inner thoughts via focalization as he contemplates how best to kill Germanicus' children. By this point, Sejanus has seduced Livilla and, with her aid, killed Drusus. Astounded by the ease of this deed and the fact that Drusus' death went unavenged, Sejanus considers how best to carry forward his plans against Agrippina and her sons:

> ferox scelerum, et quia prima provenerant, volutare secum quonam modo Germanici liberos perverteret, quorum non dubia successio. neque spargi venenum in tres poterat, egregia custodum fide et pudicitia Agrippinae impenetrabili. igitur contumaciam eius insectari, vetus Augustae odium, recentem Liviae conscientiam exagitare, ut superbam fecunditate, subnixam popularibus studiis inhiare dominationi apud Caesarem arguerent.
>
> 4.12.2–3

> Impetuous for crimes, and because the first ones prospered, he pondered how to bring down Germanicus' children, whose succession was certain. Three-way poisoning was not possible, given the unusual loyalty of their guards and Agrippina's impenetrable purity. Her defiance, then, he attacked, stirring Livia's long-standing hatred and Livilla's fresh complicity. *Arrogant in her fecundity,*

confident in popular support, she covets mastery!—these were the criticisms they should address to Tiberius.

In this passage Tacitus shows a much closer relationship between intention and the method of actual completion for the desired deeds. In the first example, we see Sejanus noting the sheer number of imperial family members that need to be eliminated, as well as the difficulties of disposing of them too rapidly. Here, Sejanus openly contemplates the use of poison against Germanicus' children and, discounting this approach as too risky, looks for another option. Tacitus also focalizes through Sejanus much more openly in this section, expressing the verb of thought (*volutare secum*), which he had omitted in the previous example.[36] The first sentence (*ferox . . . successio*) is clearly in Tacitus' authorial voice and is a simple statement of fact describing the circumstances in which Sejanus is plotting.[37] The next sentence proceeds thematically, as the problems posed by the certain succession of Germanicus' children flow into Sejanus' thoughts. Here, Tacitus focalizes through Sejanus, showing the minister thinking to himself that poison would be impossible and looking for another potential method (*neque . . . impenetrabili*). In the next sentence (*igitur . . . arguerent*), Tacitus steps back from the direct thoughts of Sejanus, providing now a quick summary of Sejanus' final decision to first discredit the children's mother Agrippina, in order to thereby leave them politically unprotected. Thus, in this section Tacitus moves the narrative extremely rapidly and subtly between his own authorial voice and the focalized thoughts of Sejanus.

Tacitus differentiates Sejanus' focalization sentence from those surrounding it through his conjugation of the main verbs. The passage uses historical infinitives (*volutare*, *insectari*, *exagitare*) in the first and third sentences.[38] The historical infinitives provide a vivid and cinematic tone, setting the stage for the important sentence that comes between them.[39] Tacitus further highlights this second sentence, containing the Sejanus focalization, by conjugating the main verb in the indicative (*poterat*). While this change from historical infinitive to conjugated verb could simply be an instance of Tacitean *variatio*, this seems unlikely. I believe that Tacitus conjugates the main verb here in order to intensify the *enargeia* in the focalization in this passage. Tacitus could have placed Sejanus' thoughts into *oratio obliqua* and entirely omitted the verb of thinking, as he did in the third Tiberian example discussed in the prior section of this chapter.[40] That Tacitus here elects to specify that we are in the mind of Sejanus makes this passage extremely powerful even at the level of the grammar.

Convincing Tiberius

A more overt example of focalization through Sejanus occurs near the midpoint of book 4, following on the heels of the famous letter exchange between Tiberius and Sejanus. In an attempt to bolster his claim for the purple, Sejanus asks Tiberius for permission to marry Livilla, the young widow who only a short time before assisted Sejanus in the murder of her own husband (4.39.1–40.7). Tiberius' response is fittingly obscure, raising the specter of public disapproval and reminding Sejanus of his many enemies. After this ominous rejection, Sejanus is seized with anxiety, worried that Tiberius might come to see through him entirely and put an end to his power. In order to forestall this potential, Sejanus quickly responds to Tiberius that he has been slandered, and begins to formulate a new plan. Eager to expand his power in Rome, and gain additional control over access to Tiberius, Sejanus encourages Tiberius to leave Rome:

> huc flexit, ut Tiberium ad vitam procul Roma amoenis locis degendam impelleret. multa quippe providebat: sua in manu aditus litterarumque magna ex parte se arbitrum fore, cum per milites commearent; mox Caesarem vergente iam senecta secretoque loci mollitum munia imperii facilius tramissurum; et minui sibi invidiam adempta salutantum turba, sublatisque inanibus vera<m> potentia<m> augeri.
>
> 4.41.1–2

> [H]e changed course to urging Tiberius to abide far from Rome in pleasant settings. His expectations were many. *I will control access and decide about most letters since they will travel with soldiers. Tiberius, nearing old age already and unstrung by the location's secrecy, will more easily transfer the responsibilites of rule. Less antipathy to myself without crowds of well-wishers and, with inanities' removal, more real power.*

Tacitus here focalizes through Sejanus as the minister considers the benefits which will accrue if he convinces Tiberius to leave the city and govern at a distance.[41] Tacitus introduces this focalization with a conjugated verb (*providebat*). Following this, however, the remainder of the passage is in indirect discourse, with verbs in the infinitive (*fore*, *tramissurum*, *minui*, *augeri*), showing that these are the eventualities Sejanus foresees. Here it is Sejanus' vision of potential acts and outcomes that we are viewing; Tacitus takes on the voice of Sejanus rather than the removed historical narrator. Both *minui* and *augeri* have a sense of futurity, but are placed into the present tense for increased vividness.[42] Tacitus' use of these verbs marks out this passage as distinct, separating it from both the preceding and following text.

In the next section, Tacitus turns from Sejanus' thoughts and expectations to focus on his actions as he attempts to consolidate his own power:

> igitur paulatim negotia urbis, populi adcursus, multitudinem adfluentium increpat, extollens laudibus quietem et solitudinem, quis abesse taedia et offensiones ac praecipua rerum maxime agitari.
>
> 4.41.3

> Therefore, increasingly, the chores at Rome, the people thronging, the multitude of visitors were Sejanus' complaint, while he extolled repose and solitude. *Tedius and annoying matters are absent and affairs of state are one's main business.*

Tacitus presents these events as fact, relying on his previous use of Sejanus-as-focalizer to explain the minister's sudden change of tactics. The main verb is in the historical present (*increpat*), its vividness strengthened by the use of a present participle (*extollens*). Sejanus is portrayed as extremely persuasive, and Tiberius is complacent as he takes Sejanus' advice without giving thought to the latter's motivations. The reader, however, has been made well aware of Sejanus' intentions through Tacitus' use of focalization. Thus, the reader is placed in the uncomfortable position of knowing more than the emperor, experiencing both a sense of anxiety for Tiberius as well as anticipation for the success of Sejanus' plans.

Much like the audience watching *The Third Man*, the reader here is drawn into the machinations of the villain while retaining his or her own moral compass, hoping for a positive outcome despite the seductive rewards promised by misdeeds. Having shared the gaze of Harry Lime, we too have considered the possibility of ill-gotten gains. Here, seeing through the eyes of Sejanus, the reader has seen his dreams of glory. We have watched as he has manipulated Tiberius and gotten away with murder. Like Holly, we are horrified, but also entranced, not entirely sure who we are hoping will come out in the lead at the end of the show. By focalizing through Sejanus, Tacitus has made us powerless observers of and passive accomplices to his deeds, making us a part of his history of the *Annales*.

Agrippina the Younger

Following on the theme of Julio-Claudian murder, Tacitus uses focalization to bring to life the history of Rome under Claudius. Specifically, Tacitus employs the device with regard to Agrippina the Younger, providing his reader with insight into her thoughts and machinations as she plans to do away with her doddering emperor husband. In this passage, Agrippina has already decided to kill Claudius and is debating about the correct selection of poison.

> tum Agrippina, sceleris olim certa et oblatae occasionis propera nec ministrorum egens, de genere veneni cosultavit: ne repentino et praecipiti facinus proderetur; si lentum et tabidum delegisset, ne admotus supremis Claudius et dolo intellecto ad amorem filii rediret. exquisitum aliquid placebat, quod turbaret mentem et mortem differret.
>
> 12.66.1

> Agrippina was long since resolved on crime and—if occasion offered—quick and well supplied with agents. She took advice on poison type. *Something sudden and abrupt will reveal wrongdoing*, she worried. *If I choose a slow and wasting type, Claudius, facing the end and perceiving the plot, will return to loving his son.* She decided on something special, to confound intellect and defer death.

Tacitus here stresses the hypothetical and academic slant of Agrippina's thoughts as the verb subordinate to the main verb of thinking (*consultavit*) is in the pluperfect subjunctive (*delegisset*) denoting an unreal or potential action, with imperfect subjunctives depending on them in each of the *ne*-clauses (*proderetur*, *rediret*), further stressing the actions' as yet unreality. The ending touch is Tacitus' macabre use of *exquisitum* to refer to the ideal variety of poison for Claudius; by casting Agrippina's selection as *recherché*, Tacitus suggests a level of connoisseurship on the part of the emperor's wife. The reader has already been informed that Agrippina is a nefarious and ambitious member of the imperial family,[43] but here with a single word Tacitus is also able to intimate her skill as a murderess.

The tone of this focalization is also instructive to our reading of the text. This entire inner monologue bears a highly academic tone that is at odds with the subject matter, indicating that for Agrippina, the decision to kill is both cold blooded and carefully planned. Rather than simply narrating these facts about Agrippina, Tacitus reveals her character much more cinematically by using Agrippina herself as a focalizer. Tacitus makes the reader see not only what, but how she thinks about poisoning her husband.

Perhaps not surprisingly, as with many literary devices, Tacitus concentrates his use of focalization in the Tiberian books, preferring instead a more omniscient and seemingly detached voice in the Neronian books.[44] This change has more to do with the shift of narrative tone between the reigns of Tiberius and Nero than with an arbitrary change in style or an infecting artlessness or laziness. Tacitus infuses Tiberius' principate with intrigue, plots, and a dark and brooding atmosphere. After the horrors of Caligula and the corruption of Claudius, unbridled evil stands unashamed in the light of day under Nero. Thus, there is less need for these techniques in the Neronian books, since Nero makes no attempt to hide his crimes. Tacitus, suiting his history to its subject, is more inclined to plainly narrate Nero's wickedness, rather than to hint at it, as he does when writing Tiberius.[45] That said, Tacitus does occasionally still employ focalization in the Neronian portion of the work, using it judiciously (and rarely) to create targeted effects. In the Neronian books there are not the formal internal monologues of characters like we saw in the Tiberian section. Instead, Tacitus' focalization is much more incisive, using small glimpses of characters' inner thoughts in order to color the narrative. Mirroring the general tone in the Neronian books, Tacitus' use of focalization becomes sudden and frantic.

The above examples are direct and relatively straightforward illustrations of Tacitus' use of focalization to place the reader in the mind of his villains in the early *Annales*. Tacitus achieves both heightened tension and a strange sense of identification between reader and character through this technique. Suspense is created via the revelation of the character's thoughts and plans, to which the reader becomes a party because of this insider access. Helpless to change or alter the narrative, the reader also shares in the focalized characters' guilt. In the final section of this chapter, we will be building on these concepts as we consider a more complicated example. In order to further illustrate the visual components of Tacitus' focalization, we will be discussing it in light of the classic Hollywood cinema technique known as the shot-reverse-shot.

The Murder of Agrippina: The Ideal Spectator and the Shot-Reverse-Shot

In film, the sudden change of perspective from one person to another in a dialogue is known as the "shot-reverse-shot." This technique enables to the viewer to maintain the ideal vantage point at all times while watching a conversation taking place. Written out textually, the technique may sound obscure, but this device has become such a standard part of cinema that it is hardly noticed by modern audiences.[46] To outline the technique in its most basic form, consider a scene in which we are watching a simple conversation between two people, a woman and a man. The first shot will center on the first character as she is speaking. The next shot is a reverse of the first, in which the camera tracks the view of the first character as she watches the second speaker while he delivers his lines. Thus, in the second shot, the camera is focalizing through the first character, showing the audience what she is seeing. It enables the audience to become a part of the conversation, taking on the perspective of the first speaker and thereby gaining access to the best view of speaker two for his moment in the conversation. Then, the third shot is employed, in which the same tracking mechanism is repeated; this time, the camera assumes the gaze of the second speaker. With the camera, the audience watches "as" speaker two. Again, the viewer receives the ideal perspective to view that moment in the discussion, as the camera is correctly positioned to watch the performance of speaker one. In the shot-reverse-shot, this back and forth trading of view may continue for many minutes and multiple cuts. This alternating device gives the audience immediate access to the reactions of each character based on what is said during the course of a scene, and shows us an additional layer of thought and reception beneath the level of mere dialogue.[47]

Strangers on a Train

The shot-reverse-shot can also be employed in scenes with both dialogue and action. For example, consider Hitchcock's *Strangers on a Train* (1951), during the scene in which Guy (Farley Granger) punches Bruno (Robert Walker). At this stage in the film, Guy has realized that Bruno is not a moral agent, and may be mentally disturbed. Bruno, wishing to be free of his father and to gain his inheritance, and knowing that Guy would like to be free from a difficult first marriage, suggests to Guy early in the film that they should assist one another. Bruno's scheme, which he refers to in the film as a "crisscross," is that he and Guy should "swap murders," thus Guy would kill Bruno's father (whom he has no motive against, making Guy an unlikely suspect for a police investigation), and Bruno would kill Guy's wife.

In the scene in question, Guy is resisting Bruno's pressure to agree to the switched-murders plan. Guy and Bruno are filmed from the third-person point of view, framing both actors in the shot as Bruno responds to Guy's pleas to leave him alone, stating "But Guy, I like you." At this point, the filming changes to capture the focalized exchange. The camera tracks as though representing Bruno's eyes; we see as Guy pulls back his right shoulder, then delivers a punch at Bruno's face (the camera). There is a white flash accompanying a punching sound, as the impact is "felt" by the viewer. The audience next sees Bruno falling after being struck, as the camera focalizes through Guy. The camera then switches to Bruno's perspective for a moment, and we watch with Bruno while Guy stands, massaging his fist and trying to comprehend what has just happened. We return to the gaze of Guy, watching as Bruno cradles his jaw and menacingly says, "You shouldn't have done that, Guy." The next shot returns us to the eyeline of Bruno as Guy urges him to pull himself together.

At this point, with the emotional climax past, the narrative returns to the more normal and sedate third-person point of view, as the audience watches Bruno straighten his collar and tie. This scene is pivotal in the film, representing the point at which Guy starts formulating plans to stop Bruno and bring him to justice. Hitchcock uses this technique later in the film for another crucial exchange, when Guy attempts to warn Bruno's father of his son's machinations, only to discover when the lights are switched on that Guy had been talking to Bruno, and not Bruno's father, in the dark.[48] In both instances, the viewer experiences the characters of both Guy and Bruno via focalization, which is critical as Hitchcock relies on the heightened level of engagement created thereby to maintain the suspense of the film. The tension in the piece relies on the interplay of audience anticipation between the two characters; at all times, the audience knows key information that would be helpful to Guy, and at times to Bruno, and it is the back-and-forth drama of watching the characters attempt to foil one another that drives the narrative of the film.

Tacitus was well aware of the power of focalization, as we have seen in the prior sections. In order to heighten tension in a particularly vivid scene in book 14, Tacitus employs the device to bring his readers into the minds of his characters during an extended and dramatic series of exchanges leading up to a murder. In much the same way as Hitchcock achieved suspense in *Strangers on a Train*, Tacitus here uses focalization like the shot-reverse-shot, enabling the reader to both understand and experience the various machinations building to the death of Agrippina the Younger.

Nero's Plan

Tacitus begins book 14 with an extended narrative of Nero's plans to murder his mother. In this scene Nero, who has wished to be free of the influence of Agrippina for some time, is urged by his mistress Poppaea to kill his mother. Tacitus shows Nero's thoughts, wherein he ponders the difficulty of selecting a method, as well as his discussions with Anicetus, the head of the fleet at Misenum. Anicetus suggests a collapsing boat as a possible option, which would give Nero the ability to claim natural accident. Nero accepts the plan, which then backfires when the boat does not sink immediately. After consulting with his advisers Burrus and Seneca, Nero orders Anicetus to take a company of soldiers and finally dispatch Agrippina. Throughout this narrative, Tacitus repeatedly changes focalizers, including both Nero and Agrippina as well as the rowers on the collapsing boat. These focalized exchanges, and the transfer of gaze between them, is reminiscent not only of *Strangers on a Train* but also of the Pompeian fresco of Ariadne, in which the gaze of the viewer is directed through both Ariadne and Dionysus. Thus, Tacitus' original Roman audience was likely prepared for and able to understand this change of gaze, making the device an effective method for heightening reader engagement and suspense. Here, as in the foregoing examples, Tacitus uses focalization to show (rather than tell) what is going on in his characters' minds.[49] This mechanism allows Tacitus to present hypothetical alternatives, and to raise the specter of deeds or events that never actually happened. Through focalization, Tacitus provides access to the innermost thoughts of his characters, giving them the opportunity to suggest alternative histories and multiple variations of motive. Thus, this device enables Tacitus to show both characters' intentions and their reactions, material unavailable to straight third-person narration.

In order to place his readers (analogous to the way in which a director places the camera, and thereby the audience) in the best position to observe a particular action, Tacitus alters the focalization between characters in order to track conversation and/or narrative flow.[50] Much like the changes in narration and focalization characteristic of the shot-reverse-shot, Tacitus' successive focalizations enable rapid direction of the reader's gaze from one participant to another. The results of these maneuvers are so effective, positioning the reader or viewer ideally at all times, that they often go unnoticed. Film scholars have long been aware of the subtle and almost invisible effect of the shot-reverse-shot, and that when well integrated these transitions are seamless.[51] Most of us take this technique for granted when watching a film and, likely, are unaware of the use of parallel mechanics when reading a text, which in a way is as it should be. Tacitus' use of focalization is meant to make a scene or character vivid, but it is not meant to be noticed or jarring. To have its greatest effect on the reader, a technique should not stand out as a mere device, but instead quietly enhance the reader's appreciation of the narrative.

The first words of book 14 set the scene for what will be one of the more memorable and visual portions of the *Annales*: "Gaius Vipstanus, C. Fonteius, consuls. A crime long contemplated, Nero deferred no longer" (*Gaio Vipstano C. Fonteio consulibus diu meditatum scelus non ultra Nero distulit*. 14.1.1). The nature of this crime (*scelus*) is left unclear for a few sentences, leaving the reader to come slowly to the realization that the crime is the murder of Agrippina. Tacitus guides the reader toward this conclusion through a recounting of the complaints of Poppaea Sabina (14.1.1–3). Tacitus then moves the narrative to a discussion of Agrippina's desperation for rule through Nero, the depths to which she may have sunk to secure her primacy of place in his eyes, and the tactics used to break her hold over him (14.2.1–2). Only then does Tacitus reveal Nero's intended crime in plain words.

> postremo, ubicumque haberetur, praegravem ratus interficere constituit . . .
>
> 14.3.1

> Eventually finding her insufferable wherever she was housed, he decided to kill her . . .

By employing a slow reveal, Tacitus builds suspense and allows the reader to guess at Nero's plans before they are explicitly stated. After giving the reader a parade of Agrippina's behavior, Poppaea's laments, and Nero's concerns, Tacitus returns to the decision which began the book: that Agrippina must be murdered (*interficere constituit*). In this passage, Tacitus has already started to focalize through Nero, as he states what Nero is thinking (*ratus*) and provides the emperor's immediate motive for murder. In the language of the shot-reverse-shot, this is the initial camera angle in which the first focalizer is established.

Having decided to kill his mother, Nero is faced with the problem of method. Tacitus here uses focalization not only for vividness, but also to explain the reasons for the *outré* murder weapon that Nero finally chooses.

> hactenus consultans, veneno an ferro vel qua alia vi. placuitque primo venenum. sed inter epulas principis si daretur, referri ad casum non poterat tali iam Britannici exitio; et ministros temptare arduum videbatur mulieris usu scelerum adversus insidias intentae; atque ipsa praesumendo remedia munierat corpus. ferrum et caedes quonam modo occultaretur, nemo reperiebat; et ne quis illi tanto facinori delectus iussa sperneret metuebat.
>
> 14.3.1–2

> deliberating only as to poison, sword or other method. He favored poison first. But if given at the Emperor's table it could not be ascribed to chance, Britannicus already having died thus. And it seemed toilsome to test the servants of a woman alert, from criminal experience, to plots. Plus, by taking antidotes in advance she had fortified her body. How sword and slaughter might be hidden no one discovered, and the possibility that someone selected for so momentous an action might defy orders was frightening.

This passage is highly reminiscent of the section in which Agrippina plots Claudius' death, and is rich in verbal echoes.[52] The discussion begins, in both instances, with the question of murder weapon.[53] Nero's first instinct, as was Agrippina's, is to use poison (*placuit primo venenum*). Nero quickly thinks better of this. He could not poison her at table, as he had already killed Britannicus that way.[54] He could not use her servants, since Agrippina was a past master in crime (*mulieris usu scelerum adversus insidias intentae*). Tacitus intrudes on Nero's thoughts with the interesting aside that Agrippina had seen to it that she was defended against poison by using prophylactics (*ipsa praesumendo remedia munierat corpus*). Tacitus then broadens Nero's thoughts to imply that he had canvassed his ministers, possibly Burrus and Seneca, since "no-one" could think (*nemo reperiebat*) how to conceal a violent death. With all sensible options exhausted, Anicetus, commander of the fleet at Misenum, suggested killing Agrippina by collapsing boat (14.3.3).

What the Rowers Saw

The plot proceeds apace; the boat is built, and Nero invites his mother to dinner during Minerva's festival at Baiae, across an inland lake from her residence. In due course the boat collapses, but there is a hitch, as the ceiling is arrested by the unexpected strength of Agrippina's couch. The steersman is killed, but not Agrippina or her maid (14.5.1). At this point, the murder has become a comedy of errors, with mass confusion on board the ship. Tacitus, to heighten the cinematics inherent in the scene, focalizes through the rowers.

> visum dehinc remigibus unum in latus inclinare atque ita navem submergere; sed neque ipsis promptus in rem subitam consensus, et alii contra nitentes dedere facultatem lenioris in mare iactus.
>
> 14.5.2
>
> The rowers' next plan was to tilt the boat to one side and sink it that way. But not even they reached quick consensus in the crisis, and the others, opposing, made an easier opportunity for going overboard.

The rowers, obviously involved in the plot, think to sink the ship by tipping it over, but there is no plan on how to do this, and so the boat sank slowly (*lenioris in mare iactus*). Thus, Nero's long-planned murder attempt is reduced to a collapsing boat that collapsed the wrong way and crewmen who had murderous intent, but no clear direction. Through focalization, Tacitus shows the reader what was in the minds of the rowers (*visum ... remigibus*). They were not simply unwitting victims, but were well aware of the plot and indeed served as unsuccessful accomplices. Readers are here granted a (rare, in the context of the *Annales*) perspective into the minds of tertiary characters. This makes the scene almost surreal and marks out Agrippina as truly alone; even her rowers are involved in the plot to kill her.

The Dangers of Knowledge

After Agrippina escapes to her villa, she has time to process the scene which she had just witnessed. The reader, already fully informed about the plot, knows exactly what was supposed to happen as opposed to the actual result. Tacitus then focalizes the narrative through Agrippina, as she attempts to put the pieces together.

> illic reputans ideo se fallacibus litteris accitam et honore praecipuo habitam, quodque litus iuxta, non ventis acta, non saxis impulsa navis summa sui parte veluti terrestre machinamentum concidisset; observans etiam Acerroniae necem, simul suum vulnus adspiciens, solum insidiarum remedium esse <sensit>, si non intellegerentur
>
> 14.6.1

> Pondering the purpose behind the invitation—*Deceitful letter!*—and the particularly honorific reception, the fact that the boat—*near shore, no wind pushing, not on the reef*—collapsed top-down like a structure on land; observing, too, the murder of Acerronia and considering her own wound, Agrippina realized that the trap's only remedy lay in not being understood.

Never in this passage is Nero mentioned by name, but the reader already knows that he is behind the attempt on his mother's life. Instead of a treacherous son, Agrippina thinks of the "treacherous letter" (*fallacibus litteris*). Thus, the reader infers that she cannot bring herself to believe that her son has attempted to murder her. She also considers how the boat collapsed close to shore like a device (*veluti terrestre machinamentum*), remembers her maid Acerrina's murder (*Acerroniae necem*) when she claimed to be Agrippina, and thinks about both her own wound (*suum vulnus*) and her close escape. As the truth of the matter dawns on her, Agrippina then comes to a very Tacitean decision: she will appear not to understand (*non intellegerentur*) the significance of what just happened.[55] The wheel has turned and now Agrippina is shown experiencing the same fears felt at points by Tiberius and the senators during the earlier books of the *Annales*. This focalization forces readers to identify with Agrippina, taking her part as they share in her thoughts, which in turn makes her upcoming murder more dramatic.

Tacitus then quickly changes the scene to Nero's chambers, where Nero is informed of what the reader already knows: both the boat and plot have failed.

> at Neroni nuntios patrati facinoris opperienti adfertur evasisse ictu levi sauciam et hactenus adito discrimine <ne> auctor dubitaret<ur>.
>
> 14.7.1

> Nero, awaiting word of deed complete, was informed: *She got away, lightly wounded but having come close enough to danger to be sure about its source.*

Nero realizes that matters are spiraling out of control, since Agrippina not only escaped (*evasisse*) but knows by now exactly who must have been behind the assassination attempt (*ne auctor dubitaretur*). The reader should note here that Tacitus has, characteristically, held the vital point of the message, the author of this crime, until the very end of the passage in order to heighten its dramatic quality. Tacitus achieves and maintains a high level of suspense through these exchanges, and this tension is again increased as the reader discovers Agrippina's and Nero's mutual suspicions. Agrippina's horror at the attempt on her life is paralleled and matched by Nero's terror as he is thrown into a complete panic.

> tum pavore exanimis et iam iamque adfore obtestans vindictae properam, sive servitia armaret vel militem accenderet, sive ad senatum et populum pervaderet, naufragium et vulnus et interfectos amicos obiciendo: quod contra subsidium sibi, nisi quid Burrus et Seneca?
>
> 14.7.2

> He was unstrung by panic, insisting: *Soon, soon she will arrive quick to avenge! She'll arm slaves or rouse soldiers, or else approach senate and people—and blame me for shipwreck and wound and murdered friends! What prop do I have against her, unless Seneca and Burrus have something?*

Nero's terror in this passage is almost palpable. Tacitus describes him as having the wind knocked out of him by fear (*pavore exanimis*), stressing the sudden and violent shock of the news of Agrippina's survival. Further, Nero is seen calling out that Agrippina would come for vengeance at any second (*iam iamque adfore*). The tension that Tacitus has been building throughout the previous sections is here intensified by Nero's lack of reserve and frightened panic. At this point, Tacitus again focalizes through Nero, signaled by the verb of speaking (*obtestans*). Following this verb, the remainder of the passage is short and clipped, reflecting Nero's flighty mind.[56] The reader senses Nero's panic, causing feelings not only of disgust at Nero's weakness and fear of Nero's disturbed mind, but also of compliance and pity. The narrative is now in a heightened and dramatic state, which Tacitus pushes to yet a greater degree through this use of focalization, unmasking a picture of the depraved and profligate emperor.

Most of the passage (*tum ... obiciendo*) is a single, disjointed sentence, which seems to parallel Nero's raving. Tacitus thus imbues the narrative with a sense of hectic, stream-of-consciousness paranoia. This mental distraction is reflected in the grammatical structure of the focalization, which is abbreviated, even for Tacitus' *brevitas*. There is no main verb, and the passage is held together by a participle (*obtestans*) introducing two indirect questions (*sive ... accenderet* and *sive ... pervaderet*), the second elaborated by an ablative phrase (*naufragium ... obiciendo*). Without any answers or conclusions, indirect question follows indirect question as Nero's frenzied mind rushes through an ascending tricolon of nightmare imaginings. The second possibility, that of Agrippina inflaming the people against him (*sive ad senatum et populum pervaderet*), is further elaborated by an ablative gerund phrase enumerating the evidence that might be used against him (*naufragium et vulnus et interfectos amicos obiciendo*). The sentence, begun loosely, keeps the reader in anxious expectation of a slower and/or ordered explanatory phrase, but the sentence merely devolves. The passage ends with a direct but rhetorical question (*quod contra subsidium sibi*), and its answer (*nisi quid Burrus et Seneca*), both lacking verbs. These direct the course of the narrative away from Nero's ranting and toward the scene in which Nero questions Burrus and Seneca.

Tacitus has deftly and skillfully navigated the reader's emotions through this passage. Beginning with a description, Tacitus shows a glimpse into Nero's mind, then, following the emperor's train of thought, moves to the next plan featuring Burrus and Seneca, who appear as if on cue. Looked at from a directorial perspective, this passage is on rails; the audience is unable to look away from the onrush of motion, sentiment, and fear. Like a skilled director of suspense films, Tacitus knows how to control the gaze.

Desertion, Murder, and Aftermath

Moving forward in the assassination plot, we see the outcome of Nero's interview with Burrus and Seneca; Nero decides to send Anicetus to kill Agrippina directly. To deflect public outcry for what will now be a very obvious murder, he publicizes that she attempted to kill him and, upon failing, chose to kill herself (14.7.6). The scene changes rapidly back to Agrippina's villa, where Anicetus has surrounded

Agrippina's house. There, he and a column of soldiers break down the doors and search the house, heading for Agrippina's room.

> Anicetus villam statione circumdat refractaque ianua obvios servorum abripit, donec ad fores cubiculi veniret; cui pauci adstabant, ceteris terrore inrumpentium exterritis.
>
> 14.8.2

> Anicetus surrounded the villa with sentries. He demolished the gate and seized the slaves he encountered, eventually reaching Agrippina's bedroom door.

Up to this point, the reader has been watching the scene unfold from Anicetus' eyes. Tacitus thus focalizes the narrative first through Anicetus and his men, and then through Agrippina. Agrippina becomes focalizer just as Anicetus is about to enter her chambers. The change in focalization is effected nicely with the use of *cubiculi* ... *cubiculo* as a transition, taking the narrative from outside the bedroom doors to the inside of the bedroom itself. Tacitus then sets the stage in the bedroom.

> cubiculo modicum lumen inerat et ancillarum una, magis ac magis anxia Agrippina, quod nemo a filio ac ne Agermus quidem: aliam fore laetae rei faciem; nunc solitudinem ac repentinos strepitus et extremi mali indicia. abeunte dehinc ancilla 'tu quoque me deseris?' prolocuta.
>
> 14.8.3–4

> In the bedroom there was a modest light, a single slave girl. Agrippina was more and more anxious at there being no one from her son, not even Agermus. *A happy outcome would look otherwise than solitude and sudden noises and indications of the worst.* When the girl started to leave, "*You too desert me?*" she cried.

The tension in this scene is dramatic. Agrippina has ceased to be merely worried and has become an object of pity, a transition reminiscent of the senatorial accounts in the Tiberian books. The reader is made to assume her position and to feel some of the loneliness implicit in her simple question to her maid. This rapid change in focalization makes us fear the worst for Agrippina, as we have already seen Nero's thoughts, as well as the actions of Anicetus. Once the narrative moves inside the bedroom, Tacitus describes the scene with cinematically poignant touches. The small light and a single maid are all that is left of Agrippina's army of slaves and freedmen (*modicum lumen inerat et ancillarum una*). Through focalization, Tacitus allows the reader to see and experience Agrippina's anxieties, again moving seamlessly from the description of a character to her inner thoughts without a verb to alert the reader to this change. As her anxiety increases, Agrippina catalogues her surroundings rhetorically in a tricolon, ascending not only in number of syllables, but in ominous nature: *solitudinem* ... *repentinos strepitus* ... *extremi mali indicia*. Already the reader can sense her approaching doom, but Tacitus gives a further emotional touch. As her maid leaves, Agrippina asks the heartbreaking "*tu quoque me deseris*?" For possibly the only time, the reader feels true pity for Agrippina, abandoned and alone, waiting for her inevitable death. Tacitus achieves, through focalization, an extremely brief but powerful character vignette just before her demise.

After her question, Agrippina looks around to see that her murderers are already beside her in the room, without the necessity of an entrance.[57]

> respicit Anicetum trierarcho Herculeio et Obarito centurione classiario comitatum: ac, si ad visendum venisset, refotam nuntiaret, sin facinus patraturus, nihil se de filio credere; non imperatum parricidium.
>
> 14.8.4

> And [she] turned to see Anicetus, accompanied by ship captain Herculeius and fleet centurion Obaritus. *If you are paying a call, report me recovered. But if you intend to accomplish the deed—I don't believe it of my son. No order has been given for kin-murder!*

Agrippina, seemingly unflustered, challenges her assailants (again without a verb of speaking). This time, however, Tacitus, removing us from the victim briefly, has put the dialogue in *oratio obliqua*. The most desperate portion of Agrippina's statement is her last clause (*non imperatum parricidium*), which recalls her fears at the murder of Britannicus ([*Agrippina*] *quippe sibi supremum auxilium ereptum et parricidii exemplum intellegebat*. 13.16.4). Immediately after these words, Agrippina is murdered.

Following Agrippina's death, Tacitus briefly sums up other accounts about Nero's treatment of the body, the funeral, and her burial. At the end of this, Tacitus relates a story which states that Agrippina knew she would meet just such an end. When Chaldaean seers had prophesied that Nero would become emperor and kill his mother, Tacitus has her reply in direct speech "Let him slaughter, provided he achieves command!" (*atque illa "occidat" inquit, "dum imperet."* 14.9.3). With these posthumous words, Agrippina leaves the narrative without even a brief summary obituary. Following Agrippina's quotable answer the scene pointedly cuts to a concluding shot of Nero, as the narrative of Agrippina's murder, which began the book, draws to a close.

> sed a Caesare perfecto demum scelere magnitudo eius intellecta est. reliquo noctis modo per silentium defixus, saepius pavore exsurgens et mentis inops lucem opperiebatur tamquam exitium adlaturam.
>
> 14.10.1
>
> Nero only realized the crime's magnitude when it was complete. The rest of the night, sometimes in silence, rooted, more often panic-spurred and witless, he awaited daylight thinking it would bring ruin.

Tacitus here paints Nero as a fearful but unrepentant murderer, recalling something of the Greek tragedies which Nero loved to enact. This description tells the reader much more than an authorial statement, showing that Nero was only sorry he might be caught for this recent crime. After this scene there is the aftermath of the murder, including the sycophancy of the senate, as well as of other cities, to the triumphant Nero.

This long series of focalizations, rapidly changing from person to person, gives the reader the optimal vantage point for the exchange and also increases narrative tension.[58] The reader is always at the center of the action, whether watching Nero as he plans, worries or laments, experiencing Agrippina's worry and terror, or seeing the haphazard boat fiasco along with the confused, though complicit, rowers. By employing a narrative technique parallel to the shot-reverse-shot, Tacitus raises the emotional level of the narrative to a high pitch, which peaks with Agrippina's last words. A master of emotion and suspense, Tacitus uses this device expertly, and, as a result, the reader does not notice the repeated and sudden changes in focalization, and is instead carried along with the emotional flow of the story. As scholars, it is instructive for us to note the deft skill with which Tacitus changes perspective and focalizers, channeling through different characters in order to deliver the best view of the scene. As has been recognized in the realm of film studies, the use of focalization is only successful when it is well assimilated into the framing narrative,[59] and here Tacitus does so seamlessly.

Final Thoughts

In this chapter, we have examined Tacitus' use of focalization to direct the reader's gaze, thereby gaining access to the thoughts and perspectives of his various characters. As we have seen, focalization has powerful effects on the reader, including the development of a relationship between reader and focalizer, the creation of empathetic sentiment, the formation of guilt or complicity, and the building of narrative tension. Often the thoughts of the character (in the *Annales*, usually a member of the rogues' gallery), are laid bare to the reader's gaze. This exposure gives the reader knowledge withheld from the other characters in the *Annales*, creating not only heightened suspense but, more problematically, a feeling of collusion with the villain focalizer. This internal discomfort, experienced by the reader, is important not only because of the emotional effect it creates in the context of the narrative, but also the subtext it offers to the historical account; specifically, the unease experienced by the reader in becoming a party to the villain's plans is in some measure the same type of discomfort felt by Roman senators living under, and forced to comply with, tyrannical emperors and their decrees.

Tacitus' adroit use of multiple focalizers, and his ability to switch rapidly between their accounts, is highly reminiscent of the shot-reverse-shot of classical Hollywood cinema. While the same kind of effect is achieved in Roman static art, such as the Pompeiian Ariadne, painted art is limited in its ability to direct the gaze on cue. Multiple, often interconnected, conversations of gaze are possible in static art, but only film provides a suitable visual context to illustrate Tacitus' tightly controlled, quickly changing narrative focalization. Through careful use of this technique, the reader is made to identify with both villain and hero, deepening his or her involvement in a scene and bringing to life the action therein described. Focalization is one of the ways Tacitus "illustrates" his *enargeia* bringing his readers into the visual and dramatic *monumenta* of his work. As illustrated by the examples of this chapter, this technique, whether called a literary device or the shot-reverse-shot, is just as powerful in the twenty-first century as it was in the second.

2

Vox Caesaris, Vox Taciti: Imperial Alignment

From the first lines of the *Annales*, Tacitus shows that his narrative, and all histories of the early principate, are inextricably tied to the Julio-Claudian emperors (1.1.2, *temporibus Augusti . . . Tiberii Gaique et Claudii ac Neronis res*). With this beginning, Tacitus signals that his *Annales* will not be the history of a people from its foundations, but instead that the stamp of each emperor will color the events of his reign. While the early principate is discussed in overall unfavorable and inauspicious terms, the emperors themselves are portrayed as highly individual and varied. The scholarly but unworldly Claudius governed by his wives and freedman is a far cry from the histrionics of Nero or the quiet legalistic menace of Tiberius.[1] Tacitus, a consummate writer as well as an outstanding historian, employs a number of intriguing and subtle narrative techniques that enable him to convey not only the surface account of his history, but to engage his readers in a level of deep, emotional, and visceral understanding of life under these rulers.

In order to provide insight into the personality and persona of the early emperors, Tacitus mobilizes the literary device which I will call "alignment." Alignment and focalization are two of the key components of what is generally (and loosely) referred to as "point of view." Alignment is specifically concerned with the question of "who speaks," and is distinct from focalization in its use and effect on the reader. While focalization allows us a brief glimpse into a character's gaze and thoughts, alignment does not alter our perspective directly, but instead colors the narrative through a twinning of the authorial voice and the interests (and, in some cases, the syntax) of a particular character. For example, alignment may occur when an author, discussing a character with private interests in gardening, includes discursive discussions on horticulture during unrelated portions of the narrative. In the *Annales* Tacitus' use of alignment occurs uniquely during digressions, which is particularly notable, since in this type of authorial aside the reader generally expects to find impartial historical material. Thus, when Tacitus instead aligns his narrative voice with that of a character, the result can be both disorienting and confusing. In these instances Tacitus' comforting authorial voice, which, following historical convention we are accustomed to trust, is subsumed by the personality of the current emperor. In this chapter, we will be looking at Tacitus' uses of this technique in order to align with, and thus speak "as if" in the position of, the emperors.

Excursus, Voice, and Alignment

Excursus and digression were very much a part of Roman rhetoric and historiography.[2] These breaks from the narrative did not substitute for notes or appendices, but were an integral and expected aspect of ancient historiography. The historian was encouraged to vary the main narrative with digressions in order to maintain audience involvement, by providing additional relevant material tangential to the narrative. Herodotus, for example, often links his excurses with the flow of his main narrative: as Persia contemplates the conquest of Egypt, Herodotus stops the forward motion of his account for a book-long digression on the country, its people, religion, and strange-but-true facts.[3] Cicero, in his *Brutus*, laments that there are no Romans who know how to please their audience with digression (*nemo qui delectandi gratia digredi parumper a causa*).[4] A particularly famous example of a lengthy excursus in pre-Tacitean Roman historiography occurs in book 9 of Livy's *History*.[5] At the beginning of this long digression, Livy denies that he intends to provide the reader with a welcome side-narrative (*deverticula amoena*),[6] but that seems precisely what he is attempting to do as he plays alternative history, questioning the likely outcome of a war between Alexander and Rome. Livy's mention of pleasure as a possible motivation for including an excursus shows that ancient readers both anticipated and appreciated these diversions in ancient historiography.

Tacitus, no less than Livy, occasionally breaks the narrative flow of his history by introducing an excursus.[7] By including a speech, trial, or descriptions, Tacitus can slow the tempo of his history, and also provide a much-needed break or change of pace from treason trials and forced suicides.[8] These excurses also allow Tacitus to vary the narrative and provide some entertainment for his readers. In some instances, however, Tacitus mobilizes his excurses to enhance the ominous tone of the surrounding narrative.[9] For example, Tiberius' reign is interrupted by a questionable sighting of the phoenix in Egypt, and Nero's is similarly paused by a farcical treasure hunt in Africa.[10] While these tangential episodes appear lighthearted, the placement of both of these examples enables

Tacitus to execute sudden and dramatic juxtapositions of the City, beleaguered by its bloodthirsty emperors.[11] Tacitus uses excurses in a wide array of situations, and is thereby able to create complex effects, but in order to fully understand the impact of each instance we must first examine Tacitus' use of narrative voice.

Alignment

As discussed in the introduction, narrative voice deals with the question of "who speaks."[12] The narrator's voice can be understood to change as different speakers take over the narrative, although the modification of narrative voice is much more common in modern fiction than in ancient historiography. In ancient historiography, the narrative is normally dominated by the historian, who is deemed master of his historical facts as well as the employed literary effects. The generation and maintenance of this historiographical authority is a central issue in historical writing of all periods, particularly in antiquity.[13] In line with the genre of history, Tacitus' narratorial voice is generally that of an omniscient third person, who is able to see the outcomes of events and occasionally enter the minds of his characters through focalization.

Tacitus uses this consistent, authoritative narrative voice during the vast majority of the *Annales*, including in many of his digressions. A wonderful example of this is Tacitus' discussion of imperial historiography in book 4 (4.32.1–33.4). Tacitus here breaks the narrative to compare imperial historiography with its Republican counterpart, to the apparent disadvantage of his own history. The fact that this is written in the historian's authorial voice is made clear by the repeated use of the first person throughout the passage: *sum ... nobis ... nos ... coniungimus ... redeo.*[14] Thus, Tacitus uses his authorial voice not only to provide a removed, third-party account, but also, by moving into the first person, to add his opinions or thoughts directly. As has often been pointed out, this excursus actually ties in thematically to the trial of the historian Cremutius Cordus, which follows immediately afterward (4.34.1–35.5).[15] Tacitus thus, like Herodotus, can use digression that seems arbitrary and merely tangential to the narrative, only to reveal its importance during a subsequent scene.

Tacitus is not restricted to these applications of the authorial voice, however, and in a number of his digressions elects, for rhetorical impact, to employ an alternative style. Another voice used in many of the excurses in the *Annales* is that of indirect speech, taken explicitly from one of the characters. An example of this would be Claudius' discussion concerning the granting of immunity from taxation to the island of Cos (12.61.1–2). Again, Tacitus marks this passage as a reported speech of Claudius with the introductory verb of speaking, *memoravit*. Note that in this digression, Tacitus is very clear about the source of the words relayed, indicating that they form a portion of Claudius' speech and are not the opinions or comments of the author. These are the usual voices of historical narrative: the author as commentator and narrator, the author in his own person, and the author relaying, either through direct or indirect speech, the thoughts or words of a character.

On occasion, however, Tacitus steps outside the normal, expected realm of historical narration. In order to add additional layers of meaning to the *Annales*, and to bring his readers emotionally (if, perhaps, only subconsciously) into the world of his history, Tacitus occasionally elides his narrative voice with that of a character during these digressions, becoming what a narratologist would term an "unreliable narrator." According to Gerald Prince, the unreliable narrator is one "whose account is undermined by various features of that account."[16] This term commonly applies to narrators who are found to be lying, forgetful, or insane, during the course of a story, forcing the reader to doubt the truth of all that has gone before. The reader, after this realization, might feel disoriented, at a loss, or betrayed in some way. Often, there is enough information revealed for the reader to know or guess at the truth that the narrator is hiding or has forgotten, or never knew. The narrator, the guide through the story, has been shown to be untrustworthy, and the structure of the narrative must change as a result. In the case of the *Annales*, Tacitus aligns his normally-authoritative voice to mirror the thoughts or feelings of a character, without employing reported speech. Thus, Tacitus "becomes" the character for a moment, which is deeply disorienting for the reader and calls into question the veracity and historical remove of the account.

Tacitus' subversion of his authorial voice intentionally causes these unsettling reactions in his readers. When a reader encounters an excursive passage told through an altered voice, the impact is vivid and effective, both because it is unexpected and because there is a shocking disruption of the implicit bond of trust between reader and historian. The reader of the *Annales*, by the time he or she encounters a narrative aside, has become accustomed to Tacitus' usual authorial voice and the level of confidence which can be placed in material encountered in this fashion. When that narrative expectation is upset through authorial alignment, as in the examples we will be considering, the reader is placed in a difficult and precarious position. The reader no longer knows whether to trust the narrator of the passage and, in keeping with the ongoing theme of the *Annales*, is placed in a position akin to the senators of history—unsure of how to interpret the words of the historian/emperor, and fearful of changes that can take place at any moment and without warning.

When employing the device of alignment, Tacitus often elides his voice with that of the emperors. The most striking examples of these elisions occur in the reigns of Tiberius and Claudius. Under Tiberius, Tacitus becomes highly concerned with Roman law and Augustan precedent, and under Claudius, rambles repeatedly over scholarly questions, often losing the main thread of the discussion in ever-spiraling digressions. In these excurses Tacitus becomes an unreliable narrator by changing his own voice into that of a specific character. Through this device, Tacitus creates a brief but effective affinity between the emperors, himself, and the reader. The reader thus enters a liminal area between modernity and history, between commentary and description. Tacitus has moved his own authorial voice into an uncomfortably close harmony with the Caesars, and his reader is caught on the edge of trust and fear as Tiberian history is experienced first-hand.

Pompeian Narcissus

The Roman viewer was also aware of the concept of alignment, which is evident from a selection of the highly nuanced and complex art images preserved from antiquity. In the first chapter, we looked at the challenged gaze in the context of a fresco painting of the myth of Ariadne, in order to illustrate the use of focalization in Roman art. Here, we will again consider an image from Pompeii, which can aid us in understanding the concept of alignment as it was portrayed in the ancient world.

One of the most interesting, and also most philosophically challenging, myth-images from the Roman world is the Narcissus, which mobilizes a number of different emotional and intellectual themes in its portrayal.[17] This is due in part to artistic influence, but also because the story of Narcissus itself questions our notions of beauty, attraction, self-awareness, and identity. In the myth, a beautiful young man fell in love with his own image reflected in a pool. Rather than find interest in any other pursuit, he wasted away in front of the pool and was transformed into a small flower which, to this day, bears his name.[18]

The depictions we have from antiquity, in the main, follow one of only a few standard types. There is Narcissus shown alone beside the pool, Narcissus and Eros, and the trio depiction of Narcissus, Eros, and Echo.[19] Narcissus is shown either fully or nearly nude, which is openly suggestive and offers the viewer an opportunity to appreciate his form. Just as Narcissus experiences sexual desire in the context of his gaze, we (the viewer) are invited to do likewise. Thus, even at this first level of engagement with the art piece, our view is aligning in important ways with that of the fully internal gaze of Narcissus himself.

The second aspect of the gaze at play is clearly visible in Fig. 2.1, a picture of the Fresco of Narcissus from the Casa di M. Loreius Tiburtinus (Pompeii, II.2.2), and this is the reflection in the pool.[20] This complex image needs to be unpacked, especially with an eye toward the problematic role of the external viewer. When approaching a work of art, the viewer experiences what is shown, and forms a mental concept of the piece. It is this subjective interpretation that guides the formation of meaning. The piece is only fully experienced on this subjective, internal level. This is important in the context of the Narcissus, since the entire purpose of the piece is to watch the subject's gaze. We see Narcissus depicted in the process of gazing longingly at his reflection in the water. The image that he sees is made meaningful within his mind, where he transforms the sensed image into an object of affection. This, Narcissus' own mental process, is what the external spectator first observes when viewing the piece.

The external viewer, however, is also engaging in the same internal-processing mechanism; the image of the Narcissus painting is internalized and considered. As Narcissus contemplates his own image, we contemplate his. He sees himself mirrored in the water, and therefore we must ask ourselves whether we see a personal reflection in our own view. By watching Narcissus, are we watching ourselves?

This question is made even more directly challenging in this rendition of the myth, as Narcissus appears to look at us rather than into the pool. In this way, the questions posed by the painting become direct and pointed; we feel uncomfortable with our own voyeurism, unsure whether we should be watching this scene, as well as concerned by what we see reflected through our gaze. This is, however, not the most troubling aspect, as we also appear to be watched by the face reflected in the pool. This reflection, by staring back at us rather than appearing to mirror Narcissus, further questions our role as viewer. If the reflection is tracking us, are we the subject that is being mirrored and, by extension, have we become one with Narcissus?

In order to understand the full impact of this image, we must also consider the context in which it was originally displayed. The Narcissus painting comes from the interior terrace of a Pompeiian house, which contained a nymphaeum flanked by two masonry dining couches. There are two frescos, with one on

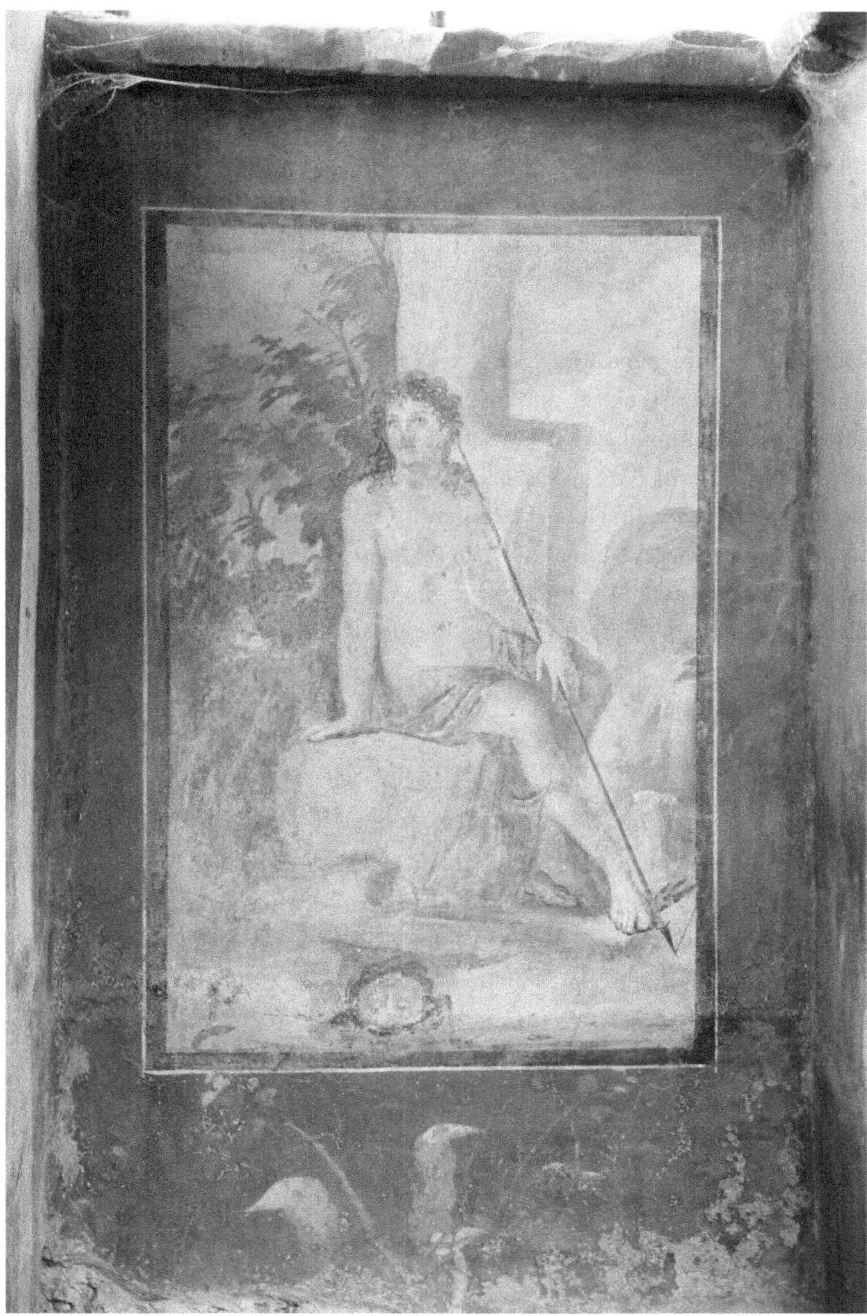

Figure 2.1 Fresco of Narcissus from the Casa di M. Loreius Tiburtinus (Pompeii, II.2.2), photograph by Yasemin Olgunoz Berber/Shutterstock.com

either side of an aedicula niche. On the right is the Narcissus, and on the left a related painting of Pyramus and Thisbe.[21] Thus, a diner reclining on the couch before the painting of Narcissus would look into the reflecting pool in much the same way as the mythical youth shown on the wall behind. The parallel between the occupant of the couch and the Narcissus of the image is evident, but complex. If a viewer were to walk into this dining room while in use, s/he would see life imitating art, and specifically, an artistic image that itself depicts the dangers of reflection and imitation.

The Narcissus painting threatens our concept of personal gaze because we, like Narcissus, are made aware of the risks inherent in viewing. By accepting the image of an external object, and internally changing it through our perceptions into a representation that holds meaning or significance, we have participated in a transformative act. We, on some level, have merged with that image and it has become a part of us. That loss of self-identity or self-boundary is directly brought into play in the Narcissus image, when we must ask ourselves to what degree we have become one with the internal viewing "other." The viewer, aligned with the doomed subject in the painting, is momentarily disoriented by, and very likely troubled with, the loss of normal boundaries. In the *Annales*, Tacitus uses alignment to this exact same effect.

Murder, My Sweet

Tacitus' use of alignment, at base, has many of the same disturbing effects on the reader that focalization has, but to a much greater degree. In a sense, Tacitus withdraws the narrative voice to which the reader has become accustomed, only to replace it with that of the emperor. The reader, as a result, is unsettled by the alignment between narrator and narrated.[22] I posit that the best analogy for modern readers of Tacitus' *Annales* as to how alignment of author and subject matter would have been understood by a first-century audience is found in certain directorial effects in film.

An example of this alignment between narrator and character is found in Dmytryk's *Murder, My Sweet* (1944). In the film, a version of Raymond Chandler's *Farewell, My Lovely*, Philip Marlowe (Dick Powell), a private investigator, is on the track of a vanished woman and a priceless jade necklace. At a crucial point in the narrative, Marlowe is knocked unconscious and subsequently drugged. When Marlowe wakes, he is lying in a hospital bed alone in a room, and the gray filaments that he describes as either smoke or spiders' webs still fill his vision.

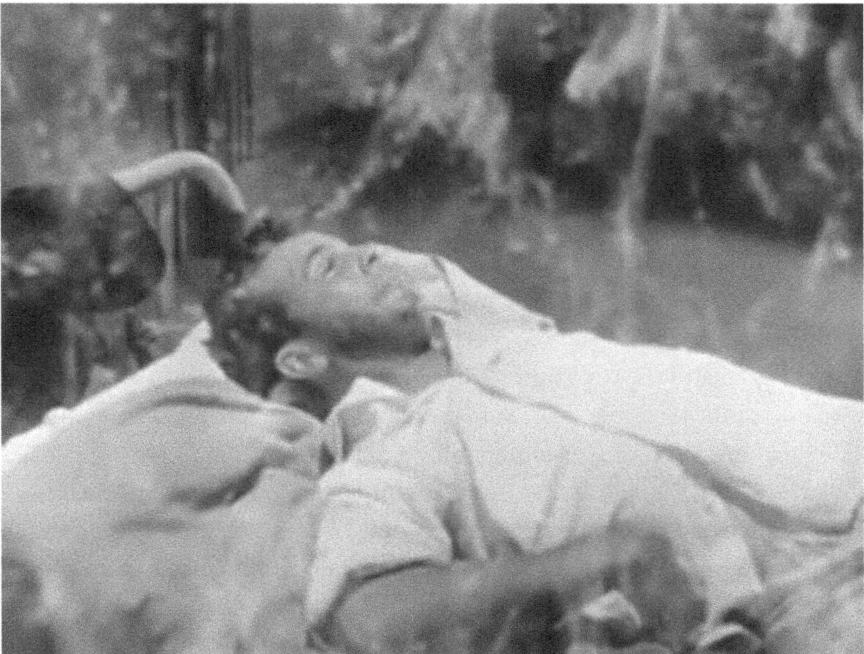

Figure 2.2 *Murder, My Sweet*, directed by Edward Dmytryk © RKO Radio Pictures 1944.

In an interesting filming choice, the viewer also sees the smoke, which overlays the shot.[23] As Marlowe's head clears, the screen clears. This sequence is not in Marlowe's point of view, but is still filmed in the usual third-person mid-range shot. The viewer, therefore, is made to feel Marlowe's visual confusion, but not to share his view.[24]

In this way, the audience's experience aligns with Marlowe's sympathetically, giving us not only a visual cue to what Marlowe is seeing, but forcing us to experience the world in Marlowe's idiom, although not through his eyes. Since we are forced to identify with the hero, this change to visual alignment is only disconcerting rather than morally repugnant, as it would be in the case of a villain. The use of alignment in this way invites us, the viewers, to consider the situation in which Marlowe finds himself, and to ask what we would do in that situation. How would we attempt to escape when our vision, too, is impaired? We experience his world alongside and with him, heightening our emotional engagement and concern for his continued survival.

Tacitus uses alignment in a very similar way, as his readers are discomfited by the sudden alignment of the trusted historian and the distrusted emperors. The result is disorienting, as the reader is no longer sure whether the account is reliable, and whether to trust the narrator's statements. This device not only places us in the position of the Roman senators, who must read through the lines to understand and interpret imperial intent, but also forces us to ask whether the perspective of the Caesars is so strange after all.

Tiberius: The (Mis)Rule of Law

The image that Tacitus conjures when he aligns with Tiberius is that of an emperor deeply interested in Roman law and its practice.[25] Tacitus quotes Tiberius, praying that the gods grant him "a quiet mind cognizant of human and divine law" (4.38.3, *quietam et intellegentem humani divinique iuris mentem*). When employing the device of alignment with Tiberius, then, Tacitus adopts the language of jurisprudence, pays particular attention to Augustan decrees, and shows a marked interested in legal affairs. This characterization, however, would only have been effective as a basis for narrative alignment if Tacitus' original audience was familiar with this proclivity of the emperor.

Tiberius and Justice

The clearest picture of Tiberius' almost slavish reliance on Augustan precedent comes from the *Annales* themselves.[26] That said, two additional authors address the issue: Suetonius and Velleius Paterculus. Suetonius, a near contemporary of Tacitus, wrote multiple biographies, most famously those of the first twelve *principes*: the Twelve Caesars. While Suetonius was a biographer rather than a historian, he also depicts a Tiberius fascinated with justice and the courts. Furthermore, his opinions on Tiberius reflect a tradition uninfluenced by Tacitus, as there is no reason to suppose that Suetonius based his own biography of Tiberius on the *Annales*.[27] In his *Life of Tiberius*, Suetonius records that Tiberius was fascinated with justice and law:

> itaque et constitutiones senatus quasdam rescidit et magistratibus pro tribunali cognoscentibus plerumque se offerebat consiliarium assidebatque iuxtim vel exadversum in parte primori. et si quem reorum elabi gratia rumor esset, subitus aderat iudicesque aut e plano aut e quaesitoris tribunali legum et religionis et noxae de qua cognoscerent admonebat.
>
> Suetonius, *Tib.* 33[28]

Thus he revoked some regulations of the senate and sometimes offered the magistrates his services as adviser, when they sat in judgment on the tribunal, taking his place beside them or opposite them at one end of the platform; and if it was rumoured that any of the accused were being acquitted through influence, he would suddenly appear, and either from the floor or from the judge's tribunal remind the jurors of the laws and of their oath, as well as of the nature of the crime on which they were sitting in judgment.

Tiberius, in this selection, sounds much like a conscientious judge as he corrects perceived judicial lapses in the courts. The emperor, says Suetonius, was so concerned that justice be done that even the rumor of impropriety would cause him to remind the senators of their obligations under the law. An emperor naturally has an interest in ensuring the laws and the courts run well, but Tiberius' judicial dedication seems to rise beyond a passing familiarity. Moreover, Suetonius is not our only evidence; the Tiberian contemporary Velleius Paterculus also recalled Tiberius' manner when listening to court cases.[29]

Cum quanta gravitate, ut senator et iudex, non ut princeps <...> et causas pressius audit!

Velleius 2.129.2[30]

With what seriousness did he listen closely to pleadings <...> as senator and jury-member not as emperor!

Velleius here describes a dual ambition of Tiberius, which is echoed in Suetonius, to be both on equal footing with the other senators during legal proceedings, and to be knowledgeable in law and justice.[31] As emperor, Velleius tells us, Tiberius was more interested in participating in law and court cases as a fellow senator and juror, rather than in weighing in as a final judge in his role as *princeps*. This image, of a just and fair *princeps*, is one that Tiberius might well have sought to have publicized about himself, either through Velleius' writing or through such media as inscriptions or coinage.

Tiberius was sufficiently interested in his reputation as a legal expert to include the adjective *iustissimus*, which appears in epigraphy, as part of his imperial titulature. An example of this comes from the via Flaminia:

Ti. Caesari divi Augusti f. Augusto pontif. maximo, cos. V, trib. potest. XXXIIII, principi optumo ac iustissimo, conservatori patriae.

ILS 159 = CIL 11.3872[32]

To Tiberius Caesar, son of the Deified Augustus, Pontifex Maximus, Consul for the fifth time, holder of Tribunicia Potestas for the thirty-fourth year, best and most just Princeps, protector of the fatherland.

While this inscription was set up by a private individual, it reflects the opinions and ideals of its time. That the phrase "most just" is included in the praises, titles, and honors associated with Tiberius is highly suggestive. It would seem, especially in light of our other evidence, that Tiberius was indeed concerned with his appearance as a fair and just law-maker, both during his own lifetime and for posterity.

Tiberius' desire to be connected with ideas of law and justice is also readily apparent in the emperor's coinage. Numismatic messages were some of the most durable and widely spread across time and space in antiquity. As long as the coin existed, the owner/viewer could be reminded of the maker's intent, either through words or through images. Two coins (examples of the same type), currently in the British Museum, show on the obverse (facing side) a large SC, surrounded on the edge by Tiberius' titulature: TI·CAESAR·DIVI·AUG·F·AUG·P·M·TR· POT·XXIIII.[33] The face of these coins tells us much about Tiberius' self-presentation. The focal point of the facing side is SC (*senatus consulto*), showing that the coins were minted by order of the Senate. Tiberius' insistence on the authority of the Senate is here reaffirmed visually. Tiberius' titles recall his own position as holder of the tribunician power, the title Augustus, and the highest Roman priesthood—all inherited from Augustus, whose relationship with his son is also celebrated. On the reverse of the coins is a woman in profile with diadem, with the legend IUSTITIA underneath. It is noteworthy that a visual representation of Tiberius does not appear on the coins. The overwhelming messages are that the Senate is in control, and that justice is paramount, with Tiberius as emperor.[34]

With all of these examples both from literature and inscriptions, we can safely infer that Tiberius' legal pretensions were familiar to the readers of the *Annales*. This is important to bear in mind when we encounter the examples of Tacitean alignment in the next four sections, as the changes between Tacitus' authorial voice and the justice-focused, law-obsessed Tiberius are often swift and abrupt.

Lex Maiestatis

Tacitus first aligns with Tiberius in an excursus near the end of the first book of the *Annales*. At this point in the narrative, Tiberius has just refused many sycophantic measures voted on him by the senate, including the title of "Father of his Country" and the oath of senatorial obedience to all of his enactments (1.72.1). Tacitus, however, is quick to undercut Tiberius' humility with the following statement: "But [Tiberius] did not thereby gain credit for a citizen-like attitude, for he had brought back the treason law" (1.72.2, *non tamen ideo faciebat fidem civilis animi; nam legem maiestatis reduxerat*). This statement encapsulates much of what characterizes the narrative of the *Annales* and Tacitus' writings more generally: swift narrative movement, instantaneous changes in tone, undercutting through juxtaposition, effective use of foreshadowing, and ending clauses with brief-but-telling phrases or statements.[35] Tacitus, seeming to continue the flow of the discussion, begins the excursus and imperial alignment with a gloss on the law of treason (*maiestas*):

> cui nomen apud veteres idem, sed alia in iudicium veniebant: si quis proditione exercitum <a>ut plebem seditionibus, denique male gesta re publica maiestatem populi Romani minuisset: facta arguebantur, dicta impune erant. primus Augustus cognitionem de famosis libellis specie legis eius tractavit, commotus Cassii Severi libidine, qua viros feminasque inlustres procacibus scriptis diffamaverat; mox Tiberius, consultante Pompeio Macro praetore an iudicia maiestatis redderentur, exercendas leges esse respondit.
>
> 1.72.2–3

> Its name was the same in the past, but the cases before the court were different: men who damaged the army by betrayal or the populace with seditions or, by conducting state business improperly, diminished the majesty of the Roman people. Deeds were accused, words had impunity. Augustus was the first to hold a hearing about libellous pamphlets under this law's pretext. He was dismayed by Cassius Severus' wantonness, which prompted defamatory attacks on notable men and women. Then Tiberius, when asked by the praetor Pompeius Macer whether to hear treason cases, replied: *Laws are to be used.*

In this passage, Tacitus begins with a description of the original law under the Republic, when *maiestas* applied only to serious matters involving betrayal of Roman arms, sedition of the plebs, and/or blanket charges of maladministration. Tacitus' description of the Republican law ends with the summary of the differences in the *lex* between Republic and Principate: critically, under the Republic, speech was immune from the effects of the law (*dicta inpune erant*). Tacitus' ominous statement thus foreshadows the later expansion (and abuse) of this law, and its unfortunate effects. Tacitus continues his comments on the law, chronicling its extension under Augustus to cover defamation.[36] This expansion underscores the Augustan perception that imperial control was necessary to maintain public morals, as well as signals Tiberius' respect for continuing Augustan legal precedent.

In this passage, the reader sees the situation much as Tiberius would have seen it at the time. Through the use of alignment, Tacitus adopts Tiberius' interests, providing the reader with a narrative voice assimilated to the voice of the emperor. Tiberius was a student of Roman law, both of the senate and the lower courts.[37] The reader can easily imagine Tiberius, skilled in Roman law as he was, using the material in this excursus in a discussion on Roman legal precedent. In much the same way as we align with the view of Narcissus as he watches his pool, Tacitus has dissolved into the mind and persona of Tiberius, leaving us (his readers) both disoriented and unsettled.

Given the Augustan precedent, Tiberius would be impelled, and justified, to follow his predecessor's legal example. The Tiberius portrayed by Tacitus could hardly answer otherwise to Macer's question: the laws must be upheld. Law and justice were of paramount importance to Tiberius, and questioning them (or looking askance at their full observation) would be disrespectful to the memory of Augustus. By answering in this fashion, Tiberius could also appear to follow in the best traditions of Republican senatorial practices.[38] Augustus' example, as Tacitus explicitly states, weighed very heavily with Tiberius, and he would be unlikely to deviate from Augustan practice without excellent reasons.[39]

An additional layer of alignment is also at play in this instance, which concerns the reader's engagement with the Tacitus/Tiberius narrator. When Tacitus' authoritative narrative voice is subsumed into Tiberian idiom, the reader is temporarily left without a guide. In this instance, having been offered an explanation for the reasons behind the change to the law under Augustus, and thus more able to understand Tiberius' potential thoughts on the subject, the reader is placed in a challenging position: does the reader adopt the views of the aligned Tacitus/Tiberius or, recognizing the unsettling nature of the passage, instead step back and reserve judgment? If the reader accepts the aligned narrator then, in effect, the reader has also aligned with the emperor Tiberius. When this occurs, the reader must question whether Tiberius was indeed so wrong in his decisions. Much as the viewer of *Murder, My Sweet* shares the perceptions of the drugged Marlowe and thereby comes to understand his situation, the aligned reader comes to accept aspects of Tiberius' reasoning through a sharing of knowledge.

The narratological effect of this passage is quickly and purposefully shattered in the next section, as Tacitus gives his own judgment (in his authorial voice) on Tiberius' motivations for re-introducing the *lex maiestatis*.[40] Moving from the aligned to the objective, Tacitus gives the externally viewed, implied reason for Tiberius' ready assent to Macer's questions:

> hunc quoque asperavere carmina incertis auctoribus vulgata in saevitiam superbiamque eius et discordem cum matre animum.
>
> 1.72.4

> He, too, was provoked by poems, published under dubious names, about his brutality and arrogance and misunderstandings with his mother.

Tacitus here returns to his own narrative voice, undercutting the excursus by the sudden revelation that the reader has been lured into Tiberian sentiments through the use of alignment. The nature of the conversation, and both the import and intended use of law, have been inverted and revealed. Viewed by an outside (and, perhaps, somewhat cynical) third party, the issue is no longer one of precedent, but a matter of insult and retaliation. Tacitus, in his own authoritative voice, portrays Tiberius as using an existing law for his own savage ends.[41] This is spelled out explicitly in the immediately following sentence, in which Tacitus gives two test cases for Tiberius' use of the *lex maiestatis*.

> haud pigebit referre in Faianio et Rubrio, modicis equitibus Romanis, praetemptata crimina, ut quibus initiis quanta Tiberii arte gravissimum exitium inrepserit, dein repressum sit, postremo arserit cunctaque corripuerit, noscatur.
>
> 1.73.1

> I am not averse to reporting the preliminary charges attempted against Faianius and Rubrius, men of modest equestrian rank, so that people know from what beginnings and with what strategy on Tiberius' part an utterly ruinous affliction crept in, was checked, then blazed forth and took hold of everything.

The judicial murders which darken and eventually consume the Tiberian principate are directly foreshadowed, and their blame is laid squarely on Tiberius' shoulders. Tacitus notes that the law would have been dangerous at any rate, but it is made lethal by Tiberius' subtlety and skill (*quanta Tiberii arte*).

In these passages, then, Tacitus has aligned his narrative voice with Tiberius, providing the audience with insight into the emperor's thought processes, values, and reasoning. Immediately after securing this connection between Tacitus/Tiberius and the sympathies of the reader, the illusion is shattered as Tacitus pulls away from the trio, castigating the motives of Tiberius and suggesting petty, selfish reasons for his actions. The reader is thus left with two strong impressions about the reasons behind, and true inspiration for, the expansion of the *maiestas* law. Through alignment, the reader has been made to see inside the thoughts of Tiberius, making his noble and worthy, idealistic reasoning for the law seem plausible, and yet Tacitus' bitingly aggressive reproach also feels believable as it is conveyed in the author's authoritative voice. The reader, then, does not know which version of "history" to trust, and is left in an extremely uncomfortable position. Unsure who is correct, the reader is thrown into a state of confusion analogous to the turmoil of the senators living under the early emperors, a situation Tacitus engineers through the expert use of narratological techniques. Nearly two millennia later, Edward Dmytryk was able to achieve the same type of effect through the use of alignment, altering the audience's quality of vision to mirror that of the recovering Marlowe. Akin to the film audience, we are left with an impression of Tiberius' thinking and beliefs when the camera cuts away to a different and disorienting perspective.

Rule of Law

The next occasion when Tacitus aligns his narratorial voice with Tiberius occurs in the third book of the *Annales*. Here, the excursus is prefaced by a discussion of the *lex* Pappia Poppaea:

> relatum dein de moderanda Papia Poppaea, quam senior Augustus post Iulias rogationes incitandis caelibum poenis et augendo aerario sanxerat.
>
> 3.25.1

> The next business was moderating the Papia/Poppaea law, which an elderly Augustus enacted after the Julian laws to encourage penalties for the unmarried and to increase revenue.

This law, part of Augustus' program to increase the number of (elite) children, was unsuccessful in its aim. Rather, the law gave a greater opportunity to informers reporting on those who violated it. The irony of this passage is especially poignant in Tacitus' use of *augendo* in such proximity to Augustus. By this pairing, Tacitus creates a *figura etymologica*, playing on the similarity between the name of Augustus and the word *augendo*, suggesting that the emperor is "Augustus-ing" the treasury in his (eventually unsuccessful) attempt to increase imperial funds.[42] Tacitus then delivers a *sententia*, one of the brief, pithy comments for which he is well-known, and proceeds immediately into a long excursus on Roman law:

> utque antehac flagitiis ita tunc legibus laborabatur. ea res admonet, ut de principiis iuris et quibus modis ad hanc multitudinem infinitam ac varietatem legum perventum sit, altius disseram.
>
> 3.25.1–2

> Before, crimes brought suffering; now, laws did. This matter prompts me to speak in more depth about law's origins and how the present infinite number and variety of laws were reached.

The excursus is marked by Tacitean *sententiae* and pessimism. Beginning from humanity's legendary past, Tacitus chronicles the development of the rule of law.[43] In this account, humanity at its origins was without fault, and so had no need for laws and punishment (3.26.1). This golden age was succeeded by various episodes of despotic rule which, on occasion, were followed by the establishment of law, instituted by such as notable leaders as Minos, Lycurgus, and Solon (3.26.3). Tacitus then traces Roman history from the Regal Period to the foundation of the Principate, the excursus thus forming a learned commentary expanding on Tacitus' brief introduction to the *Annales*, mentioning such constitutional changes as the *decemviri* and the many vicissitudes from Sulla to Augustus (3.26.4–28.2).[44] During this excursus, Tacitus uses his recitation of Roman constitutional history to provide grounding and context for his primary discussion, which concerns the alarming volume of laws enacted for the city and empire.[45]

By the final portion of the excursus, Tacitus describes a situation spiraling rapidly out of control, fueled in large part by the change from the Republic to the reign of Augustus. Granted additional power through the expansion of legal charges, the *delatores* were well-motivated to enforce the laws for their own personal gain:[46]

> sed altius penetrabant urbemque et Italiam et quod usquam civium corripuerant, multorumque excisi status.
>
> 3.28.3

> But these agents burrowed too deeply and ruined Rome and Italy and citizens everywhere. Many people saw their status demolished.

Tacitus vividly describes the situation in terms of disease and surgery. The state struggles (*laborabatur*) while the denouncers infect (*penetrabant*) and seize (*corripuerant*) Rome and Italy, only disappearing when citizens had their estates amputated (*excisi*).[47] This violent and vivid language likely reflects period sentiment, when *delatores* were viewed as a (perhaps endemic) evil, symptomatic of the changes to imperial rule.

Tacitus, having traced the state of jurisprudence from its inception to its perversion under Augustus, is back to where he began, with Tiberius confronting the state of the Papia/Poppaea law. As Tacitus tells us, Tiberius elected to soften the law, thus ending the digression with Tiberius' timely proposal:

et terror omnibus intentabatur, ni Tiberius statuendo remedio quinque consularium, quinque e praetoriis, totidem e cetero senatu sorte duxisset, apud quos exsoluti plerique legis nexus modicum in praesens levamentum fuere.

3.28.4

Terror was assailing everyone, except that Tiberius, to establish a remedy, chose by lot five ex-consuls, five former praetors, and a like number from the remaining senators. In their hands many of the law's knots were loosened—a modest and temporary relief.

Tiberius' decision is explicitly stated as a check on the expansion of legislation begun under Augustus. Metaphorically, Tiberius gives a much-needed cure (*remedio*) for the legalistic disease.[48] In this excursus, Tacitus again aligns with Tiberius' thought process and preoccupations: while the importance of precedent is unquestioned, justice requires that the laws be explained and clarified. This image of Tiberius as healer of the laws is immediately reminiscent of Suetonius' description, where he is depicted as a protector ensuring against the weakening of the laws.[49]

State of the Empire

Tacitus' use of alignment in the Tiberian books is at its most dramatic at the beginning of the fourth book of the *Annales*, when Tiberius addresses the senate (4.4.1). After commending Germanicus' son Drusus to the senate, the discussion turns to the necessity of Tiberius' leaving the city (4.4.2). Among the pretexts which Tiberius cites were the need for veterans to be settled in *coloniae* and the raising of levies. Almost as an afterthought, Tiberius listed the legions and the provinces of the Roman Empire.[50]

percensuitque cursim numerum legionum et quas provincias tutarentur. quod mihi quoque exequendum reor, quae tunc Romana copia in armis, qui socii reges, quanto sit angustius imperitatum.

4.4.3

Tiberius also surveyed quickly the legions' total and the provinces they secured. I think I, too, should track this. What were Rome's military resources then? Who the allied kings? How much narrower the Empire?

Tiberius continues, listing the locations of Rome's military forces: two fleets for Italy, one for southern Gaul, eight legions on the Rhine, three in the Spains, two in Africa, two in Egypt, four in Syria, four legions along the Danube, four in Dalmatia, and Rome was held by twelve cohorts—all of this not counting the allied auxiliary forces which roughly equaled the legions (4.5.1–4).[51] Tacitus again aligns his voice with that of Tiberius; emperor and historian are doing the same thing, in the same manner, at the same time. Tacitus states his mental alignment through linking of the emperor's thought (*percensuit*) with his own (*quod mihi quoque exequendum reor*). The reader takes the position of audience to Tiberius/Tacitus and, as before, where there is no authorial narrator to guide the reader, he or she must share the view and gaze of the aligned emperor/historian.

This digression is particularly notable because of its placement in the narrative, and the effect it has on the reader. This passage comes during an especially tense portion of the *Annales*, in which Sejanus is plotting to kill Drusus the Younger and ingratiate himself into the imperial family by marrying Livilla (4.3.1–5). Although this material is naturally interesting, Tacitus interrupts the flow of Sejanus' machinations to follow Tiberius' deliberations about the placement of the legionary forces. Through alignment, Tacitus draws the reader into Tiberius' daily activities and thoughts, making them more vivid, more pressing, and more real than the fascinating material of murder. Further, this excursus heightens the suspense of the narrative; we watch as Tiberius works tediously with the senate, entirely unaware that the "ally of his labors" is plotting his downfall. We, the reader, are made anxious by the digression, knowing what we do about Sejanus' plans. Tacitus draws out the tension by following Tiberius' thoughts, melding with him as he ignores the much more pressing material that has just been revealed to the reader.

Tiberian Rome

An additional, if somewhat more complex, example of aligned narration commences in the next section. At this moment in the narrative, Tacitus is signaling the start of the second half of Tiberius' reign, which will constitute a dramatic shift (for the worse) in the emperor's temperament and governance. This portion of the digression begins thus:

> congruens crediderim recensere ceteras quoque rei publicae partis, quibus modis ad eam diem habitae sint, quoniam Tiberio mutati in deterius principatus initium ille annus attulit.
>
> 4.6.1

> It is fitting, I am inclined to believe, to review the state's remaining elements as well, how they were handled until then, since that year initiated for Tiberius a regime changed for the worse.

Here, Tacitus signals the transition between the two portions of the reign of Tiberius, and lets the reader know in no uncertain terms that the next half of the regime will be problematic and troubled. The interplay between narrator and emperor begins to take on a strange hybrid character after this point. Tacitus next engages in a review of Tiberius' reign to date, summarizing what has already been seen in the previous years, up to the beginning of book 4. What is complicated about this passage is the questionable remove of the narrator; Tacitus appears to speak in his authorial voice, yet the narrative is highly sympathetic to Tiberius. It is as though Tacitus, more or less in his own person, were delivering the kind of exonerating and explanatory speech Tiberius would give on his own behalf. Thus, it is quite difficult to discern the location or person of the narrator. As compared with Tacitus' usual delivery, in which he is quick to undercut any perceived good action on the part of the emperor, this certainly appears to be an aligned account, but it is not as clearly delineated as, for example, the first passage noted in this section.

As this excursus is particularly lengthy, for the sake of clarity I will discuss it in detail through four excerpts (i–iv, below):

(i) iam primum publica negotia et privatorum maxima apud patres tractabantur, dabaturque primoribus disserere, et in adulationem lapsos cohibebat ipse (4.6.2)
At first, public business and the most important private business was conducted in the senate. Leading men had permission to speak, and those who lapsed into flattery were checked by Tiberius himself.

(ii) sua consulibus, sua praetoribus species; minorum quoque magistratuum exercita potestas; legesque, si maiestatis quaestio eximeretur, bono in usu. (4.6.2)
Consuls looked like consuls, praetors like praetors, and even lesser magistrates exercised their functions. Laws too—the treason court excepted—functioned well.

(iii) plebes acri quidem annona fatigabatur, sed nulla in eo culpa ex principe: quin infecunditati terrarum aut asperis maris obviam iit, quantum impendio diligentiaque poterat. (4.6.4)
The populace did suffer under galling grain prices, but not by the emperor's fault. Indeed he countered the lands' infertility and rough seas with outlay and attention insofar as he could.

(iv) rari per Italiam Caesaris agri, modesta servitia, intra paucos libertos domus; ac si quanto cum privatis disceptaret, forum et ius. (4.6.5)

> Land-holding in Italy was a rarity for Tiberius, his slaves were restrained, his household limited to a few freedmen. And for his disputes with individuals he used courtroom and law.

Tacitus goes further in this section than in the previous one, detailing not only the facts and figures relating to the legions and provinces, but also providing an overview of Tiberius' highlights as emperor: the favorable relationship between emperor and senate, the handling of taxation and provincial governance, the fair treatment of the populace, and the size and nature of the imperial household. Tacitus' tone throughout implies an admiration for Tiberius, amounting almost to a defense of the first half of Tiberius' reign. The verbiage in this section is extremely positive, and seems at odds with Tacitus' normal practice of inserting sneaky, undercutting remarks whenever praise is dispensed.[52]

In the first excerpt (i), Tacitus refers to the senators' need for correction once they had slipped into sycophancy (*in adulationem lapsos*). Further, Tiberius would restrain these senators personally (*cohibebat ipse*), a fact all the more vindicating since the emperor would be the last person expected to show sufficient modesty to stop adulation directed toward him. The verb *cohibeo* carries a connotation of containment and restraint rather than of active disciplinary correction or punishment.[53] The tone here is more akin to that of a parent correcting wayward children than to a vengeful or vindictive emperor.

The second excerpt (ii) praises the observation of Roman Republican traditions under Tiberius. The consuls and praetors retain their outer signs of rank (*sua consulibus, sua praetoribus species*) and the lesser magistrates continued to exercise their powers (*minorum . . . potestas*). The maintenance of Republican prerogatives is understood to flow from the modesty and civility of Tiberius. The next point, concerning the laws, contains the only *caveat* in this list of Tiberian virtues.[54] Tacitus states that the state ran well under existing law (*legesque . . . bono in usu*), but still the *lex maiestatis* remains in effect (*si maiestatis quaestio eximeretur*). This reminder of the *lex maiestas* foreshadows the abuse of the law which will occur in the second half of the Tiberian hexad, and also recalls the passage in book 1 where Tacitus interrupted his praise of Tiberius with a digression on the *lex maiestatis* (1.72.2).[55] Tacitus here intrudes on this praise narrative to cast the shadow of Tiberian treason trials, momentarily disrupting the semi-aligned quality of the passage and, as a consequence, causing a brief ripple of reader unease.

In the third excerpt (iii), Tacitus exculpates Tiberius for the increased price of grain. Although Tacitus begins the statement with *quidem*, marking a concession to Tiberius' detractors,[56] this admission is immediately annulled by the assertion that Tiberius was not at fault (*nulla ... culpa ex principe*) and the claim that Tiberius had done everything in his power (*quantum impendio diligentiaque poterat*) to ameliorate the situation. Tacitus thus offers an entirely positive (albeit short-lived) view of Tiberius' domestic policy, using language and sentiments that align with the self-presentation we would expect from Tiberius himself.

The last excerpt (iv) describes Tiberius' personal holdings and the imperial household. This modest picture is in marked contrast to later emperors, such as Claudius or Nero, whose households grew unchecked and, in time, included imperial freedmen who wielded more power than senators.[57] Tacitus rules on each aspect of the imperial household with a single word: Tiberius' Italian land holdings are scarce (*rari*), his slaves are restrained (*modesta*), and his freedmen are few (*paucos*). The last sentence of this excursus tells us that Tiberius is so moderate in his exercise of power that he uses public civil remedies to settle his private quarrels.

Throughout this excursus, Tacitus has defended Tiberius much as the emperor might have defended himself. The alignment between *princeps* and historian is broken only once: pointedly, at the mention of the *lex maiestatis*. During this digression, Tacitus gives his reader a last glimpse of the good qualities of Tiberius before the inevitable slow erosion in the second half of the hexad. Tacitus illustrates this change without hesitation, as he exits the excursus unceremoniously, undercutting Tiberius' image of moderation and returning to the cynical, authoritative narrative voice that characterizes the *Annales*.

> quae cuncta non quidem comi via, sed horridus ac plerumque formidatus, retinebat tamen, donec morte Drusi verterentur.
>
> 4.7.1
>
> All these things Tiberius retained, though in no affable style—he was prickly, rather, and generally alarming—until they were overset by Drusus' death.

This brief summary (*quae cuncta ... retinebat*) interrupts and undermines the rosy image left in the reader's mind at 4.6.4. Tacitus describes Tiberius' manner as not only unfriendly (*non quidem comi via*), but even prickly (*horridus*) and generally alarming (*plerumque formidatus*).[58] These adjectives mark the negative aspects of Tiberius' personality, dominant even during his good years. The death of Drusus upsets all of Tiberius' good intentions, and leaves in their stead a slavish dependence on Sejanus. With this passage, Tacitus ends his alignment with Tiberius and returns both to his normal authorial voice and the thread of the main narrative.

Tacitus' alignment during the Tiberian digressions has a dramatic and vivid narratological effect on the reader. All of these excurses are concerned with the retention of Augustan models, especially as regards imperial policies and law, subjects that would naturally be expected to hold the interests of Tiberius. Through alignment, variously with Tiberius' personal interests, voice, and sentiments, Tacitus leaves the reader wondering which depictions are true, and whose version of events to believe. The effect is similar to that experienced by the viewer of the Narcissus fresco—initially expecting to see a representation of Narcissus' self-desire, we find ourselves confused and entrapped by the mingling of gaze. We expect Narcissus to watch the pool, but by joining him in viewing, our gaze is aligned with his. The face in the pool looks back at us, not at Narcissus, and thus we must ask where we stand in relation to the meaning, and also the subject, of the painting. Here, Tacitus' elision with the persona of Tiberius dissolves the boundary between narrator and character, and we, the viewers, are left without a trustworthy guide. In that position, we must choose between disengaging with the text, and accepting the potentially flawed, character-subjugated view of history. Thus, we are forced to question who directs the gaze.

Additionally, the final disengagement from the scene, when Tacitus abruptly shocks the reader out of the aligned, optimistic, and Tiberius-centered excursus, is well-illustrated by the change from aligned view to straight, third-person filming in *Murder, My Sweet*. The viewer experiences much the same kind of disconnect as Dmytryk moves between the shots in which the camera is covered with spider-webs or smoke, representative of Marlowe's impaired vision and, moments later, resumes normal filming. This transition can provide a helpful metaphor for the jarring disconnect felt by Tacitus' readers as the historian returns to his own authorial voice. In these excurses, it is sometimes difficult to separate Tacitus from Tiberius, and in those gray moments the reader must question and reconsider Tiberius' thinking and decisions, forced to wonder whether Tiberius was indeed a villain, or simply much maligned.

Claudius: The Professor-in-Chief

In the previous section, we considered Tacitus' use of alignment in two lengthy Tiberian excurses, and have seen how the historian uses this technique to draw the reader into the narrative. There are two striking examples of Claudian digressions which employ alignment for similar effect. The Claudian examples are much easier to view and parse, as the narrative voices of Tacitus-the-historian and Tacitus/Claudius are markedly different. Throughout the Claudian books, Tacitus portrays the emperor as a bookish antiquarian ruled by his wives and freedmen.[59] This impression, regardless of its historicity, is one which is rendered and reinforced through the two Claudian digressions that will be discussed in this chapter.[60]

The Oblivious Scholar

Just as in the case of Tiberius, in order for Tacitus to effectively align his voice with Claudius through a twinning of interests and subject matter, there must have been an established consensus about the emperor's personality and proclivities. Thus, we must look to our literary and epigraphic evidence to see whether it is plausible that Tacitus' original audience would have seen Claudius as the rambling scholar-emperor.

Claudius' reputation as an antiquarian is certainly well established. The biographer Suetonius notes that Claudius had great erudition in matters of history and research,[61] listing Claudius' many literary accomplishments, including a Roman history beginning with the death of Julius Caesar and restarting at the end of the civil war, an autobiography, and two histories in Greek of the Etruscans and Carthaginians.[62] This view is reinforced by Seneca's *De Brevitate Vitae*. In this essay, Seneca points to the multitude of things that a person can do with spare time that are less worthwhile than a study of philosophy, the only proper use of leisure.[63] Among Seneca's list of relatively useless pursuits is Claudius' passion for history and antiquarian studies.

> Sullam ultimum Romanorum protulisse pomerium, quod numquam provinciali sed Italico agro acquisito proferre moris apud antiquos fuit. hoc scire magis prodest quam Aventinum montem extra pomerium esse, ut ille affirmabat, propter alteram ex duabus causis, aut quod plebs eo secessisset, aut quod Remo auspicanti illo loco aves non addixissent, alia deinceps innumerabilia quae aut farta sunt mendaciis aut similia? . . . tamen cuius ista errores minuent? cuius cupiditates prement? quem fortiorem, quem iustiorem, quem liberaliorem facient? dubitare se interim Fabianus noster aiebat an satius esset nullis studiis admoveri quam his implicari.[64]
>
> Sen. *De Brev. Vit.* 13.8–9

> Sulla was the last of the Romans who extended the *pomerium*, which in old times it was customary to extend after the acquisition of Italian, but never of provincial, territory. Is it more profitable to know this than that Mount Aventine,

> according to him, is outside the *pomerium* for one of two reasons, either because that was the place to which the plebeians had seceded, or because birds had not been favorable when Remus took his auspices on that spot—and, in turn, countless other reports that are either crammed with falsehood or are of the same sort? . . . still, whose mistakes will be made fewer by such stories? Whose passions will they restrain? Whom will they make more brave, whom more just, whom more noble minded? My friend Fabianus used to say that at times he was doubtful whether it was not better not to apply oneself to any studies than to become entangled in these.

In addition to this broadside attack on the study of historical minutiae, Seneca recalls Claudius to his reader's mind through the mention of the *pomerium*, which Claudius also extended after his conquest of Britain.[65] Seneca has this most recent extension of the *pomerium* in mind, and does Claudius one better by bringing in Sulla as a historical source for Claudius' illegality. Seneca not only categorizes most historical inquiry as useless, if harmless, but he also points out that Claudius' extension of the *pomerium* was improper, using for support the very historical inquiry that he condemns. Throughout his *Apocolocyntosis*, Seneca consistently attacks Claudius, but rarely mentions his antiquarianism, preferring to stress his physical limitations and penchant for executing people, especially family members, without trial.[66]

Claudius' antiquarian pursuits are even more evident in the material record. Modern classical scholars are unusually blessed with the epigraphic record of a nearly complete oration by Claudius. The *Tabula Lugdunensis* is a bronze tablet copy of a large portion of Claudius' speech concerning his decree to allow Gallic citizens to become senators.[67] Tacitus has included his own version of this speech at the proper point in the narrative of the *Annales* (11.24.1–7), and the two have often been compared in order to understand Tacitus' use of original documents in his historiography.[68] In this instance, however, we are not concerned with Tacitus' faithfulness to the original speech *per se*, but rather with the narrower question of whether Claudius was perceived by his contemporaries as a scholarly emperor prone to digression. In examining the epigraphic document, one is surprised by the amount of pedantic, circuitous material, particularly as this speech was delivered by the emperor before the senate.[69] Near the beginning of the speech (the first few lines are missing), Claudius attempts to show that the Roman state has undergone changes before, and so should not be shocked at his proposed legislation.[70] In support of his argument, Claudius traces Roman history under the kings, showing that many were not native to Rome.[71] Then, in the middle of this proof, Claudius begins a historical digression which is entirely beside the main point.[72]

> huic quoque et filio nepotive eius (nam et hoc inter auctores discrepat) insertus Servius Tullius, si nostros sequimur, captiva natus Ocresia, si Tuscos, Caeli quondam Vivennae sodalis fidelissimus omnisque eius casus comes, postquam varia fortuna exactus cum omnibus reliquis Caeliani exercitus Etruria excessit, montem Caelium occupavit et a duce suo Caelio ita appelita[vit], mutato nomina (nam Tusce Mastarna ei nomen erat) ita appellatus, ut dixi, et regnum summa cum rei p(ublicae) utilitate optinuit.
>
> ILS 212= CIL 13.1668, lines 16–24

> He [Tarquinius Priscus] too and his son or grandson—there is a disagreement on this point amongst the authorities—had Servius Tullius interpolated in their succession. If we follow our Roman sources Servius was born in captivity to Ocresia, but if we follow the Etruscans, he was once the most faithful comrade of Caelius Vivenna and his companion in all his adventures, and, after he was driven out through the fickleness of Fortune and was exiled from Etruria with all the surviving troops of Caelius, took over the Caelian Hill and gave it that name after his commander, changed his own name—in Etruscan his own name was Mastarna—took the name I have mentioned, and claimed the kingdom with the greatest benefit to the state.

In this short passage, itself a digression from the central argument of foreigners ruling in Rome, Claudius wanders even further. His listeners (and later, readers) are told of the varying traditions concerning Servius Tullius, including that he may have been a comrade of Caelius (namesake of the Caelian hill), and that Servius' name was Mastarna in Etruscan.[73] All of this is quite beside the point, that Servius Tullius was a foreigner, and it is this type of ever digressing tedium that Suetonius mentions and that Seneca rails against. Thus, both literary and epigraphic evidence support the view of Claudius as a doddering emperor-scholar interested in history and antiquities. Tacitus uses this characterization of Claudius to great effect in the *Annales,* in order to broadcast the use of narratorial alignment.

Altering the Alphabet

After the large *lacuna* in the *Annales*,[74] our record picks up during the last years of Claudius' reign. The narrative resumes during a discussion of Claudius' problematic and unfaithful wife, Messalina. Tacitus states that Claudius remains unaware of Messalina's activities (11.13.1, *at Claudius matrimonii sui ignarus*). Claudius' ignorance of his own household is strongly contrasted with his scholarly erudition in the following section, and Tacitus makes much of the irony of a know-it-all emperor who knows nothing about the vital subjects of his household and the empire.[75] In this passage, Tacitus provides a lengthy example of Claudian erudition, concerning the emperor's decision to add three letters to the Latin alphabet.[76] Tacitus then aligns with the antiquarian emperor during an excursus on the history of writing and letters.

> ac novas litterarum formas addidit vulgavitque, comperto Graecam quoque litteraturam non simul coeptam absolutamque. primi per figuras animalium Aegyptii sensus mentis effingebant (ea antiquissima monimenta memoriae humanae impressa saxis cernuntur), et litterarum semet inventores perhibent; inde Phoenicas, quia mari praepollebant, intulisse Graeciae gloriamque adeptos, tamquam reppererint quae acceperant. quippe fama est Cadmum classe Phoenicum vectum rudibus adhuc Graecorum populis artis eius auctorem fuisse. quidam Cecropem Atheniensem vel Linum Thebanum et temporibus Troianis Palamedem Argivum memorant sedecim litterarum formas, mox alios ac praecipuum Simoniden ceteras repperisse. at in Italia Etrusci ab Corinthio Demarato, Aborigines Arcade ab Evandro didicerunt; et forma litteris Latinis quae veterrimis Graecorum. sed nobis quoque paucae primum fuere, deinde additae sunt. quo exemplo Claudius tres litteras adiecit, quae <in> usu imperitante eo, post oblitteratae, aspiciuntur etiam nunc in aere publico [<publican>dis plebiscitis] per fora ac templa fixo.
>
> 11.13.2–14.3

> And three new letter shapes were supplied and publicized after he discovered that the Greek alphabet, too, was incomplete when new. At first animal shapes were used by Egyptians to express ideas—these exceedingly ancient monuments of human memory are visible on stone—and Egyptians claim to be letters' inventors. *From Egypt the Phoenicians, dominant on the seas, took letters to Greece and gained glory for having devised what they merely acquired.* There is indeed a story that Cadmus, who voyaged with his Phoenician fleet while Greek peoples were still primitive, was the art's inventor. Some record that Athenian Cecrops or Theban Linus or during Trojan times Argive Palamedes devised sixteen letter shapes. Later other men, especially Simonides, devised the rest. In Italy Etruscans learned from Corinthian Demaratus, native populations from Arcadian Evander. Latin letter shapes were like the oldest of the Greek. For us, too, they were few at first, with later additions. Following this precedent Claudius added three. In use while he was in power, afterwards forgotten, they are seen even now on the official bronzes used for publishing senatorial decrees to the populace and affixed in public squares and temples.

This passage is striking to anyone familiar with Tacitean style: gone are the swift summaries of period politics, the biting commentary on imperial decisions, the brief, dense prose. Instead of the expected Tacitean brevity, the reader is taken on a meandering journey through the back-annals of boring and irrelevant historical matter only vaguely related to the main narrative. Tacitus has indeed become one with the pedantic antiquarian emperor.[77]

The tone of this passage is tedious in the extreme, almost to the point of being laughable.[78] The timing of the excursus is off-putting as well (11.13.1–2), coming after a brief recitation of some of the laudable small changes Claudius made in the city.[79] The last item in this list is the mention of Claudius' newly adopted letters, which appears upon first reading to be of relatively little import. Unlike many of the excurses in the *Annales*, Tacitus does not begin this digression with a formal introduction, and instead the reader is plunged directly into a winding historical recitation beginning with the Egyptians' use of letters.[80] When the excursus finally concludes, Claudius is immediately seen pursuing his antiquarian interests, forming the college of haruspices to preserve traditional religious practices (11.15.1–3). Tacitus, Claudius-like, displays a bounty of erudition unrelated to the main narrative.

In marked contrast to Tacitus' normal narrative voice, this excursus is unusually antiquarian. Tacitus gives a wide range of specific names and includes side-tangents only vaguely related to writing systems. As though to prove his case scientifically, Claudius first notes that Egyptian hieroglyphs are still preserved in stone (*ea . . . saxis cernuntur*). Alternative theories on the origins of letters are put forward: either the Egyptians or the Phoenicians invented them. The flow of the narrative is slowed to a crawl during the rambling list of ancient Greeks who may or may not have discovered letters, including Cecrops, Linus, Palamedes, and Simonides. The introduction of writing to Italy is safely credited to Evander and Demaratus. All of this is provided as evidence that a system of letters was adopted and then supplemented in the case of both the Greeks and the Latins. The point is made twice, at the introduction (*Graecam quoque litteraturam non simul coeptam absolutamque*), and at the conclusion (*paucae primum fuere, deinde additae sunt*). In the end, the entire excursus exists solely to provide linguistic precedent for Claudius' adoption of three more letters.

The voice again becomes recognizably Tacitean in the last sentence (*quo . . . fixo*) (11.14.3). This sentence moves with Tacitean *brevitas* as time is accelerated, jumping from the adoption of the letters (*quo exemplo Claudius tres litteras adiecit*), to the remainder of Claudius' reign (*quae usui imperitante eo*), to their later obscurity (*post oblitteratae*), and then to Tacitus' own day (*aspiciuntur etiam nunc in aere publico dis plebiscitis per fora ac templa fixo*). The constructions here are markedly unlike those in the Claudian excursus. Beginning with a simple phrase, Tacitus accelerates the tempo using a descending tricolon (*quo ... adiecit*; *quae ... eo*; *post oblitteratae*), as less time is spent on each phase. Tacitus only slows the pacing at the very last phrase, in which he notes that these letters can still be seen on laws displayed in the fora or attached to temples.

Tacitus here offers pointed commentary on the fate of Claudius' letters; they are forgotten (*oblitteratae*) after his reign. Tacitus further shows the futility of this kind of scholarly pursuit, as Claudius' letters have the exact same fate as Egyptian hieroglyphs.[81] Both are now only seen (*cernuntur* :: *aspiciuntur*), carved into rock (*impressa saxis*), or into bronze (*in aere*), implying that Claudius has done nothing but add a minorly interesting linguistic relic, of as much practical use as Egyptian hieroglyphs. Tacitus seems surprised by the continued evidence of these Claudian relics (*aspiciuntur etaim nunc*), whereas he simply states that hieroglyphs survive (*cernuntur*). Tacitus, taking up the interests and language of Claudius, here recalls for his readers what was once forgotten. The rambling irrelevance of this digression highlights the frustration the reader (and, likely, the senators of Claudius' day) feels at the lack of attention to imperial business, and the time wasted on antiquarian research. The reader, through Tacitus' alignment with Claudius, experiences the disconnect between Claudius and reality. Tacitus' reassertion of his authorial narrative voice offers the reader perspective and highlights the triviality of these digressions.

Tacitus' alignment with Claudius during this digression places the reader in the maddening position of dwelling on arcane history while political murder runs rampant through Rome. The divide between the Claudian excurses and their surrounding narratives adds a level of heightened frustration and unreality. Through alignment, the reader is made to contemplate Claudian topics of linguistics while Messalina destroys leading Roman nobles, and to experience Claudius' oblivious remove from the active dangers that surround him. Like the viewer of *Murder, My Sweet*, we share the hazy and clouded vision of the aligned author/emperor, aware of the dangers lurking beyond but unable to see them clearly.

Expanding the *Pomerium*

Tacitus again aligns his voice to Claudius' in book twelve. At the beginning of the year 49, Claudius has already married Agrippina the Younger, and she has been using her power to rid herself of rivals. At 12.22, Tacitus paints a terrifying picture of Agrippina "frightening in her hatred" (*atrox odii*) as she frames Lollia, a former rival for Claudius' hand, for treason (12.22.1).[82] Claudius, rather than allowing Lollia a defense (*inaudita rea*), discourses on the illustrious history of the defendant's family: she was related to L. Volusius and Cotta Messalinus, and had been married to Memmius Regulus and (although Claudius omits it) Gaius Caligula (12.22.2). After this genealogical discussion, Claudius condemns her to exile. Later in the chapter, Agrippina sends a military tribune to Lollia to force her to commit suicide (12.22.3). Claudius, terminally pedantic, follows Agrippina's wishes as the empress gains power.[83] Claudius' failure to check the extreme behavior of his wife is significant for the reader familiar with imperial history, as Agrippina's desire for power will eventually lead her to murder her husband.

In stark contrast to political murder and power politics, Tacitus juxtaposes the mundane legislative decisions of Claudius: senators were now able to visit Narbonese Gaul without express permission, Judaea and Ituraea were made part of Syria after the deaths of their respective kings, and the augury of the god Salus was reinstated after a break of twenty-five years (12.23.1). Like the emperor and the senate, our attention is focused on the humdrum of administration while Agrippina wreaks her vengeance elsewhere. The final piece of legislation in this list is Claudius' expansion of the *pomerium*:[84]

> et pomerium urbis auxit Caesar, more prisco, quo iis qui protulere imperium etiam terminos urbis propagare datur. nec tamen duces Romani, quamquam magnis nationibus subactis, usurpaverant nisi L. Sulla et divus Augustus. regum in eo ambitio vel gloria varie vulgata. sed initium condendi, et quod pomerium Romulus posuerit, noscere haud absurdum reor.
>
> 12.23.2–24.1

> And the city's sacred boundary was lengthened by Claudius. Ancient custom permitted those who had expanded the Empire to expand the city's limits as well. Of Rome's commanders, however, despite the conquest of many great nations, none had used it but Sulla and Augustus. About the kings' ambition or renown in this connection various stories circulate. To learn the origin of its foundation, however, and what boundary Romulus established, is not, I think, preposterous.

During the first portion of this excursus, Tacitus chronicles the Roman leaders who had altered the *pomerium*: Sulla, Augustus, and the early kings of Rome.[85] Tacitus seems to include this list either to juxtapose the great military and political leaders of Roman history with the buffoonish Claudius, or to show similar Claudian erudition as that displayed in the excursus on writing. Further, Tacitus stresses that the very tradition of extending the *pomerium* is old fashioned (*more prisco*), although it had been expanded as recently as the reign of Augustus. The representation of the altering of the *pomerium* as an act tied to history and tradition accords well with Tacitus' depiction of Claudius as a learned antiquarian.

Up to this point, Tacitus has maintained his own voice, giving a brief parenthesis to the actions of the senate, which is itself a parenthesis to the narrative of power politics in the imperial household. Here, however, Tacitus aligns with Claudius, expanding the excursus to an extreme degree as he maps out the Romulean city and traces the ancient *pomerium*.

> igitur a foro boario, ubi aereum tauri simulacrum aspicimus, quia id genus animalium aratro subditur, sulcus designandi oppidi coeptus ut magnam Herculis aram amplecteretur; inde certis spatiis interiecti lapides per ima montis Palati<n>i ad aram Consi, mox curias veteres, tum ad sacellum Larum. forumque Romanum et Capitolium non a Romulo, sed a Tito Tatio additum urbi credidere. mox pro fortuna pomerium auctum. et quos tum Claudius terminos posuerit, facile cognitu et publicis actis perscriptum.
>
> 12.24.1–2

> The furrow outlining the city was begun at the cattle market where we see a bronze bull's likeness, since this sort of animal is harnessed to the plow. It goes around the Great Altar of Hercules, and from there, with boundary-stones placed at regular intervals, along the foot of the Palatine to Consus' Altar, the old Assemblies and the Lares' Shrine. The Forum and the Capitoline, people believe, were added to the city not by Romulus but by Titus Tatius. The boundary was later lengthened in proportion to our fortune. The limits established by Claudius are easily seen, and described in public records.

Tacitus, in Claudian-aligned voice, scarcely begins the circuit of Romulus' Rome when his excursus is further slowed by another digression. The path begins in the cattle market (the Forum Boarium), at the place where there is a bronze bull (*ubi aereum tauri simulacrum aspicimus*). This, Tacitus informs us, is depicted because it is the bull that draws the plow which marks the boundary (*quia id genus animalium aratro subditur*).[86] Tacitus then proceeds to complete the circuit, listing ancient monuments as landmarks such as the *Ara Maxima*, the altar of Consus, the shrine to the Lares, and the Curia, which Tacitus specifies as the Old Curia (*curias veteres*), although the Curia remained in roughly the same location throughout Roman history.[87] Following this *pomerium* route,

Tacitus enters the scholarly comment that the Forum and Capitoline were added by Titus Tatius rather than by Romulus (*forumque Romanum et Capitolium non a Romulo, sed a Tito Tatio*). The correction of Titus Tatius for Romulus seems unnecessarily bookish, as though Tacitus were weighing in on a historical debate, and thus this authoritative aside is reminiscent of the antiquarian ramblings seen in the Greek alphabet digression (11.14.2).[88] Again Tacitus uses alignment to blur the line between his own authorial voice and that of the emperor, and the reader is a captive audience to the ensuing lecture. The divergence between the real world, in which Claudius will soon be poisoned by his wife, and the comfortable complacency of Claudius' scholarship is vast indeed—to such an extent that this digression is almost humorous in its multiple nested tangents. Tacitus has not only aligned himself with the emperor, he has placed the reader into the world of the oblivious and scholarly Claudius.

In these two Claudian excurses, Tacitus shows in a vivid, dramatic fashion the kind of emperor Claudius was: scholarly but ineffectual. Particularly dramatic is Tacitus' juxtaposition of these digressions, both of which follow descriptions of the threatening and dangerous behavior of Claudius' wives.[89] Tacitus depicts a Claudius either ignorant of, or foolishly complicit in, his wives' power plays. In the case of Lollia, Claudius gives a brief digression about her familial history in lieu of allowing her a legal defense, moments later condemning her in accordance with Agrippina's wishes (12.22.2). Through these digressions, Tacitus portrays Claudius as entirely ignorant of the affairs in his own household, although erudite in such impractical subjects as the history of writing and the Romulean *pomerium*.

Tacitus' alignment with Claudius further illustrates for the reader the irritation and foolishness of Claudian pedantry, forcing his audience to wander through Claudius' meandering digressions, all the while aware of the pressing and threatening risks to the emperor and to Rome—while threats press in, Claudius lectures the senate on Etruscan history. The metaphor of Narcissus is particularly apt for Claudius, whose gaze is always inward, toward scholarly antiquarianism, instead of outward to the real dangers threatening him. Through alignment, Tacitus lulls the reader into a drowsy stupor as the interminable lecture drones on. The reader experiences the senators' fear of the real issues at hand during these alignments, but there is also a pervasive sense of oblivious boredom, no doubt also shared by the senators of Claudius' day. By aligning with his art, Tacitus can vividly display to his reader how it felt to be a senator under the Julio-Claudians.

Final Thoughts

Throughout the *Annales*, Tacitus' use of alignment contributes to the effect of *enargeia*, enabling the historian to tell his history in a vivid, personal, and realistic way. The reader not only learns the facts, but also experiences them. In the digressions examined above, Tacitus has used alignment to create a deeper dimension of reader participation in the narrative. This alignment not only of the audience, as in focalization, but also of narrator and emperor, renders these excurses highly vivid and engaging. Tacitus, just as the artist of the Pompeian Narcissus or Edward Dmytryk, has effectively aligned his audience with the subject of his work through the alteration of his narrative voice. In the case of Tiberius, Tacitus uses the quintessentially Tiberian themes of the rule of law, Augustan precedent, and imperial governance to add depth to the digressions. The reader, during these excurses, is suddenly engaged in the same activity as the emperor. During the Claudian digressions, Tacitus adopts the emperor's voice, and arguably his speeches and research, in order to make a point about imperial knowledge and ignorance. Through these excurses, Tacitus depicts the essential qualities of each emperor, deeply impressing upon his reader their imperial personalities and the risks inherent therein, at a level unreachable through mere description.

3

The Directed Gaze and the Construction of Meaning

The first two chapters of this book have dealt with the questions "who sees?" and "who speaks?" using the language of focalization and alignment. The present chapter, focusing on the object of the gaze rather than on the focalizor, asks "what are we made to see?" This is an important component of the *Annales*, as Tacitus often directs us to see what is not present, forces us to watch and interpret ambiguous character reactions, or to participate in the language and action of the threatening gaze. Tacitus directs the gaze of his readers, framing and focusing the narrative to achieve subtle effects, to ensure that the correct interpretations of events are internalized by his audience.

Readers have long wrestled with Tacitus' visual techniques, comparing him variously to a painter, moralist, or dramatist.[1] This latter analogy, while useful for discussing aspects of Tacitus' staging, backgrounds, and characters, fails to adequately describe Tacitus' ability to control his readers' gaze—a far more exact and comprehensive narrative device than those possible in the open format of a play. In the theater, the audience is able to watch the "wrong" character or action, despite correct staging, staring at Horatio rather than paying attention to Hamlet.[2] Film guides our gaze to relevant objects through cinematography and the editing process. The *Hamlet* mistake in viewing could be avoided in film by the use of a close-up, and the dialogue could be highlighted using the shot-reverse-shot. Through these editing techniques, so familiar that they now pass largely unnoticed, a director limits and specifies the audience's gaze. Depending on the subject matter shown, the types of transitions used, and the way in which the audience is obligated to experience emotionally, this guided viewing may be discussed in terms of gendered or more- or less-privileged lenses. Thus, the presentation showcased by the director (or author) keys to one of several types of gaze.

The elite Roman male gaze is the usual register in ancient Roman art and the majority of ancient Roman literature. This gaze is described by modern scholars as aggressive and objectifying, consuming the visual world as a source of pleasure, and is highlighted in sexualized descriptions—whether in Latin poetic ekphrases or in Pompeiian frescos—in visual images or vivid descriptions.[3] Even more explicitly, Bartsch discusses the male gaze as not merely consuming, but penetrating and violent towards its recipients.[4] This objectifying gaze is the normal register in the *Annales* as the reader watches, with varying emotions, the depictions of Julio-Claudian Rome.

This elite Roman gaze has resonances in the male-dominated classical Hollywood cinema, wherein the audience is regularly invited to share the perspective of a male protagonist, or to co-participate in the experience of male-pleasurable images. In film studies, the male objectifying gaze was discussed by Laura Mulvey, who describes the two great pleasures of male viewing as the projection of sexual fantasy onto the female form and the empowering association with an on-screen male avatar who makes things happen and drives the narrative.[5] Thus, the male gaze is inherently, even if subtly, voyeuristic and, in this way, the viewer consumes the visual images present on the screen from the comfortable anonymity of a darkened theater. In some instances, however, both in classical Hollywood cinema and the *Annales*, the normal gaze of the viewer/reader is itself attacked and challenged or subverted and replaced. Mulvey explains how this happens in film, when the male objectifying gaze subverts its own fantasy by transforming the feminine object into a sexual image which is, in turn, challenging to the viewer. The object thereby "freezes the look, fixates the spectator and prevents him from achieving any distance from the image in front of him."[6] The spectator is left without the psychological distance and safety between self and the threatening object. Thus, according to Mulvey, the male gaze's quest for pleasure is defeated at the point of being challenged by its object.

This objective challenge to the gaze is also mobilized by Tacitus, when the true relationship between senators and emperor destroys Augustus' false image of the emperor as a first among equals. As will be shown in the first two sections of this chapter ("Imperial Close-Ups and *Touch of Evil*" and "*The Maltese Falcon* and the Threatening Gaze"), Tacitus depicts the once-powerful Roman elites as forcibly cowed by their failure to interpret the emperor's visual cues and thereby made passive recipients of a threatening imperial gaze. We, as readers, join the senators as their consuming/understanding gaze is met and challenged by the emperor in an emasculating act of hostile vision.

In the third section ("*Damnatio Memoriae*, *Rebecca*, Watching the Invisible"), I examine Tacitus' mobilization of the subordinated feminine gaze. Following Laura Mulvey's discussion of the psychology of male viewing, scholars such as

Mary Ann Doane and Tania Modleski have investigated the feminine viewer and viewing, especially in 1940s films marketed to women, such as *Suspicion* (Hitchcock, 1941), *Gaslight* (Cukor, 1944), and *Rebecca* (Hitchcock, 1940).[7] In these films, Mary Ann Doane argues, the central female character, rather than a mere fetish or sexual object, becomes the active protagonist functioning in a problematized domestic sphere. This character's active gaze, which would be disconcerting to the 1940s audience accustomed to the masculine/active, feminine/passive viewing structure, is often subverted at crucial moments and assimilated to that of a male supporting character. In effect, the woman sees what the male characters disclose.[8] Although Tacitus is an external narrator, the subversion of the readers' gaze at the level of the story functions in an analogous manner. In the world of Tacitus' *Annales*, the reader's vision can be replaced by the dominant gaze of the historian/narrator, revealing what the powerless reader is incapable of discovering.

Although Tacitus is not unique in directing our gaze, he often controls it to a greater degree than do other historians. By controlling the images shown, the order in which they appear, and the way in which the material is presented, Tacitus can guide his reader to forge a subtext under the surface facts of his history. This narrative subtext, seldom overt or noticeable, permanently colors the impressions and interpretations of his audience. Tacitus forces us to experience viewing that is challenged, disempowered, and subordinated first to the imperial gaze, and then to his own. Through these various but related devices Tacitus is able to make the invisible visible, and to construct meaning from enigmatically silent images.

Imperial Close-ups and *Touch of Evil*

In film, the cinematic technique of focusing on the face of a particular character is known as a close-up, which generally forces the viewer to "read" the face of a character in order to determine what that person may be thinking or feeling. Classic Hollywood cinema avoids close-ups except in moments of extreme emotion or to reveal aspects of a character's personality.[9] When faced with a close-up, the viewer's task is to correctly read emotional information from the face that dominates the screen—usually a simple task as the character broadcasts an emotion—which the audience interprets in the context of the film.

In certain films, however, the task of reading the close-up is actively disrupted when a character displays an ambiguous or unemotional expression. The ambivalence of the character's expression forces an initial misreading by the viewer, only to be corrected on a second viewing. In these cases, the initial misreading happens by design to drive the narrative and create suspense. Famously, Lev Kuleshov, in his early work with montage, showed viewers a seated man with an ambiguous expression, then other images (e.g., food, a reclining woman, etc.) and asked for their reactions. His audience commented on the amazing ability of the actor in portraying lust, hunger, and revulsion. The audience, forced to construct meaning from an ambiguous close-up, used the context of the surrounding images to create meaning by interpreting the narrative.[10] The task of meaning-making lies with the audience of the close-up, just as in Kuleshov's montage.

A film that uses the close-up to great narrative effect is Orson Welles's *Touch of Evil* (1958).[11] In the film, a corrupt police detective, Hank Quinlan (Orson Welles), tries to pervert justice by framing a man for murder by planting evidence in his apartment. Welles' directing is marked by repeated close-ups of Quinlan's face as his schemes are slowly unraveled by a Mexican police detective, Miguel/ Mike Vargas (Charlton Heston). Quinlan is visually defined by his outsize dimensions, especially those of his face.

The viewer, and many of the characters who know Quinlan, continually try and fail to read his emotions during close-ups, even though Quinlan's actions

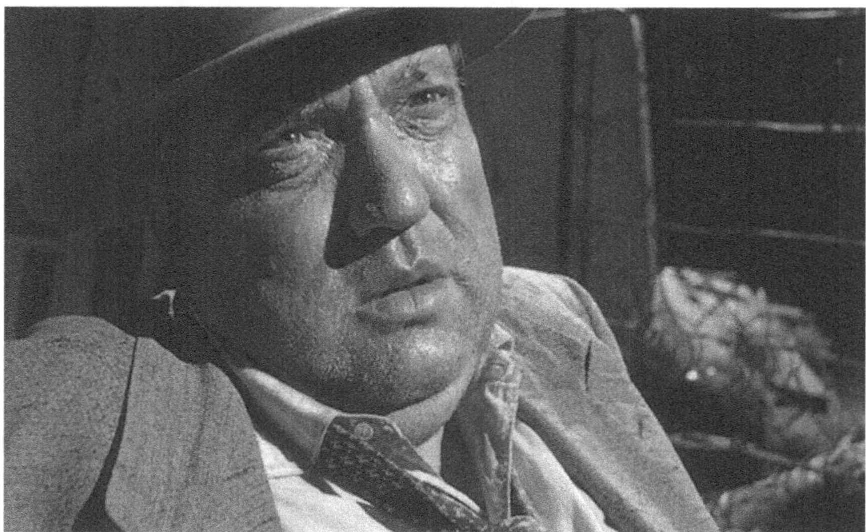

Figure 3.1 *Touch of Evil*, directed by Orson Welles © Universal Pictures 1958. All rights reserved.

and thoughts are often very clear from context in other scenes. The ambiguous and "blank" expression of Quinlan chewing the inevitable cigar eludes the viewer's reading, and adds suspense to the mystery.[12] Even after the conclusion has been reached, the audience, and most of the film's characters, could not explain or contextualize who Hank Quinlan was emotionally. His ambiguity and unknowable character are carried throughout the film.[13]

This same effect is achieved in the *Annales* when Tacitus interrupts the narrative to give a visual description of a central character, usually an emperor. Just like a close-up in film, this device forces the audience to pay singular attention to the image of a character without the added benefit of commentary on his/her thoughts. Unlike focalization, the close-up does not generally offer insight into the thoughts of the character under scrutiny, and the audience is forced to construct the character's emotions and motivations from the outer facial aspect alone. This effect is powerful because it breaks the flow of narrative and, through the suppression of information, renders the scene almost entirely visual. The close-up is even more disconcerting when the viewer's gaze is challenged by an answering gaze, which problematizes the creation of meaning as the viewer is objectified by the image on the screen. Welles' mobilization of the ambiguous and challenging close-up parallels Tacitus' direction of the reader's gaze to the impassive and dissembling faces of Tiberius and Nero.[14]

Tiberius

Tacitus' Tiberius is purposefully ambiguous in almost all of his actions. He not only fails to be read, but actively tries not to be read correctly.[15] Tacitus' senators, moreover, realize that reading the emperor correctly is dangerous and, as a result, they hide their knowledge as a way of securing their own safety (1.11.2–3). The senators must also hide their personal feelings while making sure that they appear unable to read Tiberius' thoughts from his expression. This cat-and-mouse game of intentionally hiding knowledge plays out in Tacitus' use of the close-up of Tiberius.

The Trial of Calpurnius Piso

The first of these close-ups occurs in book 3 when Cn. Calpurnius Piso is on trial for his life before the senate, with Tiberius as his judge (3.12–14). Piso had been Tiberius' close associate and, the narrative implies, an agent for the emperor.[16] At the start of the trial, however, Tiberius is carefully ambiguous in his speech concerning the accused (3.12.1, *die senatus Caesar orationem habuit meditato temperamento*). The emperor, by turns, seems to blame Piso, then Germanicus' friends on the prosecution, and seeks to cast himself as a fair and balanced judge more interested in the public good than his personal loss. After the prosecution presents its case, Tacitus records that the senate and Tiberius remained committed to conviction. Tiberius, however, orders those who had torn down Piso's statues and dragged them to the Gemonian stairs—in anticipation of his conviction and execution—to replace them (3.14.4). The emperor's ambiguity was not lost on the Roman people, and rumors were plentiful near the end of the trial:

> igitur inditus lecticae et a tribuno praetoriae cohortis deductus est, vario rumore, custos saluti an mortis exactor sequeretur.
>
> 3.14.5

> So Piso was put in a litter and escorted home by a Guard officer to rumours various. *Is that a security guard—or an executioner—behind him?*

The people see the guard as a signal or clue to Tiberius' mind, and, like Piso, are unable to decipher it—is this a guard or executioner? Again, Tiberius' behavior is depicted as carefully ambiguous and implicitly threatening. Tacitus informs us that Plancina, Piso's wife, was saved by a backroom agreement with Livia and had separated her defense from her husband's (3.15.1). Piso, knowing that he would be convicted without his wife's inroads to imperial favor, thinks of suicide, but is convinced by his son to face the senate (3.15.2). As Piso's trial resumes, Tacitus alters the narrative voice, shifting from a historical third-person perspective to one focalized through Piso. In this way, the reader shares Piso's experience of encountering a hostile senate and emperor:

> redintegratamque accusationem, infensas patrum voces, adversa et saeva cuncta perpessus, nullo magis exterritus est quam quod Tiberium sine miseratione, sine ira, obstinatum clausumque vidit, ne quo adfectu perrumperetur.
>
> 3.15.2

> Renewed recrimination, hostile senator words, opposition and brutality everywhere caused him pain, but nothing so alarmed him as seeing Tiberius without compassion, without anger, stubbornly closed against any feeling's breach.

As Piso enters the senate, we enter with him and are assaulted (*perpessus*) auditorily by the senators' accusations and shouting (*accusationem, infensas patrum voces*). In the Latin, Piso is struck by everything hostile and savage (*adversa et saeva cuncta*). Tacitus piles on these verbal attacks in rapid succession, without conjunctions to slow the onslaught. After this auditory overload, the description moves into the visual, as Piso gazes upon the crowning horror: the impassive face of Tiberius (*Tiberium ... vidit*). The sight of Tiberius' expressionless countenance overshadows everything that Piso has suffered in the senate. Tacitus compels the reader to visualize Tiberius' threatening image. Piso, and we as readers, attempt in vain to read Tiberius' emotionless and opaque face.

In this rhetorically powerful close-up, Tacitus spends considerable time and care on the presentation of Tiberius, especially as compared with the general and non-specific verbal attacks of the senators. Grammatically, Tacitus places Tiberius within a *quod*-clause that is in apposition to the entire first half of the sentence. Within the clause, Tacitus focuses the reader's attention on Tiberius; he is the object of the verb and the focus of not only Piso's gaze, but our own. All of the adjectives refer to Tiberius, and Tacitus presents them in a rhetorically structured manner, using anaphora and alliteration (*sine miseratione, sine ira, obstinatum clausumque*). Tacitus highlights Tiberius' disturbing lack of emotion, either positive or negative (*sine miseratione, sine ira*). The emperor's face is described as unmovable (*obstinatum*), closed-off (*clausum*), and like an unbreakable wall (*ne . . . perrumperetur*). Tacitus creates an indelible image for the reader: not of Piso the insurrectionist, but rather of Tiberius the cruel judge. Tacitus thus makes Tiberius' apparent impartiality terrifying. Piso, we are led to believe, is left helpless before the impassive and silent Tiberius.

After Piso's ordeal in the senate he returns home, and is found the next morning with his throat cut and a sword lying beside him (3.15.3). While Tacitus leads the reader to believe in Piso's guilt,[17] we still feel pity for the former minister. Tacitus' use of the close-up places the Piso story into perspective through an emotional appeal and, most importantly, the gaze of the reader.

The Persecution of Nero Caesar

Another example of Tacitus' use of the emperor's close-up occurs later in the Tiberian books, when Sejanus and his informants seal the fate of Germanicus' son Nero Caesar. In this episode, Tacitus slowly shifts from disinterested third-person narration to a more engaged and focalized voice as he lists the young Nero's sufferings, bringing the reader into sympathy with the beleaguered character and adding a visual component.[18] The passage is organized as a list, with additional elements piling up on Nero Caesar until both he and the reader are overwhelmed:

> nam alius occursum eius vitare, quidam salutatione reddita statim averti, plerique inceptum sermonem abrumpere, insistentibus contra inridentibusque qui Seiano fautores aderant.
>
> 4.60.2

> One man would avoid his encounter, some would exchange greetings, then immediately turn away; many broke off conversations in progress, to the urging and jeering of the Sejanus-promoters present.

After this passage, Tacitus notes the detailed reports made about Nero for the benefit of Sejanus, delivered to the minister first by Nero's wife and then her mother, Livilla. Sejanus even corrupts Nero's brother into joining the conspiracy (4.60.2). Thus, unlike in the case of Piso, the reader feels a strong sense of empathy for Nero, as Tacitus focalizes through the swirl of people turning away from the doomed prince.

At the grammatical level, Tacitus highlights the passage in various ways. Through the use of historical infinitives (*vitare, averti, abrumpere*), Tacitus adds a vivid tone and gives it a sense of breathless speed.[19] The use of historical infinitives is a technique common to ancient rhetoric, and serves to increase the pacing of a narrative by simplifying the grammatical construction. Although the subjects of sentences remain in the nominative case, the verbs are not conjugated, as though the author is moving so quickly, and is so caught up in the story, that he (or she) does not have time to bother with the formalities.[20] The reader should also note the use of *fautores* for Sejanus' henchmen, as the term can mean "theatrical supporter" in addition to "political supporter,"[21] which adds a hint of filmic staging to the scene.

After a lengthy description of Sejanus' followers and sycophants, Tacitus signals a break in the narrative with the intensifier *enimvero*, drawing the reader's attention to the next statement: the description of Tiberius' face in close-up.[22]

> enimvero Tiberius torvus aut falsum renidens vultu: seu loqueretur seu taceret iuvenis, crimen ex silentio, ex voce.
>
> 4.60.2

> But Tiberius was grim or deceptively beaming in expression. Speaking or silent, Nero was blamed for silence or speech.

The vision of Tiberius' close-up is much more frightening in this instance than in the Piso example of book 3. In book 4, under the evil influence of Sejanus, Tiberius is becoming more brazen in his cruelty, occasionally allowing it to show in his face. The carefully unemotional and impassive Tiberius of the Piso episode is now gone, and has been replaced with a grim face (*torvus . . . vultu*) that falsely smiles back at the viewer (*falsum renidens*). The dangerous and internally conflicted image of an emperor smiling threats is especially abhorrent to Tacitus, and he makes it so for his reader. Not only is the emperor ambiguous both in smiling and looking cruel, but the smile is obviously lying. At this point, the reader is watching from Nero's point of view, and Nero is able to tell that Tiberius is dissimulating, making the emperor's false but projected ambiguity all the more awful. Throughout the *Annales*, Tacitus is extremely vocal about the distaste that senators felt for disingenuous emperors (e.g., 1.11.3). Even at the level of the grammar Tiberius has become more threatening; no longer the accusative object of Piso's gaze, he is now watching and showing expression in the nominative case.

The placement of the noun *iuvenis* between the introductory clauses (*seu . . . seu . . .*) and the causes of the charge (*ex . . . ex . . .*) gives the reader the visual effect of the young man trapped, alone, with his charge (*crimen*). Moreover, Tacitus employs a chiastic (ABBA) pattern with speech and silence, where Nero is walled in first by silence (*taceret . . . silentio*), then by speech (*loqueretur . . . voce*). Tacitus' use of parallelism and anaphora in this section (*seu . . . seu, ex . . . ex*) is unusual, and serves both to highlight the isolation of Nero and the "stacking" of the charges. Via anaphora, which removes the usual conjunctions employed in Latin, Tacitus suggests the piling up of insurmountable charges against the accused. The reader is left with a sense of futility; there is nothing Nero Caesar can do to free himself. This placement highlights both the inescapable nature of the charges, and leaves us with the image of Nero as a young man already imprisoned by the futility of his actions. Tacitus directs the reader's gaze once again to the deceitful face of Tiberius as we share Nero's horror of the imperial close-up.

In both of these examples, Tacitus deploys the close-up to force his readers to share in, and experience for themselves, the emotional turmoil felt by senators and nobles during the reign of Tiberius. Like Welles' staging of Hank Quinlan, the inscrutably malign force behind *Touch of Evil*, Tacitus presents Tiberius in close-up as the emotionless, ambiguous, and fatally unreadable emperor.

Tacitus' narrative changes drastically after the Tiberian books, as each emperor is portrayed in a different manner and register. Claudius, at least in the surviving portions of books 11 and 12, is portrayed as bookish and entirely subject to the will and plots of his wives and freedmen. While Tacitus showcases the brazenness of Messalina and the cold calculations of Narcissus, any focus on the emperor Claudius ends in derision rather than terror. Claudius, therefore, is not a fitting subject for the kind of close-ups that reveal so much about the characters of Tiberius and Nero.

Nero

Tacitus' Nero is constantly theatrical and increasingly divorced from reality.[23] Nero is ever the performer whose only fear is an inattentive audience. Through the course of the Neronian books, Nero becomes more tyrannical and dramatic as he removes the people (his Praetorian Prefect, his sister, his mother, and his tutor and ghost-writer) who have checked and restrained his behavior. Matching the emperor's love of the performance and the *outré*, Tacitus stages a close-up of the emperor, in which the viewer becomes privy to Nero's play-within-a-play internal machinations.

Following the failure of the conspiracy to replace the emperor with C. Calpurnius Piso, Nero grew increasingly paranoid and bloodthirsty. After executing the conspirators and those implicated in the plot, Nero began destroying the senators against whom he held grudges. Among these was the consul M. Vestinus Atticus, whom Nero ordered arrested during a dinner-party the accused was hosting (15.69.1). Rather than face arrest and trial, Vestinus committed suicide, leaving his guests surrounded by Nero's guards (15.69.2).

> circumdati interim custodia qui simul discubuerant, nec nisi provecta nocte omissi sunt, postquam pavorem eorum, ex mensa exitium opperientium, et imaginatus et inridens Nero satis supplicii luisse ait pro epulis consularibus.
>
> 15.69.3

> Surrounded meanwhile by a guard, his guests were held until late at night, when their panic—they expected destruction after dinner and Nero laughed to imagine it—was, Nero said, *Sufficient punishment for dining with a consul.*

After showing the preemptive suicide of Vestinus in a series of rapid staccato sentences, the narrative unexpectedly remains at the party. We are subjected to further terrors as we imagine the increasing fear of the dinner guests, anticipating their own executions at the emperor's command. The scene is restless and active—the guests are described only in verbal terms: the guests who had sat down together (*qui simul discumbuerant*) are surrounded (*circumdati*) and eventually released (*omissi*).

Our focus on the diners is changed at the *postquam*, as Tacitus directs our gaze to fear (*pavorem*) and its causes (*ex mensa exitium opperientium*). The subject of this part of the sentence is postponed, and is only revealed after the verbal adjectives (*imaginatus*, *inridens*). In this way, the reader knows, before the subject's identity is revealed, that the fear of the senators is being imagined (*imaginatus*) and laughed at (*inridens*). The reader is left to imagine the warped sensibilities of an individual who would intentionally daydream of, and find amusement in, others' panicked fear. Immediately following these paired verbal ideas, the subject of these actions is revealed to be Nero. The reader must visualize not only these dinner guests through Nero's imagination, but we must also gaze at Nero as he enjoys the diners' suffering. Nero, however, cannot enjoy the senators' terror directly, and must visually reconstruct the scene in his own mind in order to extract the greatest pleasure from the scene. Tacitus is exceptionally vivid in his verb choice, using *imaginor*, which occurs only here in Tacitus' extant works, for Nero's visualizing.[24] By using this word, which deals with bringing an image literally before the eyes, Tacitus gives the reader a striking depiction of Nero's virtual voyeurism.[25] The reader, then, imagines Nero delighting in his own visual picturing of the pain and fear he is causing.

Tacitus, through the use of the close-up, shows his reader images of the potential horrors inherent in the face of an emperor. On each occasion, his close-ups inspire dread, mistrust, and hatred for that emperor. We have seen how Tacitus can make impassiveness, as well as expressive hatred and delight, similarly terrifying. Just as Hank Quinlan horrifies the viewer through his expressionless (and therefore ambiguous) power, Tacitus allows Tiberius and Nero to gaze back at the reader, forcing an engagement in the same visual interplay.

The Maltese Falcon and the Threatening Gaze

Tacitus' close-ups of Nero demonstrate the horrors of Neronian theatricality and multiple levels of viewing—themes that dominate the murder of Britannicus. Tacitus elaborates on his use of the ambiguous and challenging close-up, introducing a complex conversation of gazes. By focusing on the vision of each character in turn, the reader is forced to interpret the scene, through multiple focalizations, with each audience member as they attempt to possess and obscure knowledge through the gaze.

In film, this technique is used well in John Huston's *The Maltese Falcon* (1941).[26] Near the end of the work, the private detective Sam Spade (Humphrey Bogart) demands a "fall guy" for the film's several unaccounted-for murders as part of his price for handing over the Maltese falcon to the criminal Caspar

Gutman (Sydney Greenstreet). After Spade suggests Gutman's hired gunman Wilmer Cook (Elisha Cook, Jr.) as a possible candidate, Wilmer attempts to kill Spade and is knocked out. At this point, Spade demands that Wilmer take the fall or Spade will turn the whole gang over to the police. Gutman reluctantly agrees. Spade then demands to know the truth about all of the deaths so that he can better arrange the story fabricated for the police. Gutman candidly gives Spade the history of the murders, finishing his narrative as Wilmer begins to wake.[27]

The scene, up to that point filmed in the usual medium shot showing Spade, Gutman, and Wilmer, cuts to a close-up of Wilmer's face as he slowly regains consciousness. Matching Wilmer's gaze, we cut to Gutman from a low-angle shot as he looks threateningly at Wilmer and at us. The scene cuts back to Wilmer, who remains motionless except for his eyes as he looks to his right. Huston then cuts to reveal Cairo (Peter Lorre) pitilessly looking down at Wilmer over the end of his cigarette and, like Gutman, shown to menacing effect from a very low angle.

The scene returns to Wilmer as he glances to his upper left, cutting to Spade, who is leaning in and matching Wilmer's glance by looking off-screen. Probably because Huston wanted to keep Spade's face reassuring to the viewer, his is the only answering gaze that does not look directly and threateningly back at the camera. We cut to Wilmer one last time as he swivels his eyes directly to the viewer, and his gaze is matched by a cut to a close-up of Brigid O'Shaughnessy (Mary Astor) staring back at him (and us).

During this conversation of gazes, the camera follows each of Wilmer's apprehensive glances, with an answering close-up as each character returns his gaze malevolently. After each gaze, rotating through all of the characters in the scene, the camera returns to the ever-more-terrified face of Wilmer.[28] Wilmer, at first uncertain as he wakes, reads menace in Gutman's face, which prompts him to look at the other characters, hoping for a non-threatening answering gaze. After the last close-up, the scene returns to normal mid-distance filming as Wilmer, realizing his fate, puts his head in his hands. The probability that Wilmer's character is coded as homosexual makes his gaze particularly susceptible to subversion and challenge in 1940s cinema, even by Gutman and Cairo, who are also coded in sexually problematic ways.[29] Wilmer's homosexual coding allows Spade's (heteronormative) masculinity to dominate through negative definition against women and homosexual men, who, in accord with the 1940s detective genre, are punished in the film.[30] Huston's deployment of the language of the gaze narrates in a few seconds not only Wilmer's abandonment

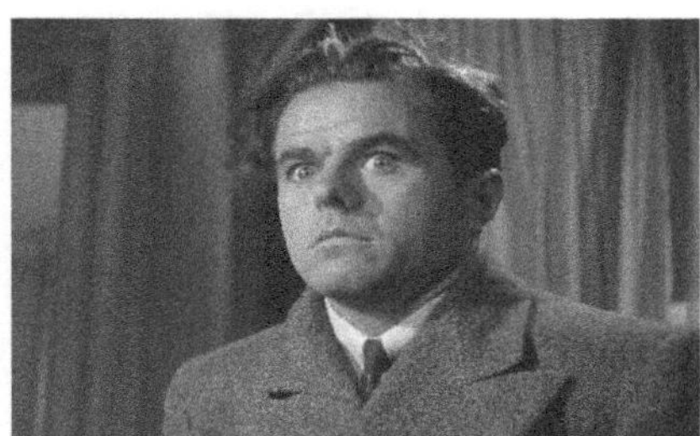
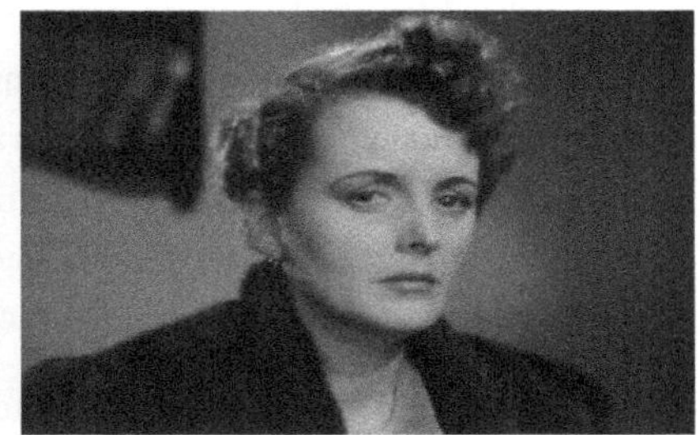

Figures 3.2 to 3.9 *The Maltese Falcon*, directed by John Huston © Warner Brothers Pictures 1941. All rights reserved.

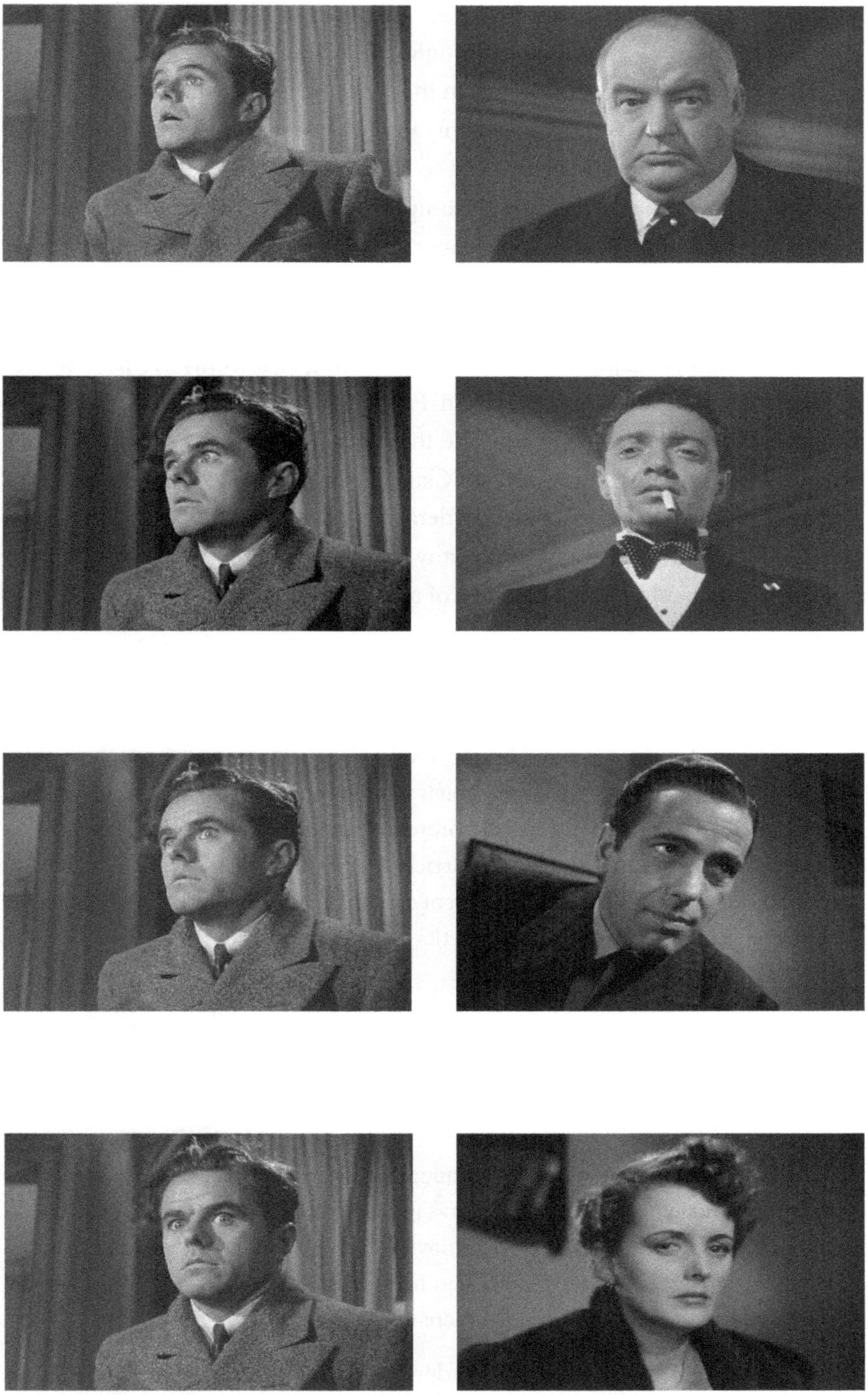

by his erstwhile accomplices, but also the violence that results from ever-changing loyalties, a major theme throughout the film. This visual interchange is one of the very few uses of close-ups in the film, and is made the more powerful as there are no intervening scenes or auditory input. The information that Wilmer will be sacrificed is conveyed to him (and us) directly through visual cues and the reading of faces in close-up. During the murder of Britannicus, Tacitus also mobilizes a language of gazes, creating a scene of "spectators turned spectacle"—at the same time watching and aware of being watched.[31]

Early in book 13, Nero had recently been named emperor after the murder of his adoptive father, Claudius. As Nero began acting against his mother's wishes by removing the influential freedman Pallas from power, Agrippina became terrified at losing political control. She then threatened that she could transfer her power and support from Nero to Claudius' only son, Britannicus (13.14.2–3). Nero, in an unexpected move, orders Britannicus poisoned at a banquet, attended by the imperial family and many powerful senators.[32] After Britannicus falls dead, Tacitus shows the reactions of all present.

> trepidatur a circumsedentibus, diffugiunt imprudentes: at quibus altior intellectus, resistunt defixi et Neronem intuentes. ille ut erat reclinis et nescio similis, solitum ita ait per comitialem morbum, quo prima ab infantia adflictaretur Britannicus, et redituros paulatim visus sensusque. at Agrippina<e> is pavor, ea consternatio mentis, quamvis vultu premeretur, emicuit, ut perinde ignaram fuisse <quam> Octaviam sororem Britannici constiterit: quippe sibi supremum auxilium ereptum et parricidii exemplum intellegebat. Octavia quoque, quamvis rudibus annis, dolorem caritatem, omnes adfectus abscondere didicerat. ita post breve silentium repetita convivii laetitia.
>
> 13.16.3–4

> There was alarm among those near, flight by the unwise. Those with deeper insight stayed in place and watched Nero. He, remaining at ease and as if unwitting, said: *This is normal for the alarming disease that from his first infancy has afflicted Britannicus. Sight and feeling will return gradually.* For Agrippina, such panic, such consternation—although their expression was repressed—flashed out that people agreed she was as ignorant as Octavia, Britannicus' sister. Indeed, she saw her last support removed, and the family-killing precedent. Octavia, too, though of raw youth, had learned to hide grief, affection—every emotion. Thus, after a short silence, there was a return to the party's gaiety.

When examining this passage, the reader should be mindful of the interaction between spectacle and spectator-participants. Tacitus changes focalizor and visual object repeatedly during this scene, altering not only who we watch with, but where our gaze is directed. This scene is extremely complex due to the large number of gazes present. Tacitus, however, tightly controls the reader's gaze as he not only describes but also interprets this scene. Each gaze is answered, while every focalizor/actor is trying to acquire information and, simultaneously, to not reveal any emotion or knowledge.[33]

The nature of the initial spectacle, is not in doubt: everyone present knows that Nero has finally killed his adoptive brother and only rival to power.[34] Tacitus had repeatedly hinted that Britannicus would be killed and, with Nero ambitious for power, Britannicus' death seemed likely to follow on the heels of Claudius'.[35] The vital point of this passage is, therefore, not the fate of Britannicus, but instead how convincing a display each viewer presents as an actor.[36]

Bartsch, in her discussion of this passage, is primarily concerned with the ways in which Nero scripts the drama that is played out at his dinner, and the fact that he is the only real spectator of that drama.[37] Each participant then fails (Agrippina) or succeeds (Octavia) in playing their part. In the following discussion, I add another layer to Bartsch's reading by following the gaze of all of the participants as they take cues, gain knowledge, and immediately conceal that knowledge in front of their imperial audience. The guests are not merely actors playing out scripted roles for their emperor/audience, but fellow viewers and interpreters of the scene, which deepens the emotional tension and disquiet. Tacitus not only offers a glimpse of Nero's machinations but, through the visual interplay of the internal audiences, draws his reader into the drama. Since the scene is rather convoluted, I address each individual spectator/actor in the order that Tacitus introduces them and follow the transmission/concealment of knowledge through the gaze: the *nobiles*, Nero, Agrippina, and Octavia.

The *Nobiles*

The first set of spectators, the elite consular senators, should be addressed in two groups: those who fled and those who stayed. The former is composed of the innocents not versed in acting (*imprudentes*), who watch as Britannicus collapses and realize that he has been murdered. Again, they are not unique in their knowledge, only in their reactions. This inexperienced group scatters suddenly, rushing off in different directions (*diffugiunt*). Tacitus' use of *diffugio*, which appears only here in Tacitus' works,[38] gives the reader a dramatic and lively idea of the group's sudden flight. Their tactless action betrays their knowledge which, according to Tacitus, is their great mistake. They have not misread the event, but broadcast their understanding by an ill-considered flight. These senators forgot that, while watching, they were also being watched and evaluated.

The group of *nobiles* who stayed understood much better how the political game was played with Nero as *princeps*. Tacitus clearly identifies this group as possessing deeper knowledge, referring to them as possessing *altior intellectus*. What they are more intelligent about is the need to control their reactions. Reading the situation correctly, they understand that Nero has just murdered Britannicus in front of them. Rather than show their fear and horror, as did the first group, the experienced *nobiles* try to fashion the correct response by taking cues from Nero. These senators, aware that they are being watched, understand that they must assume masks when performing for their emperor.[39]

Another factor in gauging the senators' reactions is Tacitus' privileging of their view.[40] Readers of Tacitus' histories quickly become educated in the mechanics of high politics through identification with the senatorial elite by means of such narrative techniques as focalization. In effect, Tacitus aligns his narrative focalization and ours, as experienced interpreters of Roman imperial politics, with this recreated audience at the court of Nero. By focalizing through the gaze of the experienced senators, Tacitus gives the reader access to the knowledge not only of what has just transpired, but how to read that information. The flow of this passage is extremely fast; the *prudentes* furtively look around the room while trying to keep their gaze fixed on Nero. The identification of Tacitus' audience with Nero's makes the passage especially moving and realistic: this is the essence of *enargeia*.[41] The reader sees the scene as it transpires.[42]

Tacitus conveys the particular horror of being watched by an emperor ever ready to expunge dissidence. The visual and emotional effect that Tacitus conveys during this scene, and through his imperial close-ups, may well have been inspired by his experiences under the emperor Domitian. In a passage from Tacitus' biography of his father-in-law Agricola, the reader is offered a first-hand description of the trauma that Tacitus experienced when forced to perform before a tyrannical emperor:

> praecipua sub Domitiano miseriarum pars erat videre et aspici, cum suspira nostra subscriberentur, cum denotandis tot hominum palloribus sufficeret saevus ille vultus et robor, quo se contra pudorem muniebat.
>
> *Agr.* 45.2[43]

> The worst of our torments under Domitian was to see him with his eyes fixed upon us. Every sigh was registered against us; and when we all turned pale, he did not scruple to make us marked men by a glance of his savage

> countenance—that blood red countenance which saved him from ever being seen to blush with shame.

This kind of experience could not fail to make a deep and lasting impression on Tacitus. Having played the charade for a cruel emperor in his own life, Tacitus is able to make the sensation vivid and terrible for his reader.

This same sensation, of performing before a vengeful ruler, is illustrated in great detail in the passage concerning Britannicus' death. In order to bring to bear its full horror, Tacitus interprets the scene for us, drawing attention to the key actions and reactions of the imperial family. The deep and penetrating gaze of the *nobiles* lingers in turn on Nero, Octavia, and Agrippina. This is conveyed through a brief, but tight description of each character's actions and posture. Tacitus is extremely economical with his directing, giving the reader only a quick, but critical, glimpse at every character. Again, Tacitus shows, rather than tells, this dangerous language of gaze.

Nero

Nero, the primary focus of attention in the room, is the only actor who is prepared for this scene. Nero's explanation of Britannicus' death in monologue (Nero's is the only voice in this passage) foreshadows Nero's further thespian aspirations in the later books of the *Annales*.[44] Tacitus reveals, through the gaze of the knowing senators, that Nero remains reclining at table (*reclinis*) and that he was acting as though he had no knowledge of the murder (*nescio similis*). With these two descriptors, the reader visualizes the *princeps*: Nero is at ease on his couch, reclining and not moving to assist his dying brother, thus presenting a picture of apathetic and cultured evil. As Tacitus describes him, Nero is also lying with his appearance, in that he actively pretends to be unaware of what is going on.[45] Nero's theatrics have become murderous even before he appears on stage. His audience, however, is unimpressed either by his studied performance or the story about Britannicus' fictive epilepsy. Unlike Tiberius, Nero is flagrant, with no real interest in whether anyone is convinced by his acting.[46]

Nero is also implicitly watching his audience. While Nero-as-viewer is not directly addressed in the passage, the emperor's gaze provides the necessary context for the dual responses of the noble senators. Those who fled would not be acting foolishly, except that they are themselves being judged. Additionally, the senators who remained, as well as Octavia and Agrippina, are controlling their reactions for the implicit and assumed gaze of the emperor.

Agrippina

By the time that Britannicus has been murdered, Tacitus' reader knows Agrippina as a consummate politician. In this scene, however, Agrippina makes the mistake of allowing her emotions to be visible for a brief moment before she regains self-control. Tacitus heightens the language here in order to bring its visuality to the fore. As the senators' gaze moves from Nero to his mother, the emotions that overcome her expression take precedence. Tacitus implies here that these emotions have drawn the gaze of the senators by placing the emotions, panic (*pavor*) and alarm (*consternatio*), in the nominative case, leaving Agrippina in a referential dative. The importance of these emotions is further heightened by the parallel and anaphoric intensifying demonstratives (*is pavor, ea consternatio*), which further draw the reader's attention. In this way, Tacitus makes it very clear that Agrippina's reaction has a force of its own, outside of Agrippina's agency. The reaction flashes forth violently (*emicuit*)[47] from her face, even as she is attempting to suppress it (*quamvis vultu premeretur*). Terror has overcome Agrippina, to the extent that the senators can read the innocence in her countenance. Further, her lack of foreknowledge is compared with Octavia's. Tacitus' reader knows that this murder was intended as a direct message from Nero to Agrippina, as Nero removes his mother's last safeguard and support. While the watching senators (and we) can read innocence on Agrippina's face, Nero, we are led to believe, would be delighted with the visual evidence that his dramatic message had been received.

After Agrippina's reaction, the narrative gaze moves outside of the senators' ability to see: into Agrippina's mind. Through focalization, Tacitus reveals Agrippina's thoughts and fears to the reader, as well as the full importance of what has just happened. Until this point in the narrative, Agrippina had been ruling through her young son with the aid of his tutors and freedmen. With the death of Britannicus, however, Agrippina understands that Nero is much more politically ruthless than she had previously thought: Nero now has a paradigm for parricide.

While the term *parricidium* strictly means the killing of one's father or mother, its definition can be stretched to include all family members.[48] Tacitus' use of the term here seems odd at first glance, given that Britannicus is only Nero's adoptive brother, with whom he shares no parent. The use of *parricidium*, however, does bring to the foreground other familial murders in Nero's family—the past murder of Claudius, Nero's adoptive father, and the future murder of his mother, Agrippina. Tacitus has constructed the scene, including Agrippina's focalization, to be read back on the past and forward on the future.

The temporal suggestion is especially pointed, since Britannicus dies in much the same way as his father Claudius. Even the insignificant details concerning failed poisoning attempts, due to the releasing of the bowels, are included in both cases.[49] This backshadowing is especially effective since the narrative at this point is focalized through Agrippina, who is well aware of the details of her husband's murder since she herself was its instigator. Britannicus' murder, however, is more than a reminder to Agrippina (and to the reader) of past familial murder. For Agrippina, the true horror is that the death of Britannicus is an *exemplum* of murder within the family.

Tacitus' use of *exemplum* here is highly charged, recalling the preface of Livy's monumental *Ab urbe condita*, wherein Livy promises a history full of behaviors to emulate or avoid (Livy, *praef.* 10). As Feldherr points out, Livian *exempla* can only exist as long as the oligarchic senatorial regime continues.[50] In Tacitus' nightmare world of Neronian Rome, the behavior to emulate is the murder of inconvenient family members. Nero now has a precedent to follow, and nothing is sacrosanct. Agrippina, dramatically deprived of her last defense, begins to actively fear for her own life, and rightly so, as Nero engineers her murder at the start of the next book (14.8.5).[51] Agrippina, reminded of the past, and fearful of the future, attempts to wipe the emotions from her face, and to thus remove them from the gaze of all present.

Octavia

After the complex viewing of (and, through focalization, with) Agrippina, the senators' gaze moves to Octavia. Here the narrative is again in close-up, as the senators study Octavia's face. Unlike their realization of the falseness of Nero's dramatic performance, the senators' view of Octavia is poignant and touching. Tacitus has already mentioned Octavia, noting her innocence during his description of Agrippina's reaction. The full discussion of Octavia, however, is delayed until after the description and focalization of Agrippina, and the reader is expecting the pathos of an emotional outburst at the death of her brother. This desire to view Octavia's grief or sisterly emotion is frustrated: Octavia's expression is not described at all.

Tacitus explains her lack of visible reaction by stating that she has learned to bury emotion (*dolorem caritatem, omnis adfectus abscondere*) below her expression. This skill, which the senators have also learned, explains why her face is unreadable. Octavia's youth serves as an additional source of sympathy, since she has had to learn this painful acting lesson at such a young age (*quamvis rudibus annis*). Thus, the image that Tacitus creates (and that we and the senators see) is one of a young, but long-suffering innocent, whose death is also not far away.[52] Tacitus depicts Octavia's emotionless mask as the best self-presentation against the gaze of a tyrannical emperor. She has learned, through the experience of multiple deaths within her family, to betray no fear or emotion despite her understanding of the situation. The shock at Britannicus' death would be the greatest for Octavia, who at this point has no family outside of Agrippina and Nero, with both her father (and now brother) murdered and her mother, Messalina, executed. She has been taught comportment through the sorrow and terror of living at the court of Nero.

Tacitus ends this scene with classic Tacitean brevity (*ita post breve silentium repetita convivii laetitia*).[53] It is as though, with the horrors of the evening over, the petrified guests can resume the pleasures of the banquet. The reader should note the placement of *laetitia* at the end of the sentence (and, indeed the entire passage), much like the punchline of an epigram or satire. The image created is heavily sardonic, paradoxically giving away Nero's true feelings concerning his brother and, at the same time, showing how monstrous those feelings are. This picture, emphasized by the epigrammatic *bon mot*, ends the scene on a disjointed and unnerving note, as everyone ignores the elephant (or, in this case, the cadaver) in the room.

This passage is one of the most visually complex scenes in the *Annales*. The reactions and descriptions of all present, complete with a separate foray into Agrippina's thoughts and Tacitus' sardonic ending commentary, comprise only six sentences. Almost all of the narrative techniques which have been discussed thus far appear here. The passage begins with a sustained focalization through the senators' eyes and the scene is described as they scan the room. Their gaze includes several close-ups, another focalization (through Agrippina), and temporal suggestion. The senators' vision takes in not only the emperor, but, like Wilmer's frightened glancing from one person to the next, reads emotion and knowledge in Octavia and Agrippina.

Through communication of gazes, Tacitus seamlessly creates a world in which the slightest glance can betray, and where more is seen than can be voiced. Just as in *The Maltese Falcon*, each group of characters must both gaze and also receive the gaze of all others in the room. In Tacitus, the full import of what has just occurred is both experienced and interpreted, as well as concealed, through the interplay of gaze. The experienced senators watch the faces of Agrippina and Octavia to determine what they are thinking. As the *nobiles* watch they are also targeted by Nero's gaze, aimed at discovering whether they are aware of what they have just witnessed. Agrippina's momentary lapse is noted by her son, and the message of murder is delivered. All the participants in the room, as well as Tacitus' reader, gaze at Nero, his court, and his crime, and are unsurprised to find Nero's gaze returning their own.

Damnatio Memoriae, *Rebecca*, and Watching the Invisible

Tacitus, as we have seen, can direct the vision of his reader to close-ups of Tiberius and Nero, allowing us, along with the doomed characters of the *Annales*, to attempt to read their expressions. He can also direct sight-driven scenes, such as the death of Britannicus, forcing the reader in turn to assume the perspective of the knowledgeable senators and experience the apprehensions of Agrippina. This ability to direct the reader's visual perceptions can be taken a step further, when Tacitus controls the gaze of his reader to such an extent as to show the invisible. At points in the *Annales*, history is told through absence, when the lack of a character or image is the center of focus. While some images in the *Annales* are visually accosting, such as Tiberius' false smile, Tacitus also applies his authorial lens in scenes where the truth would be unseen without his intervention.

The need for this deeper level of understanding—of a historian's ability to show the invisible—is most clearly illustrated by the Roman practice of what has been called "*damnatio memoriae*."[54] After the death of a prominent Roman found guilty of treason, or an emperor vilified by the senate, memory sanctions were often imposed. These punishments against the memory of the dead often extended to the destruction or alteration of statuary representations[55] and physical inscriptions of the person's name. These inscriptions, once altered, were sometimes allowed to remain in place. The original dedicatory purpose of the inscription was thus changed: instead of recalling the person in an honorific context, it serves as a lasting monument to shameful sanctions. The inscription thus becomes a memorial to the erasure, rather than of the individual. In some instances, epigraphic erasures were carried out in such a way to preserve both the name of the condemned and the visual evidence of its destruction. The viewer is simultaneously reminded not only of the individual, but of the crime. The power of memory sanctions exists only as long as the viewer remembers whose name or image has been eradicated. By supplying the names, faces, and facts to fill these erasures—that is, by showing the invisible—Tacitus prolongs the memory of his readers.

A powerful example of this kind of erasure can be seen in Fig. 3.10.[56]

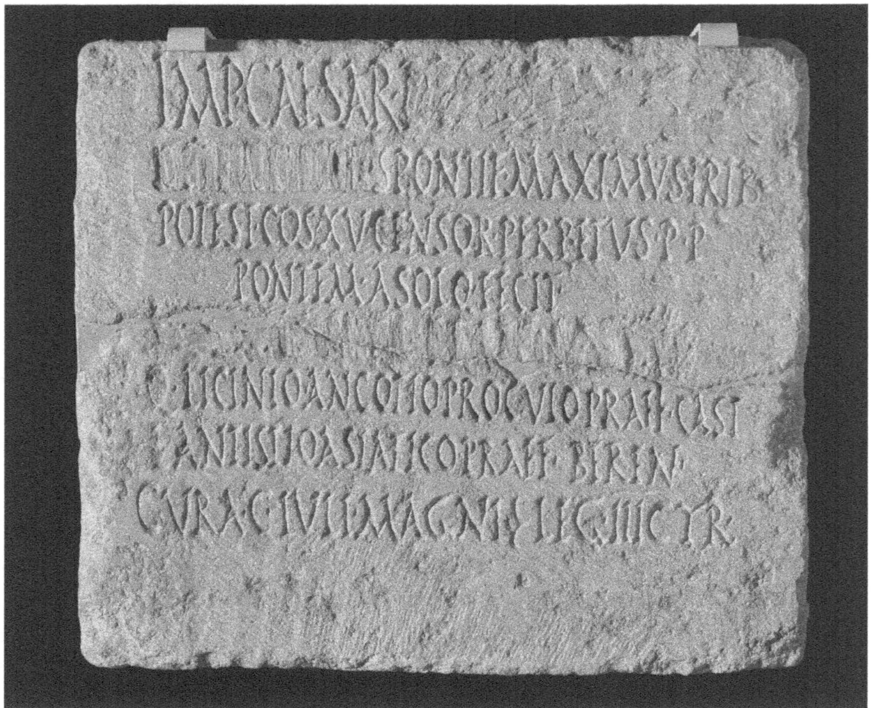

Figure 3.10 CIL 3.13580, image © Trustees of the British Museum.

In this inscription, now in the British Museum, there have been two erasures, both as the result of memory sanctions.[57] The original inscription reads:

> IMP CAESAR ~~DOMITIANUS AUG~~
> ~~GERMANICU~~S PONTIFMAXIMUS TRIB
> POTEST COS XV CENSOR PERPETUUS PP
> PONTEM A SOLO FECIT
> ---[58]
> Q LICINIO ANCOTIO PROCULO PRAEF CAST
> L ANTISTIO ASIATICO PRAEF BEREN
> CURA C IULI MAGNI y LEG III CYR

The names of both the emperor Domitian (after 98 CE) and the praefectus Aegyptus M. Mettius Rufus are both erased. The praefect suffered memory sanctions under Domitian, and then Domitian suffered the same fate under Nerva. As Flower points out, however, the erasure of Domitian's name did not restore that of Rufus—both are lost in through memory sanctions.[59] It is against this exact kind of memory loss that Tacitus writes his *Annales*: so that the reader can remember both the good and the evil who have become invisible.

Tacitus' interest in preserving the memory of the victims of the emperors is one of the central goals of the *Annales*. After the mass of deaths following the Pisonian Conspiracy, Tacitus seems to feel the need to catalog the final moments of the senators who lost their lives under Nero. For this, he offers the following rationale and explanation:

> detur hoc inlustrium virorum posteritati, ut, quo modo exsequiis a promisca sepultura separantur, ita in traditione supremorum accipiant habeantque propriam memoriam.
>
> 16.16.2

> Let us grant this to the legacy of notable men: just as they are distinct in their funerals from common burial, so let them receive in the record of their final hours, too, lasting possession of a particular remembrance.

Tacitus considered his *Annales* to be, at least in some fashion, a memorial for those who could not receive traditional Roman funerary rites and remembrances. The *Annales* serve as a commemoration for an otherwise unrecoverable and unremembered past, repressed by either the senate or the emperors.[60] In both contexts, Tacitus crafts the *Annales* as a secret history of the Julio-Claudians, a necessary commentary without which the reader would misinterpret the past by accepting the version left in the wake of the emperors. Tacitus alters memory in the *Annales* by helping posterity to recall the deeds that resulted in memory sanctions. In effect, Tacitus reminds his readers what caused the villains of the past to deserve being forgotten.

A film that shows the invisible to similar dramatic effect is Alfred Hitchcock's *Rebecca* (1940).[61] Near the end of the film, Maxim de Winter (Lawrence Olivier) tells his new wife (Joan Fontaine) about the death of his first wife, Rebecca. When Maxim indicates that Rebecca began her final conversation sitting on a certain divan, the camera follows his gesture, and the new Mrs. de Winter's gaze, to the now empty divan but does not cut back to the two living characters. Rebecca remains the focus of the scene, although she is only shown through empty blocking and staging, as the camera adjusts for where she would be, if she were visible. At this point, the second Mrs. de Winter's gaze is supplanted by Maxim's as the narrative focalizor aligns with his character. This scene has been discussed by film studies scholars as the transfer of the gaze from the second Mrs. de Winter to Maxim, and the forcible replacement of her own look with his.[62] In the "woman's films" of the 1940s, the feminine searching and curious gaze were often avoided by a similar appropriation of the gaze by a male character.[63] Maxim contextualizes this scene in authoritative voice-over, narrating how Rebecca moved and spoke to him, quoting her as the camera tracks and focuses on the visually absent Rebecca.[64] As Maxim supplies her dialogue and the camera places her within the scene, Rebecca is hauntingly resurrected. According to Modleski, this highlights the horror of absence, which the viewer must "experience . . . as an active force."[65] This visual effect continues until Maxim recalls how Rebecca stumbled and fell to her death. The camera moves rapidly to catch this invisible action, then cuts to Fontaine's character as she gazes, horrorstruck, at the invisible corpse. The camera follows Fontaine's character's gaze back to the floor, panning upward to Maxim as he backs away, his eyes also fixed on the absent body on the floor. The scene then returns to shot-reverse-shot as Maxim and Fontaine's character continue to talk.

This is the key scene of the film, as the plot has been building to the reveal of Rebecca's true character and the nature of her death since the beginning of the narrative. The power of Rebecca's personality and sexuality is destroyed during this scene, which is possible only after the substitution of Maxim's subjective gaze for his wife's, and the effacement of the second Mrs. de Winter's personal judgment.[66] One of the main themes in *Rebecca* is the continuing presence of Rebecca as a character who, though absent, is far stronger and more powerful than the consistently visible second Mrs. de Winter.[67] Hitchcock, by showing the invisible Rebecca through Maxim's eyes, stresses that the most important events in the story happened in the past and are invisible to those in the present.[68] Hitchcock's subversion of focalizor into another character's focalization mirrors Tacitus' subversion of the reader's gaze with his own as he reveals the invisible in Julio-Claudian Rome.

Tacitus tells the secret and hidden history of the Julio-Claudians when he brings alive the lost action of events and commentary that cannot be seen without his assistance. This occurs at several points during the *Annales*, and gives the audience an opportunity to see beyond the veneer of recorded history. The reader is guided to imagine the scene as described by Tacitus, and is made aware only later that parts of that scene did not exist. The reader is then able to view both halves of the history: the evident, and the erased. In much the same way as a viewer interprets an instance of *damnatio memoriae*, the missing parts of the picture are filled in by Tacitus' commentary. This double-exposure of the invisible onto the visible leaves a ghostly image on the reader's imagination. Moreover, these invisible objects are usually the focal points, and key to the understanding, of these passages. Tacitus becomes an interpreter, showing the unknown to the audience and enabling them to understand history in a way that would not otherwise be possible.[69]

Invisible *Cursus*

One of the most visible proclamations of a Roman senator's career is the listing, often in inscriptions, of the offices that he has held during his life, the so-called *cursus honorum*. Normally, we would expect that a senator with a long list of public offices, achievements, and service would be a citizen concerned primarily with his civic duty to Rome. As so often in Tacitus, however, these expectations are subverted and challenged. In the world of the principate, where honors are awarded for sycophancy and political control, Tacitus forces us to question whether a full resume is really indicative of an honorable senatorial career.

Following annalistic historiographical tradition, Tacitus ends book 3 with obituaries of prominent Romans.[70] Here Tacitus recounts the death of L. Ateius Capito (3.75.1), a man of humble background,[71] whose career had been accelerated by the imperial favor of Augustus. Tacitus implies that imperial favor is the only requirement for power, the attainment of which is undeserved or at least questionable.[72] In addition to showing the reader Capito's means for achieving the consulship, Tacitus provides Augustus' motive: the emperor wanted Capito to defeat Antistius Labeo in their competition for the consulship, presumably so that Capito could further Augustus' interests in the senate (3.75.1).[73] Tacitus then reveals the respect that the two senators enjoyed afterwards:

> namque illa aetas duo pacis decora simul tulit; sed Labeo incorrupta libertate et ob id fama celebratior, Capitonis obsequium dominantibus magis probabatur. illi, quod praeturam intra stetit, commendatio ex iniuria, huic, quod consulatum adeptus est, odium ex invidia oriebatur.
>
> 3.75.2

> The age produced two paragons of peacetime pursuits simultaneously. Labeo kept his independence unsullied and was accordingly more celebrated of reputation; Capito's deference won more approval from despots. For Labeo, who was limited to the praetorship, plaudits accrued from injury; for Capito, who had held a consulship, hatred arose from envy.

The senators' condemnation of Capito's toadying (*obsequium dominantibus*) is clear in this passage, as is the groundswell support that Labeo received from his colleagues, if not from the emperors. Tacitus draws a severe contrast between the two senatorial types. On the one hand, the sycophants who praise whomever is in power are promoted and despised; on the other, senators true to their own opinions and their freedom to speak truth, even to power, attain praise rather than rank, even if only posthumously. The character of senators, Tacitus implies, can still be reconstructed by the *cursus honorum*, but only with an important *caveat* about the new ways by which high office could be earned.

Thus, the cases of Capito and Labeo illustrate the two systems of achieving honors (*duo decora*) under the empire. Capito follows the old *cursus honorum*, in which the attainment of the consulship was the height of senatorial success, but in the new fashion, relying on imperial favor rather than political merit for advancement. Labeo realizes that the consulship has become an empty title only given to imperial sycophants, and due to his Republican love of freedom of speech (*libertas*), does not seek the meaningless office.[74] Capito and Labeo receive different portions of the rank and esteem of the consulship, which were united under the Republic, but under the principate have become separate. Capito has achieved the consulship, but is censured for this office as it is undeserved. Labeo fails to win the office, but is praised for the very *libertas* that prevented him from reaching it. This theme is one that the reader increasingly encounters in the *Annales*: imperial selection of sycophants for office and the persecution of senators with Republican sensibilities.[75]

Tacitus, however, achieves more than the juxtaposition of two senatorial careers in the obituary of Capito. Through the introduction of the *duo decora*, Tacitus posits both a *cursus honorum* warped by the principate and the creation of an invisible *cursus* for senators who valued *libertas* over sycophancy.[76] Whereas a senatorial career during the Republic could be gauged simply by counting the offices held, this evaluation method becomes increasingly problematic under the principate. No longer do offices imply merit, but can instead show collusion; the winners in a race to the bottom. On occasion, as Tacitus shows, the consulate became a mark of imperial subservience and the surrender of senatorial *libertas*.[77]

The antithesis of this warped *cursus* is the invisible *cursus* of offices unattained as a mark of free thinking, free speech, and a certain independence from the controlling favor of the *princeps*.[78] Through this gloss on the obituary of Capito, Tacitus makes the reader aware of the new tools needed to analyze imperial history. Under the principate, a less illustrious senatorial resume may be more indicative of honor, respect, and merit.

That said, as a matter of history rather than historiography, this simplistic dual-*cursus* system should not be taken too far.[79] The traditional *cursus* was obviously still followed by senators,[80] including Cornelius Tacitus himself, who, at least according to the dual rubric of Labeo and Capito, followed the latter rather than the former in achieving promotion under both Vespasian and Domitian (*Hist.* 1.1.3). Tacitus' main point, however, is that the truth of history and senatorial politics under the principate is often invisible. The blurring of vice and virtue in the cases of Labeo and Capito becomes increasingly emblematic of a principate more concerned with appearance than substance, and illusion over reality.

Inverted Thanksgivings

After bringing to light the invisible *cursus honorum* and the hidden subtext of career advancement through sycophancy, Tacitus reveals the inverted nature of senatorial thanksgivings to the gods in Nero's Rome.[81] Near the end of book 14, Nero's principate has plunged into one crime after another under the malignant influence of Poppaea. The book both begins and ends with Poppaea's machinations: first against Agrippina, and then against Octavia.[82] In a scene full of pathos, Tacitus recalls Octavia's last words and the manner of her death. Octavia pleaded with Nero for her life, recalling their marriage, their common ancestry, and the name of Agrippina (14.64.1). Following her vain pleas for mercy, Tacitus, in an uncharacteristic departure, spares the reader none of the gory details. All of Octavia's veins were opened. Then, after this method of execution proved too slow, she was killed by exposure to extremely hot steam (14.64.2).[83] The final indignity was that her head was severed and brought to Poppaea, as though Octavia were a traitor or a foreign enemy and Poppaea were a Roman general responsible for this conquest. After detailing this grotesque execution, Tacitus describes the senatorial reaction to this heinous crime.

> dona ob haec templis decreta que<m> ad finem memorabimus? quicumque casus temporum illorum nobis vel aliis auctoribus noscent, praesumptum habeant, quotiens fugas et caedas iussit princeps, totiens grates deis actas, quaeque rerum secundarum olim, tum publicae cladis insignia fuisse.
>
> 14.64.3

> Gifts decreed to temples—what point recording them? Whoever comes to know the events of that age from me or another authority must assume that whenever the Emperor decreed exile or killing, the gods got thanks and every former emblem of good fortune. (At that time, they were emblems of public disaster.)

Rather than the expected reaction of shock and outrage at the brutal death of Octavia, or total inaction and apathy, the senate offers votives to the gods for saving Rome from Octavia. At this point, Tacitus makes a rare first-person interruption on the narrative with an exasperated outburst of frustration with his material. Tacitus does the senate the favor of not compounding their guilt by listing every sycophantic action. Rather, Tacitus gives the reader a general rule (*praesumptum habeant*) for Nero's principate: whenever Nero ordered death or exile, the senate thanked the gods. While the reader is spared the specific instances of the senate's servile toadying, Tacitus arguably does more harm to the Order's reputation by making their behavior the general rule rather than a sad exception.

In this scene, Tacitus shows the invisible by discussing what thanksgivings to the gods used to mean (*olim*), and what they mean under Nero (*tum*). Formerly, a Roman could refer to the times that the senate offered public thanksgiving to the gods as moments when Rome had escaped destruction at the hands of an enemy or famine, or when it had conquered in war.[84] Under Nero, however, senatorial thanksgiving meant that a Roman citizen had been either exiled or executed, both of which Tacitus refers to using the loaded term *clades*, a disaster. The senate continued offering ritual thanks to the gods, but the meaning had changed into a twisted inversion of the original.

Tacitus here, as elsewhere, interprets the outward signs (*insignia*) of senatorial behavior for the reader unfamiliar with Nero's reign. The outer veneer of the Republic has not changed, but the manner of its interpretation has become warped by the principate. Tacitus shows the invisible in this instance by explaining the reason behind the ritual, and laying bare the obsequies of the senate under a tyrannical *princeps*. In directing the reader's gaze toward what is important, but invisible, Tacitus gives the reader a new way of interpreting events in the nightmarish world of the *Annales*.

Invisible Ancestors

We now return to the death notices at the end of book 3, Tacitus' most striking illumination of the invisible, with the funeral of Junia, sister of Brutus and wife of Cassius.[85] As has been noted, Tacitus often ends his years (and books), with omens, marriages, and deaths of elite Romans. The placement of Junia's funeral at this point in the narrative assigns even greater significance to this passage since it ends not only a year and a book, but also a triad in Tacitus' annalistic structure.[86]

Before the discussion of the actual funeral, Tacitus notes Junia's will. Unlike the privacy surrounding most of today's final testaments, Roman wills, especially those of the extremely wealthy and powerful, were well known and public. This publicity gave ancient Roman testaments the possibility of open social and political commentary.

> testamentum eius multo apud vulgum rumore fuit, quia in magnis opibus, cum ferme cunctos proceres cum honore nominavisset, Caesarem omisit.
>
> 3.76.1

> Her will was the subject of much popular talk. *Although her resources were huge and she honored almost all the leading men by name, she omitted Tiberius!*

Tacitus again shows us what is most important to the will by revealing what is not there. The document, if it were presented in full, would strike the reader for the large amount of wealth involved (*in magnis opibus*) and the long list of specifically named bequests (*cum . . . nominavisset*). Tellingly, for Tacitus, and the Romans of Junia's day, the most important and visually arresting aspect of Junia's will is an absence—the name of Tiberius. Again, insult and political statement through omission reads much the same way as a name lost to *damnatio memoriae*. Tacitus reminds us that often the most important aspects of imperial history are not self-evident, but must be noted and explained.

The funeral of an elite Roman was a public affair, providing a venue for self-presentation by the family of the deceased. From the house of the deceased, the cortege entered the Forum, where the funeral itself was held from the Rostra. The youngest male family member who had come of age would deliver the eulogy, rehearsing the entire history of the family, with the visual aid of people dressed as the ancestors of the family, wearing masks and insignia matching that person's achievements.[87] As a member of Rome's senatorial elite and a practiced orator, Tacitus would have been aware of the power that public funerals offered for political statement and presentation, as his description of Junia's funeral makes clear:

> quod civiliter acceptum neque prohibuit quo minus laudatione pro rostris ceterisque sollemnibus funus cohonestaretur. viginti clarissimarum familiarum imagines antelatae sunt, Manlii, Quinctii aliaque eiusdem nobilitatis nomina. sed praefulgebant Cassius atque Brutus eo ipso quod effigies eorum non visebantur.
>
> 3.76.2

> This he took citizen-like, not preventing her funeral's distinction by a eulogy from the Rostra and the other customary marks of honor. Twenty portrait-masks from

> the most illustrious families preceded her: Manlii, Quinctii and other names of equal renown. But Brutus and Cassius outshone the rest, precisely because their likenesses were not on display.

Here, Tacitus enables the reader to see the hidden detail that gives meaning to the entire scene. While the busts of the other families are illustrious, only a well-informed observer would have been able to tell what was missing from the funeral display. Tacitus thus directs the gaze of the audience to the absent busts of Cassius and Brutus.

The effect of this technique on the reader is complex. Tacitus does more than reveal what was hidden—he does so in a dramatically cinematic way by building up a visual image, only to deny its visibility. We are informed that the portrait-masks of Cassius and Brutus greatly outshone (*praefulgebant*) the other statues. This would be expected, as Tacitus has already made it clear that Junia was related to both men. Only at the end does Tacitus let the other foot fall, revealing that the busts were not even present (*non visebantur*).[88] The reader then is forced to grapple with the antithesis of how busts can be visually preeminent in their absence. The Roman concept of *damnatio memoriae* works in a very similar way. The removal of a person's name from public inscriptions, or the destruction of representations reinforces the memory of the malefactor, since *damnatio memoriae* can only be effectual if people remember how that person had been, but no longer is, remembered. As the reader understands the complex points that Tacitus is making about memory, history, and their reception under a tyrannical regime, the pace of the reading slows and the book ends.

But Tacitus is not finished. Through the directed gaze, the reader is compelled to reconstruct a narrative of Tiberius' reactions to this last public statement of Junia, one of the last figures of the Roman Republic. The initial insult of being omitted from Junia's will registered on the emperor, but Tiberius accepted it with a civility that we imagine is grudging (3.76.2). Tiberius' true response was the tyrannical suppression of Republican martyrs, forbidding even their images at a family funeral. Further, this is not the only time that Tacitus enlists Brutus and Cassius as ciphers for senatorial freedom in the face of tyranny.[89] Tiberius' opinions on Brutus as Cassius are made entirely overt during the trial of the historian Cremutius Cordus,[90] who is condemned precisely for mentioning Brutus and Cassius as the "last of the Romans" (4.34.1).[91] Tacitus contextualizes the erasures by Junia and Tiberius as political commentary and part of a struggle over memory.

Tacitus, as we have seen, is adept at directing the gaze of his reader, through imperial close-ups, the communication of the threatening gaze, and the revelation of the invisible. By deploying the visual register to color his story, Tacitus brings his reader deeply into the narrative. By revealing what would otherwise be hidden from the reader, Tacitus achieves a similar effect to Hitchcock's in *Rebecca*, showing the ghost of the truth hidden in the past.

Final Thoughts

We have examined how Tacitus uses multiple varied, and yet connected, narrative techniques to control the gaze, showing not only the visual, through the imperial close-up and the interplay of knowledge in the language of looks, but also the invisible, thus revealing the true nature of people and events. Tacitus deploys *enargeia* in these techniques as the reader must envision the scene in order to comprehend the full importance of the narrated events. By obliging the reader to engage visually with his *Annales*, Tacitus renders his narrative much more powerful, and creates a lasting and visual, if inverted and admonitory, *monumentum* of the Julio-Claudians. Through the *Annales*, Tacitus is able to re-craft the past and direct the gaze of his readers, causing them to remember what the emperors had tried to repress.

Part Two

Transition and Connection

4

Shadows over Rome: Temporal Suggestion

The concept of temporal suggestion, and the ways in which narrative may be motivated, obscured, or mobilized via alterations to a narrative timeline or suggestion of distant events is one that has been with storytellers since antiquity. By signaling upcoming events in the plot, or mentioning important images from prior points in the story, an author is able to provide continuity, suggest the influence of fate, or raise the specter of prior mistakes in order to contextualize the narrative. The use of temporal elision, in any form, breaks the anticipated flow of the narrative and calls attention to the importance of the atemporal material.

Two of the most well-known types of temporal suggestion are foreshadowing and backshadowing, and Tacitus employs both of these to great effect at points in the *Annales*. The techniques of foreshadowing and backshadowing share some important elements; both are used to highlight the significance of an object or event, and to connect disparate points of the story through secondary meaning. In foreshadowing, the reader is given partial information about an upcoming event or reality that is only fully explained when that distant point in the narrative is reached. Backshadowing, which is less common but extremely effective, activates a reminder of the past which serves to "haunt" the present. Where history has been repeated or tragedies not averted, backshadowing can be used to suggest inescapable fate, intensify horror, or suggest human failure. In order to illustrate the use of these visual narrative techniques, we will start with an investigation into classic Hollywood cinema, and move on to the use of temporal suggestion in the art of Roman sarcophagi.

There is a wealth of potential examples from which to draw when browsing through classic film, as well as a wide array of methods for employing these techniques. In order to help focus the upcoming discussion, I will be considering Billy Wilder's *Double Indemnity* (1944), which uses foreshadowing in ways that closely mirror Tacitus' technique, employing temporal suggestion to emphasize elements or themes such as fatalism, looming authority, inevitable outcome, and secret machination.[1] Thus, unlike movies which employ foreshadowing for more sanguine effect, the tone of *Double Indemnity* parallels and encapsulates the fear-ridden and ulterior-motive-driven world of the early empire.

Double Indemnity and Roman Narrative Sarcophagi

The first picture we will be looking at to provide a comparison for Tacitean temporal suggestion is *Double Indemnity*, which follows insurance broker Walter Neff (Fred MacMurray) as he records a message via dictaphone to his long-time boss and friend Barton Keyes (Edward G. Robinson). It is not immediately clear what has happened, but the viewer soon detects that something is wrong. Neff is sweating, out of breath, and holding his hand inside his jacket, suggesting a wound. He speaks into the recorder, talking ostensibly to Keyes and by extension to the audience. He suggests that although Keyes might call his statement a confession, he doesn't like the term and immediately begins to hedge that his actions might be, if not justified, at least understandable. Thus, the audience knows from this point that it is their job to decide whether or not he is indeed to blame for a murder, and also that he has failed in his attempt at some as-yet-unexplained goal. As he tells his story, the viewer's gaze is transported back in time, to watch the events as they happened. At select points during this telling, authorial voice-over (suggesting the narration Neff is providing to his recording device) or a short segment flashing forward to Neff wounded in his office, reminds the audience that we are viewing an extended account of memory.[2] When the scene comes in which Neff is shot by his jealous lover and co-conspirator, the foreshadowing from the beginning of the piece is harmonized, and we are with him in the present moment as he finishes his story before a suddenly present Keyes.

This use of foreshadowing, as we will be discussing in later sections with regard to the *Annales*, is especially helpful as an illustration of Tacitus' technique due to the slow pacing of the reveal, the sense of an inevitable fate created by the telling of the story, and the additional elements of horror added to what we, the audience, know to be the outcome. Just we are aware that Keyes' prophesy, that co-conspirators are tied to each other forever on a one-way line to the cemetery, has already come true.

The technique of backshadowing will be discussed in the section below, "Backshadowing in the *Annales*," but as an introduction to the concept I will here outline the effect of the mechanism. In both foreshadowing and backshadowing, two distinct events occur. In foreshadowing, the initial occurrence is often vague, incomplete, or poorly understood by the critical character of the story. It is only when the second event comes to pass that the meaning of the initial occurrence is fully understood, and the full horror of the dual crises is realized. Looking back, the characters often realize (only too late) what the warning foretold. In backshadowing, however, the first event of the series is fully viewed and understood. There is often little to suggest, at the close of the initial key scene, that there will be a recurrence of this theme later in the film or text. Thus, when the first signs of the second event arise, the audience is fully prepared for the threat, and often worries alongside the characters as they attempt to prevent the cycle's completion. We will see this illustrated in the context of Victor Fleming's film *Gone with the Wind* (1939) later in this chapter.[3]

Both foreshadowing and backshadowing are methods of temporal suggestion, and deal with the transmission of information across disparate points in the narrative. Time is a critical aspect of storytelling, and moving elements through or across the timeline draws attention to their importance. This is true whether dealing with a motion picture, static art, or text.

That temporal suggestion is possible in static art, specifically during Tacitus' time period, is clear from an examination of narrative sarcophagi.[4] Although not all of these intricate bas-reliefs employ atemporal depictions, the fact that some do suggests that Romans were aware of the ability to tell, and understand, the elements of a visual story free from the confines of timeline order. In Roman sarcophagi, myths are often presented out of their sequential and temporal order, forcing the reader to move backward and forward within the narrative, reading more for theme than linear progression. As Koortbojian has noted, the sculptors of these sarcophagi were adept at altering the order of the sculptural friezes in order to achieve rhetorical effects.[5] This alteration of temporality can be clearly observed in certain Roman sarcophagi that illustrate the story of Adonis, most notably the Vatican sarcophagus depicted in Fig. 4.1.

This sarcophagus presents key elements from the myth of Adonis: his departure from Aphrodite who is reluctant to let him leave, the fatal boar hunt, and his death in Aphrodite's arms. This is the chronological sequence of the events in the myth, but, as can be seen from the image, not the order in which it is here told. The Vatican sarcophagus does not present the myth according to sequential time. Rather, the first scene (reading left to right) is Aphrodite holding the wounded Adonis. This is followed by the departure scene, wherein Adonis leaves for the hunt. This second scene is only separated from the first by the

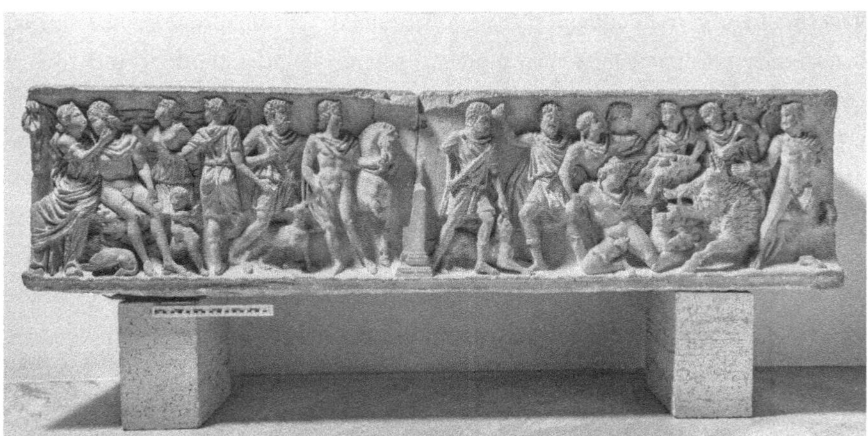

Figure 4.1 Vatican Sarcophagus depicting scenes from the myth of Adonis, image © Vatican Museums.

turned posture of two male figures. The final scene, which is much more elaborate and set off from the other two by a column, shows the boar hunt and the wounding of Adonis. Thus, the ending of this visual narrative is depicted in the first image shown, which is conjoined to and linked with the beginning scene. The left side of the sarcophagus, which comprises scenes 3 and 1, is thus balanced against the pivotal and dramatic scene 2, which takes up the entirety of the right half of the frieze.

As these scenes are arranged on the sarcophagus, the image of Adonis dying in the arms of Aphrodite foreshadows the narrative of the following myth. The viewer knows what will happen from the first scene and then, reading from left to right, watches that result come to pass. This is the same narratological effect used at the beginning of *Double Indemnity*, where the audience knows from the first moments that Neff is injured and has committed some form of criminal act. Tacitus is also highly adept with temporal suggestion, and deploys it to motivate and color his historical account, as we shall see.

Foreshadowing Tiberius

Tacitus was an artist of rhetorical effects, and the nature of foreshadowing accords well with his penchant for innuendo and allusion.[6] The first variety of foreshadowing that we will examine concerns Tacitus' use of personal names. By strategically selecting the name by which to refer to an historical character,

Tacitus subtly foreshadows that character's actions. This is made possible by the Roman naming convention, wherein multiple figures in the same family share some or all of these elements. For example, the Emperor Claudius' full name was Tiberius Claudius Drusus Nero Germanicus. Thus, if Tacitus were to refer to him as "Germanicus," it would suggest the character's connection to his father, a generally popular and benevolent figure. If Tacitus, instead, were to call him "Tiberius," it would bring to mind overtones of his sinister uncle.

This variety of foreshadowing can be difficult to extract from the surrounding narrative, particularly for first-time readers of the *Annales* who are struggling to determine which historical figure is under discussion at each point. It is helpful to study each instance in which Tacitus elects to use a less-common component of a character's name and to parse through the resultant rhetorical effect. This may be done to signal the future behavior or character traits of an individual later in the narrative, and in other cases it is used to cast a pall of suspicion over the motives or deeds of a character in the present moment by raising the specter of a difficult relative.

Foreshadowing can also be achieved by bringing to the reader's mind a character who is not yet part of the narrative. Tacitus does this in two ways, either by dropping the name of an as-yet unintroduced figure whose name (and reputation) would undoubtedly be familiar to his second-century audience, or by referring to a character who shares a name with another infamous individual. The use of name-play to suggest connections across characters is subtle but highly effective, and gives the reader not only insight into the present moment, but also sets him or her up to expect elements of the coming narrative.

What's in a Name

The ability of a name to summon both the image and the notable deeds of an individual makes it a powerful device for temporal suggestion. The name of a person inherently suggests an image—whether drawn from life or pieced together from impressions. As with all aspects of the gaze, it is this internal conception that is controlling, and that guides a viewer to interpret and understand narrative. Names are compact vehicles for the delivery of information, much of which is received visually. Basic narratology does not offer us the tools needed to explore image-based temporal suggestion, but Roman atemporal sculpture and film provide helpful illustrations.

Although the use of names is employed with good effect by other ancient historians, at certain points Tacitus takes this convention a step further.[7] Tacitus shows an unusually slight regard for the classical three-part system of Roman names and, in the entirety of the Tacitean corpus, there is only a single instance of the *praenomen*, *nomen*, and *cognomen* of an individual presented in their proper sequence: Gnaeus Iulius Agricola (*Agricola*, 4.1).[8] The need for Tacitus to give Agricola's entire name is perhaps obvious at the beginning of a laudatory biography, and this sole exception to the rule shows that Tacitus was well aware of the importance and power of names in historical narrative. At a character's first appearance, Tacitus usually provides two of the three names, while one is omitted. In addition, these names are often out of order, with *nomen* following *cognomen*.[9] While these naming practices certainly serve to keep the audience both unsettled and attentive to the narrative, Tacitus seems to be undercutting his reader's expectations at one of the most basic levels: the name of every character in the *Annales* is in some way altered or truncated. Moreover, the connections suggested by the names Tacitus employs are often driving forces in themselves, leading the reader to anticipate dark deeds or tragic failings.

It is important to keep in mind the temporal component of this mechanism, particularly as it works in this case to elide and move through history. All instances of foreshadowing and backshadowing deal with temporality, as a connection to an earlier or future event is suggested. With the use of an individual the effect is greatly strengthened, as the reader's thoughts about that person are likely to include elements of the figure's relevant historical context. Thus, foreshadowing via names not only brings to mind the image of the individual, but also "brings forward" the history surrounding him. In this way, Tacitus is able to suggest dramatic jumps across the timeline of the *Annales*, and to forge connections between characters and events often books apart.

Nero: Tiberius by Another Name

Tacitus' use of names for the purpose of foreshadowing begins early in the *Annales*, with the emperor Tiberius. Although Tiberius was born Tiberius Claudius Nero, Tacitus repeatedly refers to him simply as "Nero."[10] While it has been suggested that Tacitus needed a variety of names when referring to members of the imperial family, I posit that Tacitus recalls Tiberius' *cognomen* for other reasons.[11] Tacitus refers to Tiberius as "Nero" four times in book 1, and then only in a single instance in each of books 2 and 3.[12] Tiberius had already been adopted into the Julian *gens* by Augustus in AD 4, and his name had been formally changed to Tiberius Julius Caesar, which suggests some ulterior motive for the use of his former moniker. The only references to Tiberius as "Nero" that are logical at this stage in the *Annales* are those at 1.3.1; 2.3.2; and 3.56.2, which refer to the early period of Tiberius' life before his adoption into the imperial family.[13] Every other time in book 1 that Tacitus elects to refer to Tiberius as "Nero" must then be both pointed and intentional, especially as Tacitus usually refers to the emperor as either Tiberius or Caesar. The majority of these instances are found close together, near the beginning of the *Annales*, thus offering Tacitus an ideal opportunity to foreground the character of Tiberius. By linking Tiberius in his first appearances with the acts and deeds of a well-known and highly ominous figure, Tacitus is able to foreshadow Tiberius' character and behavior. In this way, the reader is invited to see Tiberius as the forerunner, and early incarnation, of Nero.[14]

Some scholars have suggested that the reason for Tacitus' repeated use of "Nero" for Tiberius is to stress the emperor's adoption into Augustus' family.[15] In support, they have noted that Tacitus' insistence on "Nero" for Tiberius is echoed later in the *Annales*, when Britannicus reminds Nero of his (Nero's) non-Claudian birth. I agree that this is a point of comparison between Tiberius and Nero, but Tacitus could just as easily and correctly have referred to Tiberius as Claudius before the adoption.[16] While the similar circumstances of imperial adoptions are important in both the Tiberian and Neronian narratives, I contend that Tacitus is making a more subtle comparison between Tiberius and Nero. Tacitus deftly foreshadows the fall of the Julio-Claudian house under Nero at its very inception, as he begins the discussion of Tiberius' principate. The connections between Tiberius and Nero are many and replete with meaning. Martin has noted the parallels between the two figures, especially with regard to their successions and mothers.[17] While I generally agree with Martin's reading, I also believe that Tacitus is capitalizing on the mention of Nero in his original listing of the emperors (at 1.1.3) to foreshadow the later emperor at the start of the Tiberian narrative.

If Tacitus were merely seeking another way to refer to Tiberius through the use of Nero's name, then the reader would expect to see similar substitutions with Nero, who was also adopted into the Julio-Claudian family. Nero was born Lucius Domitius Ahenobarbus, but after his adoption into the Claudian *gens* he took the name Nero Claudius Caesar Augustus Germanicus.[18] When indicating Nero, Tacitus refers to him either as "Nero," "princeps," or "Caesar."[19] The sole reference to Nero by his former name occurs after Claudius' marriage to Agrippina the Younger, when Nero is openly preferred to Britannicus. Feeling slighted, Britannicus insults Nero by calling him "Domitius" (12.41.3).[20] This incident was reported to Claudius immediately afterwards, to the detriment of Britannicus. That this was an event worth reporting, which incurred the displeasure of the emperor, suggests that names held an important status for a Roman audience, and misuse of them was both powerful and charged. This argues for the force and intentionality of Tacitus' decision to substitute the correct name of Tiberius, and suggests that the use of "Nero" not only recalls Tiberius' adoptive status, but more importantly signals the reader to Tiberius' impending misdeeds and fate.

In order to see how this foreshadowing mechanism works in the *Annales*, we will consider examples running the length of the work. During the exposition of the last acts of Augustus, Tacitus sets the stage for the adoption of Tiberius by cataloging the deaths within the Julio-Claudian family.

> ut Agrippa vita concessit, L. Caesarem euntem ad Hispanienses exercitus, Gaium remaneantem Armenia et vulnere invalidum mors fato propera vel novercae Liviae dolus abstulit Drusoque pridem exstincto Nero solus e privignis erat.
>
> 1.3.3
>
> Then Agrippa passed away. Lucius Caesar, en route to Spain's armies, and Gaius Caesar, returning from Armenia wounded and weak, were taken either by premature but fated death or by the guile of their stepmother Livia. Since Drusus was already gone, Tiberius alone of Augustus' stepsons remained.

In this abrupt and upsetting passage, Tacitus quickly shows the shattering of all of Augustus' plans for the succession. In one sentence, either through early death or Livia's trickery, Tiberius has become the only viable option. This sentence is also fascinating structurally. As soon as Agrippa dies, both Lucius and Gaius Caesar (listed in the accusative, signaling that they are the receptors of another's action) fall prey to death. Death and Livia's trickery are the joint subjects of the sentence, thus directly focusing our attention on murder. Drusus, Tiberius' brother, is removed in a passing and almost dismissive ablative absolute and we are left, in the flash of a moment, with only Tiberius before the succession of Rome. Tacitus deftly manages the narrative flow of the Latin here by laying the stress on Livia's possible actions and Tiberius' situation, not only through the use of main clauses, but by placing each after a subordinate clause. Tacitus, in this powerfully charged passage, uses not only verbal signposting, but also the mention of Livia's dynastic plots (*novercae Liviae dolus*) before referring to Tiberius simply as "Nero." This use must surely be pointed, as Tacitus sums up two decades worth of imperial deaths, leaving us in one sentenced faced with a situation where "Nero," here in his current (and foreshadowed by his future) incarnation, is the only possible choice for the leadership of Rome. Even in book

1 of the *Annales*, the image of the decadent, tyrannical, and theatrical Nero is already on stage in the minds of the audience.

Another telling example occurs in the next section of text, following a brief discussion of the state of affairs in Rome. With Augustus ill, Tacitus recounts the views of the nervous populace while the question of Rome's leadership remained unsettled (1.4.2). Agrippa Postumus was considered unfit, particularly after years of banishment. With Gaius and Lucius tidily disposed of, the sole choice is Tiberius. Tacitus provides a look at the unpopular opinion of Tiberius amongst his fellow countrymen.

> Tiberium Neronem maturum annis, spectatum bello, sed vetere atque insita Claudiae familiae superbia, multaque indicia saevitiae, quamquam premantur, erumpere.
>
> 1.4.3
>
> *Tiberius is mature in years and tried in war, but has the old inborn Claudian arrogance. Many signs of brutality, though repressed, are emerging.*

Here, the reader should notice that Tacitus is mobilizing images and themes in a very short space. Tiberius is praised briefly as a good general (*spectatum bello*), but this virtue is immediately eclipsed by his vices, *superbia* and *saevitia*, which are characterized as latent and hereditary (*insita*). In this way, Tacitus suggests that any laudatory actions by Tiberius will be undercut by his inherent nature. Roman writers often stressed the familial nature of character traits, which is here reinforced by the (now defunct) "Nero" component of Tiberius' name. Examples of these vices, Tacitus tells us, are occasionally visible (*erumpere*), hinting that Tiberius' nature is susceptible to his family's shortcomings.[21]

The final example of Tacitus' renaming of Tiberius that we will consider is also the last use of the alternative name for Tiberius in the *Annales*. This passage, which occurs just one section after the previous excerpt, occurs at the point in the narrative where Tiberius arrives at Nola during Augustus' fatal illness. Just prior to this episode, Tacitus recounted the rumor that Augustus had favored Postumus Agrippa for the succession and that the emperor had actually gone to Planasia to visit his exiled, adopted son (1.5.1). The only alleged witness to this rumored visit (Fabius Maximus) died mysteriously and we are given an account of his wife, who berates herself for having told Livia about the trip. She accuses herself of having, in effect, murdered her own husband, as Livia informed Tiberius of the situation and, we and the bereaved widow infer, Tiberius ensured that the witness was rendered unable to testify about the event. In this passage, we note that Tacitus refers to as Tiberius as "Caesar" (1.5.2). Tacitus has placed

Tiberius and Livia together in this scene, showing them plotting together and planning a murder to conceal their political machinations and to control the succession of the empire. It is this Livia and, more importantly, this Tiberius that Tacitus wants his reader to recall during the following passage.

> vixdum ingressus Illyricum Tiberius properis matris litteris accitur; neque satis compertum est, spirantem adhuc Augustum apud urbem Nolam an exanimem reppererit. acribus namque custodiis domum et vias saepserat Livia, laetique interdum nuntii vulgabantur, donec provisis quae tempus monebat simul excessisse Augustum et rerum potiri Neronem fama eadem tulit.
>
> 1.5.3–4

> Tiberius had scarcely reached Illyricum when he was summoned by a hurried letter from his mother. It has not been ascertained whether he found Augustus still breathing at Nola or lifeless. For a strict cordon was placed around the house and its approaches by Livia and happy news was occasionally broadcast. Once provision was made for the occasion's demands, word went out simultaneously that Augustus was gone and Tiberius in control.

Tiberius is indirectly blamed for the death of Fabius Maximus, and Tacitus implies that Livia and Tiberius managed the death of Augustus through spin control.[22] Whether Tiberius saw him alive in Nola or not, Tacitus would have his reader believe that Livia either smoothed the way for, or subtly engineered, the succession of her son. Tacitus again pointedly refers to Tiberius by the now long defunct name of Nero as he finishes off the Augustan mini-narrative. Again, Tacitus employs ring structure and foreshadowing as Tiberius achieves the throne in much the same way that Nero will, later in the *Annales* and in history, following the murder of Claudius (12.68.2).[23] These sections of text that concern the end of Augustus' life are all strikingly dark in tone, signaling the decline of open discourse and the descent into the terrors of empire. We have now finished with the *pauca et extrema* of Augustus and entered the *Annales* proper, and the end/beginning for Tacitus is the word "Nero." Tiberius is subsumed into this looming image, and becomes engulfed both by his own heritage and the specter of the future.

As with all instances of foreshadowing, the true import of temporal suggestion is not clear until the narrative unfolds. While a reader well versed in Julio-Claudian history (which describes most of Tacitus' original audience) would be aware of Nero's character during the Tiberian books, Tacitus does not, at least in this instance, absolutely rely on his reader's prior knowledge for the technique to be effective. Tacitus' use of Nero's name achieves its full effect only when the reader reaches the Neronian books, and sees clearly what was only hinted at in book 1. Tacitus makes these early references to Nero both short and infrequent, and thus they are not particularly intrusive on the surrounding narrative. The Neronian references provide a sense of disquiet at the start of the *Annales*, setting the reader up for a reveal of their hidden meaning. Much like in *Double Indemnity*, the reader knows something is wrong and there is a mystery of sorts to solve starting from the very first moments of his or her encounter with the narrative. In the film, we are given clues—an apparent chest wound, the reference to a "confession"—which tell us what we should be focusing on in order to understand the story and, in Tacitus, we are given the hint "Nero" to help us on our ongoing quest for the author's secret history.

Like Mother Like Daughter: The Two Agrippinas[24]

Tacitus uses a similar variety of foreshadowing to draw comparisons between Agrippina the Elder and her daughter, Agrippina the Younger.[25] Agrippina the Elder was the wife of Germanicus, a grand-daughter of Augustus, and the mother of six children including the future emperor Gauis (Caligula). She was a political force, able to raise support amongst her husband's troops and the populace of Rome. Agrippina the Younger is best known to history in her role as the mother of the emperor Nero and the last wife of the emperor Claudius. She was also Claudius' niece and played a role in his murder, and is portrayed throughout the *Annales* as a calculating political player who had no scruples in resorting to murder to achieve her ends. Throughout the *Annales*, Tacitus uses the same name for both women, without the convention of a diminutive to differentiate the daughter (i.e., Agripinilla), commonly used by other authors such as Suetonius. Since the women cannot be distinguished by name in the *Annales*, each naming of one has the power to imply the other.[26] The notion of shared familial traits was not new to Roman historiography, as Suetonius makes very plain in his summary of the Claudian *gens*.[27] These two powerful women dominate much of the extant *Annales*, and are notable for the strength of their characters.

The extent to which Tacitus intended his reader to infer references between the two historical characters at each instance in which the common name "Agrippina" is used is an interesting question, and one to which a blanket answer cannot be applied. A helpful starting point for parsing these comparisons is to look at the specific language Tacitus uses to describe each woman. For example, Tacitus describes Agrippina the Elder as having an "untamed spirit" (1.33.3:

indomitum animum) and "defiance" (2.72.1: *ferociam*), as being "contemptuous" (1.40.3: *aspernantem*), and "intolerant" (2.75.1: *intolerans*) of delay. After the death of her husband Germanicus, Agrippina the Elder is described by Tacitus as being "violent in her grief" (3.1.1: *violenta luctu*). When she is faced with Tiberius' charges of immorality, Tacitus sums up her character by stating that "Agrippina—intolerant of equality, greedy for mastery, masculine her concerns—had shed women's vices" (6.25.2. *Agrippina aequi impatiens, dominandi avida, virilibus curis feminarum vitia exuerat*). Therefore, Tacitus depicts Agrippina the Elder as a very strong character who is out of place under the Principate. Many of these traits, including those of being proud in spirit and harboring an unwomanly desire for power, are echoed and expanded with regard to Agrippina's homonymous daughter. The mother is mobilized to foreshadow the daughter, particularly in the sections following the death of Germanicus. After the death of her husband, Agrippina the Elder's outlook and desires appear to darken, both signaling her own change within the narrative and also serving as a literary herald for her mirror and child.

Agrippina the Younger enters the narrative of the *Annales* shortly after the execution of Messalina, and upon her arrival she is already at the central nexus of imperial affairs. She is in competition with two other *matronae* for the position of Claudius' wife. Tacitus uses similar kinds of descriptors to outline the personality of the younger Agrippina as he previously did for her mother. Agrippina the Younger is open in her "severity" (*severitas*) and "haughtiness" (*superbia*) (12.7.3). Tacitus refers to her anger using the charged term *ira*, which is reminiscent of Juno's character in the *Aeneid* (12.22.3, *unde ira Agrippinae citra ultima stetit*). In describing the younger Agrippina, Tacitus is very explicit about her lust for power, as well as the overt nature of her ambition. After the death of Claudius, Tacitus shows Nero's councilors (Burrus and Seneca) struggling against Agrippina's fierceness (*ferociam*), and states that Agrippina is "aflame with an evil regime's every desire" (13.2.2, *cunctis malae dominationis cupidinibus flagrans*). Later, in the early portion of book 14, at the stage in the narrative where Nero is plotting to kill Agrippina the Younger (his mother), Tacitus records an account wherein Agrippina attempted to reinstate her favor with her son by offering to sleep with him because she was "desirous of retaining power" (14.2.1, *ardore retinandae . . . potentiae*).

In addition to the similarity of these descriptions, Tacitus goes a step further to link the two Agrippinas in the mind of his reader. In order to ensure that the description of one calls to mind the image and impressions associated with the other, Tacitus assigns the same adjective to each woman: *atrox*.[28] Agrippina the Elder is referred to as "always savage" (*semper atrox*) as she rounds on Tiberius, calling him a hypocrite for sacrificing to Augustus while persecuting his progeny (4.52.2).[29] Agrippina the Younger is called "savage in her hatred" (*atrox odii Agrippina*) as she begins to persecute Lollia, one of her rivals for Claudius (12.22.1). In this latter case, *atrox* modifies the character of Agrippina the Younger, rather than the hatred itself. It is striking that he selects so violent a term to describe both women, making it all the more likely that the connection will be remembered by his reader. Had he selected a term normally associated with Roman female behavior, it might easily go unnoticed. *Atrox*, however, is normally reserved for references to war, battle, military leaders, or wild animals, and is jarring to the reader when paired with a Roman wife and mother.[30]

This linking of mother and daughter is well-crafted and intentional, and has the effect of drawing the reader through time, both to expect the excesses of the daughter, and also reminding us of the legacy left by her vengeful parent. In this way, Tacitus foreshadows the younger Agrippina through his description of the vices of the elder which, like other echoes in the *Annales*, recur in much worse manifestations. Thus, the foreshadowing through names begun in the Tiberian books is continued through the *Annales*. Whereas, in the Tiberian books, early references to "Nero" remind the reader of the dark days to come, Tacitus' use of "Agrippina," devoid of specific identification markers, immediately calls to mind the twinned images of mother and daughter, forcing the reader to draw collectively on the cruelty and misdeeds of both.

Prophecy and Prediction

In this next section, we will look at two additional figures whom Tacitus takes special care to foreshadow and predict: Gaius "Caligula" and Claudius. Unlike Tiberius and Agrippina, in these cases Tacitus does not employ the convention of name-mediated foreshadowing, but instead offers direct insight into the deeds and future errors of these characters. While more in line with traditional foreshadowing, these hints are often visual in nature due to the way in which the episodes are presented. In the cases we will examine, Tacitus provides these "reveals" in the course of mini vignettes, during which he breaks the moment of the narrative in order to bring the reader into the mind of—or at least to align the reader in sympathy with—the interlocutor who offers insight. Much like the *tableaux* of Livy, these imagistic narrative pictures provide visual entry into the episode, and allow the viewer to experience a snatched glimpse of future history along with the characters depicted in the *Annales*. As in *Double Indemnity*, we are given hints as to the story to come, along with suggestions as to how we should feel about and interpret what we see.

Gaius Caligula: A Monster Foretold

The portion of the *Annales* that deals directly with the emperor Gaius "Caligula's" reign, likely book 7 or books 7–8, is unfortunately lost to posterity. In the portion of the *Annales* that does survive, however, there are a number of foreshadowing references to him and his deeds which give scholars some insight into Tacitus' now-lost account. Unlike Tiberius and Agrippina, Tacitus does not employ a pairing with any other striking figure in the *Annales* to signal the coming misdeeds of Caligula, and instead provides direct hints at the type of behavior that we, the reader, can expect from him.

While Caligula's reign has been mentioned earlier in the Tiberian books, the first hints at the negative attributes of his rule do not occur until book 6.[31] The first reference to Caligula's immorality concerns a case for slander against him. In this instance, a senator named Sextus Vistillius apparently wrote some accusatory materials that suggested Caligula (still a young man at this point in the narrative) was guilty of some form of immorality (6.9.2, *causa offensionis Vistilio fuit, seu composuerat quaedam in C. Caesarem ut impudicum, sive ficto habita fides*). In an attempt to secure the mercy of the emperor Tiberius, Vistillius slit his own wrists and then rebound the wounds, awaiting the sentence of his ultimate fate. Instead, the emperor responded harshly, and Vistillius removed the bandages and completed his suicide. This episode, which on its face serves to highlight the cruelty of Tiberius, additionally offers a hint at the nature of Rome's next leader. At this stage in the *Annales*, near the end of Tiberius' rule, the reader is aware of and sensitive to Tacitus' dark hints, especially those concerning the imperial family. The suggestion of Caligula's impropriety before assuming the purple foreshadows a reign similarly criminal. While Tiberius' management of Rome became awful through the emperor's over-zealous application of law, Tacitus suggests that Caligula will become an immoral monster when further corrupted by power.

By the end of book 6, Tiberius has grown old as *princeps* and in his advanced age has gained some prophetical capabilities (6.46.3). Tacitus records Tiberius' predictions in quick succession before continuing the narrative of Tiberius' decline and death. During this portion of the *Annales*, Gaius Caligula is still little more than a name, as Tacitus has provided only a few glimpses into his coming reign. At this point in the account, the now-prophetic Tiberius overhears Caligula mocking the Dictator Sulla, and he speaks out to his younger relative.

> omnia Sullae vitia et nullam eiusdem virtutem habiturum praedixit. simul crebris cum lacrimis minorem ex nepotibus complexus, truci alterius vultu, "occides hunc tu" inquit "et te alius."
>
> 6.46.4
>
> A prediction: *You will have all of Sulla's vices, and nothing of his virtue.* Also, embracing with many a tear the younger of his grandsons while the other looked grim: "You will kill him," he said, "and another, you."

Tiberius, who has attained wisdom through a long life and exposure to such astrologers as Thrasyllus, predicts accurately the blood-soaked reign of Caligula, by comparing him with the notoriously bloody Cornelius Sulla. The name of Sulla would have been startling to a second-century Roman reader, as the brutal wars of Marius and Sulla were well known. That the character of Tiberius goes on to prognosticate that Gaius as emperor will be worse than Sulla was as Dictator is deeply unsettling, and sets the reader up for the reign of terror yet to come.

The next prophecy offers additional insight. While Tiberius embraces Gemellus, Caligula gives him a cruel look (*truci vultu*), full of hatred for his cousin. Tiberius notices Caligula's gaze and makes his prediction, foretelling that Caligula will indeed kill Gemellus, but that he will be killed in turn. Thus, the reader expects Caligula's murder long before he becomes emperor. In fact, the reader has already been told that Cassius Chaerea will achieve fame as Caligula's assassin (1.32.2). Thus, as in *Double Indemnity*, the viewer is told early in his or her acquaintance with the character of Caligula that he will be killed, and given only a small hint as to the reasons why. The reader, as the viewer of the film, must continue with the story in order to piece together the "why" of these end results, driving both interest in the characters and building suspense for the narrative. Additionally, the use of Sulla's name to foreshadow Caligula's future provides a hint as to the kinds of deeds and treachery that might place him in his ultimate and unhappy end.

Just a few sections after Tiberius' prophetic revelation, Tacitus again takes an opportunity in the narrative to foreshadow the coming horrors of Caligula. On this occasion, the remarks are even more pointed and clear. Macro had accused a senator, Lucius Arruntius, of being one of the adulterers of the promiscuous Albucilla (6.47.2–3). Unlike his co-defendants who chose to argue in an attempt to prolong their lives, Arruntius elected to kill himself, despite the pleas of his friends (6.48.1). He declared that he had no regrets, except having incurred the unwarranted hatred of both Sejanus and Macro. He then foretold why Rome under Caligula would fare worse than during Tiberius' rule.

> sane paucos ad suprema principis dies posse vitari: quem ad modum evasurum imminentis iuventam? an, cum Tiberius post tantam rerum experientiam vi dominationis convulsus et mutatus sit, C. Caesarem vix finita pueritia, ignarum omnium aut pessimis innutritum, meliora capessiturum Macrone duce, qui ut deterior ad opprimendum Seianum delectus plura per scelera rem publicam conflictavisset? prospectare iam se acrius servitium, eoque fugere simul acta et instantia. haec vatis in modum dictitans venas resolvit. documento sequentia erunt bene Arruntium morte usum.
>
> 6.48.2–3
>
> *No doubt the few days until the Emperor's last can be survived, but how to escape the vigorous age of the one looming? If Tiberius, with his vast experience of affairs, was riven and remade by the power of mastery, will Gaius, his boyhood scarcely ended, himself utterly ignorant and evilly raised, manage better under the guidance of Macro, who, as a worse man than Sejanus and therefore chosen for his suppression, has harried the state with more numerous crimes? The prospect now is sharper servitude, so I am simultaneously fleeing things done and coming.* Speaking thus, prophet-like, he released his veins. What followed will be proof that Arruntius put death to good use.

This section, in indirect speech, foreshadows the reign of Gaius and intimates it will, necessarily, be worse than that of Tiberius. Arruntius spells out in a logical and philosophical manner why no one should look forward to Caligula as *princeps*, comparing Macro unfavorably to his predecessor Sejanus and suggesting that Caligula will have a much worse "handler" than Tiberius. The reader should note that Arruntius, in his parallel between the two emperors, has used the term *dux* to describe Macro, but states that Tiberius' vices came through the force of ruling (*vi dominationis*). This suggests that Caligula will indeed be worse than Tiberius, since he is like him in every way, but while Tiberius was a ruler, albeit warped, Caligula would be subservient to Macro. Arruntius, foreseeing the prospect of being a slave to a servant emperor, notes that this iniquity will be much worse (*acrius servitium*) than was suffered under Tiberius.

Tacitus ends this episode with an authoritative confirmation of Arruntius' fears, moving into authorial voice and directly approving of Arruntius' choice to die rather than live under Caligula. This foreshadowing, mixed with pathos at the death of an apparently noble Roman senator, is made all the more significant by Tacitus' validation. This confirmation provides a level of finality; the future history is now set in stone, and nothing will intervene to prevent Caligula from fulfilling these terrible prophecies. Just as Aphrodite cradles the dying Adonis in the first scene of the Vatican sarcophagus, we know from the beginning that Caligula is bound to his fate. The reader, like a captive audience, must watch the scenes of history unfold, and experience with the Roman people the horrors of the early empire.

Claudius: The Forgotten Emperor

The future emperor Claudius is largely ignored by Tacitus in the Tiberian books of the *Annales*.[32] Tacitus mentions him on occasion but without making any hint as to his future role in the empire, until the narrative following the trial of Gnaeus Calpurnius Piso in book 3.[33] In this instance, the reader is made privy to a senatorial meeting, watching a vote to honor the imperial family and their part in handling the tragic death of Germanicus. Messalinus suggests that the senate give thanks to Tiberius, Livia, Antonia, Agrippina, and Drusus, but forgets to mention Claudius. Another senator corrects this error, and Claudius was added to the vote of thanks as an afterthought (3.18.3–4).[34] Tacitus then stops the narrative in order to comment on the unpredictability of fortune.[35]

> mihi, quanto plura recentium seu veterum revolvo, tanto magis ludibria rerum mortalium cunctis in negotiis obversantur. quippe fama spe veneratione potius omnes destinabantur imperio quam quem futurum principem fortuna in occulto tenebat.
>
> 3.18.4

> But the more I reflect on events recent and past, the more I am struck by the element of the absurd in everything humans do. For judging by people's talk, expectation and expressions of respect, anyone was more "destined to rule" than the future emperor Fortune was hiding.

With this comment, Tacitus very neatly foreshadows Claudius' reign, which did not take place until well into the second hexad, after the murder of Caligula. Tacitus here introduces Claudius while also emulating the forgetful senator, referring to him obliquely without actually naming him.[36] Even in Tacitus' account, Claudius' name is kept hidden (*in occulto*). Instead, Tacitus forces his reader to decipher who is meant in the last relative clause (*quem futurum principem*). Tacitus only hints at the identity of this *princeps* during the previous discussion, in which Claudius was forgotten, and, even when remembered, is mentioned late and last. Through his visual absence from this passage, Tacitus foreshadows Claudius as an emperor who is likewise invisible and subordinate to his wives and freedmen.

At the end of the first hexad, Tacitus again mentions Claudius in relation to Tiberius' choice for his successor. Tiberius had very few eligible candidates to select from, despite the importance and weight of this decision. After considering Gaius Caligula and Gemellus he briefly thought of Claudius, but only for a moment before moving on men outside the Julio-Claudian family.[37]

> etiam de Claudio agitanti, quod is composita aetate, bonarum artium cupiens erat, imminuta mens eius obstitit.
>
> 6.46.1

> [Tiberius] even considered Claudius: age settled, desirous of virtue's attainments; impaired mind an obstacle.

Except for an occasional reference, Tacitus does not involve Claudius in the unfolding of the Tiberian narrative, holding him in reserve until the second hexad. Here, nearly halfway through the *Annales*, Tacitus provides a brief reminder of Claudius' eventual ascent, almost as an aside while Tiberius considers his choices for successor. Tacitus suggests a moment of deliberation on the part of Tiberius, in which he considers Claudius' positive qualities. The reader is given a moment to consider what might have happened if Tiberius had chosen Claudius as emperor, and to speculate on the potential state of Rome had it been spared the intervening years of Caligula.[38] Such was not to be, however, as Tacitus immediately reminds his audience (6.46.4). By failing to seriously consider Claudius as a viable choice, Tiberius allows the succession of the worst potential candidate, Gaius Caligula (6.46.3). At this point in the narrative, Claudius is little more than a name. Even his future role as *princeps* is rejected by Tiberius, which is foreshadowed by Tacitus and guessed by the reader. The foreshadowing employed for Claudius, then, is both subtle and complex. Tacitus signals through the use of examples how others forget Claudius and fail to take him into account, thus suggesting to the reader that Claudius is easily overlooked, and just as easily forgotten. In this, we read a prequel of the man to come; unseen by his peers, and nearly eclipsed in the history of his own time.

Impending Doom

Tacitus foreshadows directly and ominously the future events of imperial history throughout the course of the *Annales*. Unlike the examples discussed in the first two sections of this chapter, the foreshadowing used in these instances is extremely targeted, either suggested by the affected character himself or, as in the case of Sejanus, the events foreshadowed are linked ironically to the character in question. Additionally, the narrative time elapsed between the instance of foreshadowing and the fruition of its predictions is much shorter; whereas the examples of the first section span full hexads of the *Annales*, those in this category are generally resolved within a book or two. These instances of foreshadowing all occur in moments of narrative vignette, where Tacitus has taken a moment in the narrative to illustrate a specific scene with his characters. This device, which has the effect of slowing the progression of events and drawing reader attention, provides added weight and importance to the foreshadowed suggestions. The encroaching fate signaled in these episodes is the death of positive characters, such as Germanicus and Drusus the Younger, and an encapsulation of the rise and fall of a troublesome minister (namely, Sejanus).

This kind of foreshadowing is quite similar to that used in Victor Fleming's *Gone with the Wind* (1939). Throughout the film, Scarlett (played by Vivian Leigh) is shown in unrequited love with the timid and largely disinterested Ashley Wilkes (played by Leslie Howard). During the Reconstruction, Scarlett finds herself in need of an ally, and agrees to marry Rhett Butler (played by Clark Gable). Things seem idyllic as the young couple tours Europe while, at home in the American South, the early stages of The Reconstruction are underway. During a night in London, Scarlett is awakened from a horrible recurring dream in which she found herself wandering in the fog, looking for something she had lost. Rhett comforts her, and promises that once she becomes used to safety, she will stop dreaming that dream. The marriage between Scarlett and Rhett slowly deteriorates, due in large part to Scarlett's continued affection for Ashley Wilkes. At the end of the film, Scarlett finally discovers that she has always loved Rhett. As she rushes back to her house deep fog is setting in, and Scarlett arrives to find Rhett leaving. Rhett delivers the infamous, "Frankly, my dear, I don't give a damn," dismissal and walks off into the fog. The dream stands in as an episodic encapsulation of the marriage theme for the film, and foreshadows the fruit of Scarlett's folly. It is Scarlett who is the originator of the dream image, and in it the reader sees something of what will have to come to pass.

As we will see in the following sections, the same type of short, image-driven message telling the viewer of future events can be embedded in textual narrative in much the same way. In the examples we will consider, Tacitus uses not only the mechanism of dream-images to convey future events, but also the device of a fateful speech (in which a character seems to call down his misfortune by ill-chosen words), as well as the suggestion of later history by a very compact and well-chosen placement of language.

Germanicus

One of the most heavily foreshadowed events in the *Annales*, whose exploits dominate much of the narrative of the first two books, is the death of Germanicus, who is charismatic and well liked, depicted as the exact opposite of the brooding Tiberius.[39] Numerous scholars have noted Germanicus' romantic and epic nature—a nature quite out of place in the reality of Tiberius' Rome.[40] Regardless of Germanicus' intended place within the moral economy of the *Annales*, his death is recorded as an unreserved tragedy and one that had been heavily foreshadowed throughout the preceding narrative.

During the portion of the *Annales* that deals with Germanicus' expedition across the Rhine, Tacitus relates a dream, which Germanicus initially heralded as a positive omen.[41]

> nox eadem laetam Germanico quietem tulit, viditque se operatum et sanguine sacri respersa praetexta pulchriorem aliam manibus aviae Augustae accepisse.
>
> 2.14.1

> The same night brought Germanicus happy repose. He saw himself after sacrificing—consecrated blood spattered his robe—in possession of another sacrifice, more beautiful, from the hands of his grandmother Livia.

This dream is understood by Germanicus as an omen and he calls for auspices (2.14.1, *auctus omine, addicentibus auspiciis*). The dream is interpreted positively, and the Roman army is indeed victorious in its next engagement (2.17.3–18.2). But Germanicus fails to correctly interpret this sign, as adequate weight is not given to the enigmatic figure of Livia Augusta. The mention of Livia seems out of place at this point in the narrative, and particularly odd in the context of a religiously charged dream. As the narrative of the *Annales* goes on to show, Livia is no great admirer of Germanicus; she would not be present at the return of Germanicus' ashes to Rome, and her friendship for Plancina allowed Piso's wife to escape punishment during Piso's trial.[42] By including Livia, Tacitus reminds the reader of the unseen dangers Germanicus faces, and foreshadows disaster for him via the dream narrative. Not only should Germanicus fear the more obvious Tiberius, but also the ambiguous Livia, whose presence here puts the reader on notice that additional layers of meaning are in play.[43]

Following his successful but truncated campaigns, and believing the omen to be both positive and fully concluded, Germanicus returns to Rome to celebrate his long-delayed triumph.[44] After listing the subjugated German tribes, Tacitus moves quickly to the triumph itself:

> vecta spolia, captivi, simulacra montium fluminum proeliorum; bellumque, quia conficere prohibitus erat, pro confecto accipiebatur.
>
> 2.41.2

> [Germanicus] parading plunder, prisoners and representations of mountains, rivers and battles. The war, since finishing it was forbidden, was considered finished.

After this vivid description, in which the parade seems to pass quickly in review as Tacitus narrates, Tacitus continues to paint his literary picture by focalizing through the populace.

> augebat intuentium visus eximia ipsius species currusque quinque liberis onustus. sed suberat occulta formido, reputantibus haud prosperum in Druso patre eius favorem vulgi, avunculum eiusdem Marcellum flagrantibus plebis studiis intra iuventam ereptum, breves et infaustos populi Romani amores.
>
> 2.41.3

> Increased onlooker attention came from the exceptional beauty of the man himself, and from the chariot, five children its load. But underneath there was the hidden alarm, as people reflected. *No success attended the crowd's favor for his father Drusus. And his uncle Marcellus, despite the blaze of popular enthusiasm, was snatched away still young. Brief and unlucky are the Roman people's love affairs.*

Commentators have paid scant attention to the dramatic change in tone from jubilation to one of impending disaster, but this juxtaposition of mood and image provides an excellent look into the Tacitean subtext.[45] In this remarkable moment, Tacitus turns from a vivid description of one of the grandest spectacles in the Roman world to the dark forebodings by which the onlookers, much like Tacitus' reader, are suddenly overwhelmed.

Tacitus not only uses a moment of victory to showcase the contrast between Roman glory and the acts of treachery practiced in the early empire, but also mobilizes an upset in reader expectation. With the start of a new year at 2.41 the reader might well expect a change in tone, which the triumph of Germanicus seems to herald. The reader is prepared for a long ekphrastic description of the tumultuous procession, both due to Tacitus' apparent set-up for a digression and to the popularity of triumph scenes in Roman historiography. But Tacitus disappoints expectations, plunging the reader directly into the *milieu* of disturbing thoughts experienced by the spectators in the crowd. Although watching the spectacle before their eyes (as are we, in the position of external viewers), the crowd is aware of some sense of foreboding, and guesses at Germanicus' coming ill fortune. Tacitus' sudden change in tone adds both weight and depth to this instance of foreshadowing, hinting not only at coming events, but also at the way it will feel for those living under an empire in which political power is worthy of murder.

Tacitus' reader, along with the audience at Germanicus' triumph, tries to discover what is behind this break in the narrative, like Scarlett trying to discover what was lost in the mist. Tacitus does not spell out exactly how Germanicus will meet his end, simply hinting at the author of the deed and allowing rumor and suspicion to guide history. Intentionally undercutting the presentation of a highly visual spectacle makes the transition more powerful, as the reader feels his or her gaze pulled away from the bright lights in order to better catch at the whispers in the crowd.

The last time that Tacitus foreshadows Germanicus' death occurs in book 2, when Tiberius has withdrawn Germanicus from his campaigns across the Rhine and sent him on a mission to the East to settle affairs in Armenia and Illyricum. Germanicus saw in this an opportunity for a leisurely tour of the eastern provinces of the empire, including Greece, Troy, and Egypt. While in Greece, Germanicus visited the oracle of Clarian Apollo at Colophon.

> et ferebatur Germanico per ambages, ut mos oraculis, maturum exitium cecinisse.
> 2.54.4

> The priest was said to have intoned for Germanicus, riddlingly—oracular habit!—*imminent departure.*

Tacitus here foreshadows Germanicus' death, this time through the device of an ambiguous oracle. In both ancient historiography and epic, it is common for oracles to be misread and misinterpreted; what may at first blush seem to herald good fortune is often capable of being read in a directly contrary way.[46] In this instance, Tacitus relies on the inherent potential meanings in the adjective *maturum*, which could be interpreted as either a timely (i.e., in good time, when Germanicus is an old man), or an impending death.[47] With this cryptic portent, Germanicus continues on his way and Tacitus turns his attentions to Piso.[48] This sudden change seems striking at first, but when the reader recalls that Piso was blamed by many (including Germanicus himself) for Germanicus' death, it is clear that this is not a narrative break but a continuation of the foreshadowing subtext.[49] Thus, Tacitus signals the event both directly and indirectly.

Drusus the Younger

The death of Drusus the Younger, while more precipitate than that of Germanicus, is foreshadowed in a scene replete with irony. The instance occurs in the course of a short vignette during the narrative of book 3. A member of the senate, Severus Caecina, proposed the motion that senators should not be allowed to be accompanied by their wives while serving in the provinces (3.33.1–4). Valerius Messalinus spoke against the motion, highlighting the contrary dangers of leaving wives unsupervised in such a corrupting city as Rome. Drusus the Younger then weighs in and gives his opinion.

> addidit pauca Drusus de matrimonio suo; nam principibus adeunda saepius longinqua imperii. quotiens divum Augustum in Occidentem atque Orientem meavisse comite Livia! se quoque in Illyricum profectum et, si ita conducat, alias ad gentis iterum, haud semper aequo animo, si ab uxore carissima et tot communium liberorum parente divelleretur.
>
> 3.34.6
>
> Drusus added a few words about his own marriage. *Emperors will often need to visit distant parts of the Empire. How often Augustus traveled to west and east with Livia his companion! I myself went to Illyricum and, if it serves, will go to other peoples, rarely calm of spirit, however, if torn from my beloved wife, parent of our numerous children.*

The sentiments expressed by Drusus are normal and fitting for a Roman husband, but his points are less well argued than Valerius'. Regardless of what was actually said in the senate during this particular meeting, Tacitus had no need to mention Drusus' brief and self-referential statements in order to show why Caecina's measure did not pass the senate. Indeed, Tacitus notes, even before Valerius took the floor, very few senators approved of the measure (3.34.1, *paucorum haec adsensu audita*). Additionally suggestive, both Caecina and Valerius made their arguments in general, impersonal terms while Drusus explicitly mentions his wife, whom he describes as "dearest" (*carissima*).[50] This stress placed on Livilla ironically foreshadows her later betrayal of Drusus and her help in his murder, which occur early in the following book.[51] Tacitus uses this opportunity to keep the relationship between Livilla and Drusus in the forefront of his reader's mind, and employs the rare superlative (*carissima*) to cast doubt on the nature of the marriage.[52] This episode serves to foreshadow Drusus' own impending demise as well as Livilla's faithlessness as a wife, both of which play key roles in the narrative of book 4.[53]

Tacitus' foreshadowing is darkly ironic as Drusus miscasts his wife, thus betraying his own ignorance of the fate that awaits him. Livilla, in fact, destroys her husband and nearly ruins the imperial household in the narrative of book 4. The story of Livilla's betrayal and murder of Drusus was common knowledge in antiquity well before Tacitus wrote the *Annales*. For example, Pliny the Elder makes a reference to Livilla's affair with Drusus' doctor, Eudemus, in connection with his general castigations of physicians.[54] That even Pliny was familiar with this minute fact, the reason for her affair with Eudemus (to procure Drusus' fatal poison), suggests that the story would have been well-known to Tacitus' second-century readers.[55]

As in the case of Tacitus' appellation of "Nero" for Tiberius, however, Tacitus does not rely solely upon the reader's knowledge of the Julio-Claudian story when constructing a visual narrative. The tone of the passage suggests a departure from the surrounding text, and the sudden change of reference to personal attestation signals that something unusual is going on. The moment is likely to stay in the back of the reader's mind, becoming fully apparent in the course of the following book. As in *Gone with the Wind*, the reader knows something is amiss but may not be able to put all the pieces into place. In both cases, those familiar with the story see the horror that the episode portends, as well as the inevitability of the fated character's coming fall.

Sejanus

Tacitus, as we have seen, foreshadows the death of many of the central characters of the *Annales*. Neither Drusus nor Germanicus escaped the fates foretold for them. Tacitus uses temporal suggestion in a somewhat different manner when he foreshadows the rise of Lucius Aelius Sejanus, hinting at both the lofty heights and the deep plunge destined for him. Fittingly, Tacitus also employs a slightly different mechanism in setting up these foreshadowing episodes. Sejanus was an extremely savvy political player, working behind the scenes to orchestrate and secure his position under Tiberius, and working through Livilla on a (ultimately unsuccessful) bid for the purple. Accordingly, Tacitus' foreshadowing of Sejanus occurs in very brief, tight glimpses. Unlike the comparatively lavish visual episodes used to showcase the fates of Germanicus and Drusus, Tacitus makes his comments about Sejanus compact, erudite, and easy to overlook.

While Sejanus dominates much of the second half of Tiberius' reign, he first appears in the *Annales* in book 1 as a companion for Drusus the Younger. At this point in the narrative, Sejanus shares the prefecture of the praetorian guards with his father. Tacitus wastes no time in casting a sinister shadow across Sejanus by foreshadowing his future trajectory.

> simul praetorii praefectus Aelius Seianus, collega Straboni patri suo datus, magna apud Tiberium auctoritate, rector iuveni et ceteris periculorum praemiorumque ostentator.
>
> 1.24.2

> Likewise the Guard commander Sejanus, who had been made his father's colleague and had great authority with Tiberius: a guide for Drusus and, for the rest, a broker of dangers and rewards.

Sejanus' appearance here as Drusus' mentor (*rector*) is heavily ironic, since Sejanus later has Drusus poisoned while having an affair with his wife, Livilla (4.3.3–5). As discussed previously with regard to Drusus the Younger, Tacitus' irony would be immediately apparent to those familiar with the story of Livilla and Drusus, which was commonly known in the second century.[56] Furthermore, as Sejanus' power over Tiberius is a central theme in the latter half of the Tiberian books, Tacitus seems to foreshadow his role as mentor to Tiberius by depicting him as the mentor for the emperor's son (e.g., 4.1.2).

While the murder of Drusus is not expressly foreshadowed in this passage, the rise and fall of Sejanus is. Tacitus mobilizes a dual meaning by referring to Sejanus in terms of both dangers and rewards (*periculorum praemiorumque ostentator*). Certainly, Sejanus is a broker of rewards (*ostentator praemiorum*) at this point in the narrative, with his rise to tenure of a joint prefecture with his father. The dangers spoken of are not apparent at this point in Sejanus' career, and thus this dark hint is both surprising and unsettling. Tacitus calls attention to this passage not only via the unusual atemporality (perils before prizes) of the word order, but also through the use of alliteration (p*ericulorum* p*raemiorumque*). Tacitus is not highly given to the use alliteration, and where he uses it the effect is dramatic.

Not only did Sejanus have a meteoric rise to the praetorian prefecture, but he was destined to become a true "demonstrator" of his own rise and fall.[57] As is often the case with Tacitus, the reader who is knowledgeable in Julio-Claudian history would be familiar with the story of Sejanus, and for a Roman audience the ominous overtones of this passage would be unmistakable. In this section, Tacitus gives only a brief introduction to the character of Sejanus, saving his biography for a more dramatic, structural point in the *Annales*, and yet his future fate is already established for the reader.[58] Tacitus foreshadows and introduces the twin elements of danger and reward, which in the narrative of the *Annales* are reversed; Sejanus' high-point is in book 4, and his fall is likely recorded in the lost portion of book 5. In three words, Tacitus is able to encapsulate Sejanus' rise to imperial hopes, and his sudden fall and execution. Particularly with regard to Sejanus, Tacitus' temporal suggestion is often extremely tight, confined to a few short words that receive their full import from other events in the narrative.

Although as Sejanus only becomes a central character in books 4–6 of the *Annales*, Tacitus mentions him seven times in the first three books before his major entrance at 4.1.1.[59] Even these early passages, however, are replete with meaning, echoing the events of later portions of the work. In one example, Tacitus foreshadows Sejanus' later prominence in the context of a discussion concerning Germanicus' campaigns in Germany. At this point in the narrative, Germanicus has been away from the Roman camp on the German frontier for an extended time, and the troops are growing restless. Concerned about the possibility of attack, the legionaries begin to dismantle the Rhine bridges, in order to prevent the German tribes from assaulting their position. Agrippina famously stood up to them, commanding the troops to desist the destruction of the bridges, asserting that Germanicus would return shortly (1.69.1). Tacitus moves from this scene back to Rome, showing Tiberius' point of view and interpretation of the incident. Tiberius mistrusts Agrippina and questions her motive for these actions, commenting upon her general character.[60] The reader then learns that this opinion is fueled by Sejanus, who has his own plans to discredit Agrippina's family in order to make room for his personal ambitions.

> accendebat haec onerabatque Seianus, peritia morum Tiberii odia in longum iaciens, quae reconderet auctaque promeret.
>
> 1.69.5

> Thoughts that were inflamed and aggravated by Sejanus, with his knowledge of Tiberius' character, sowing hatreds far afield to cover, and then, when grown, bring forth.

Again, Tacitus makes the reader aware of Sejanus as a character who had powerful control over Tiberius, a theme which becomes defining in the second half of the Tiberian hexad. The language in this passage is highly visual, using two metaphors for Sejanus' machinations and Tiberius' thoughts: a burning pyre and an unwholesome crop.[61] The first image shows Sejanus building a pyre in Tiberius' mind, one that he must keep fueled and burning (*accendebat … onerabat*). This metaphor is very striking, as Tiberius' mind is the locus of this conflagration. Furthermore, Sejanus will eventually be responsible for the funeral pyres not only of Agrippina's family, but also of Tiberius' son. The second metaphor casts Sejanus a malignant horticulturalist who plants hatreds in

Tiberius' mind, hidden for a time (*in longum iaciens ... reconderet*) and only revealed when they have increased (*aucta ... promeret*). Sejanus' harvest is not ready until much later in the *Annales*, in book 4.

Using foreshadowing, Tacitus is able to suspend temporal order and to link the narrative in book 1 to a central theme of book 4; namely, Sejanus' control of Tiberius to the detriment of the Julian family. This jumping ahead to highlight a critical element of the coming tale is paralleled in *Double Indemnity* where, speaking into his recording device at the beginning of the narrative, Neff tells the audience that he committed murder for the sake of money and for a woman, and that in the end the gamble didn't pay off. In both instances, we see only selected information about a key character, dropped hints within the otherwise expected narrative flow. We also know some elements of each man's forthcoming attempts at glory, and the tragic ends that will befall them. In each case, the viewer is directed to the later and thematically more important moments in the narrative, signaling the key elements that warrant close attention. In this instance in the *Annales*, Tacitus is able to instruct his reader not only about what will happen, but how to understand and interpret Sejanus' motives. Similarly, we are given hints as to Neff's personality and motivations, coloring how we will judge him as his story unfolds.

The second example of foreshadowing concerning Sejanus that we will be looking at occurs in book 4. By the early portion of this book, Sejanus has gained great ascendancy over Tiberius and, in the role of evil minister, dominates the narrative albeit behind the scenes. Near the end of the book, Tacitus describes a perverse situation that occurs when Sejanus is the only path of admittance to Tiberius; the praetorian prefect has become more powerful than proconsuls and senators (4.74.3, *eo venire patres, eques, magna pars plebis, anxii erga Seianum*). At this time, Tiberius had gone into self-imposed retreat on Capri, and Sejanus in effect ruled the empire from Campania by controlling all letters and communications to and from Capri. Sejanus decided who was allowed into the imperial presence, and what mail was permitted to reach Tiberius' gaze. Tacitus portrays this sudden alteration in the imperial hierarchy both as an inversion of government and as a cause of shame for the senators who attempted to gain access to their absentee emperor. Those who visited Sejanus and were turned away were often terrified, while those who gained admittance were delighted. Tacitus, however, foreshadows the illusory character of their joy.

> et revenere in urbem trepidi quos non sermone, non visu dignatus erat, quidam male alacres quibus infaustae amicitiae gravis exitus imminebat.
>
> 4.74.5

> People returned to the city atremble if not found worthy of a conversation or glance. And some had mistaken enthusiasm: over these an unlucky friendship's grievous result impended.

The reference to "unlucky friendship" refers to the fallout from Sejanus' condemnation later in the Tiberian books, when those who had secured the friendship of Tiberius' minister were liable to share in his fate. In this way, Tacitus, a book ahead of its narrative moment, suggests the destruction (*gravis exitus*), which overhangs (*imminebat*) Sejanus' supporters. Even Tacitus' choice of words is suggestive of impending doom for these unwisely happy senators. Martin and Woodman note that the phrase *gravis exitus* is Vergilian (*Aen.* 10.630), used of Turnus by Juno.[62] Tacitus further foreshadows Sejanus' fall by referring to those senators who had gained admittance to the minister as mistakenly joyous (*male alacres*). It would be natural for those selected for an audience to be pleased, as they have secured the opportunity to meet with the emperor. Tacitus' use of *male* is therefore jarring, and only later understood in terms of their unpropitious (*infaustae*) friendship with dire consequence (*gravis exitus*). Thus, Tacitus relates that their joy is out of place, in light of events which are clear only in light of the coming narrative.

Tacitus' use of temporal suggestion and narrative movement is extremely varied and versatile. Whether foreshadowing through names, in the context of character-driven vignettes, or ominous suggestions, Tacitus is able to shape reader expectation and prefigure the tone of the coming account. Whether the reader is familiar with Roman historical records or not, these passages are marked out in order to create an impression whether through their incorporation in visually memorable descriptions, linked images of individuals, or alliteration or unusual word order. When the moment in which these foreshadowed hints come to fruition, Tacitus is able to rely on memory to reactivate those impressions; doubly so for those familiar with the underlying stories.

In much the same way as the sculptor of the Vatican Sarcophagus, by placing critical elements from late in the narrative at the beginning of the presentation, Tacitus draws the reader into the account. Keyed to look for elements leading to that result, the viewer is driven to put the pieces together, to create meaning and to solve the mystery. Much like Billy Wilder in *Double Indemnity* provides early clues to the critical components of Neff's account and his tragic downfall, Tacitus leads the reader to find the important elements of early imperial history, putting together not only the "what" of his account, but also the "why" and "how." This type of construction, whether employed in physical media, text, or on screen, creates a vital narrative that places the viewer at the center of the action alongside the characters. Knowing what may happen ahead of the present action creates suspense, drawing the viewer toward an inexorable and often seemingly inexplicable conclusion. For Tacitus, this device offered a way to bring his second-century audience into the reality of life under the early empire, unwitting accomplices to the deeds of the past.

Backshadowing in the *Annales*

In the first three sections of this chapter, we have looked at Tacitus' numerous uses of foreshadowing and the varied ways in which he employs the technique to suggest connections, align characters, and drive reader engagement. Now we will turn to another mechanism for temporal suggestion, and look at how backshadowing in the *Annales* enables Tacitus to suggest inevitable fate and the repeating cycles of fame and destruction.

Just Like Pa

The technique of backshadowing is distinct from foreshadowing. Although both mechanisms rely on the pairing of a narratively "early" and "late" event, foreshadowing focuses on predictions for the future whereas backshadowing represents a repetition or suggestion of the past.[63] Generally speaking, in foreshadowing, the event is suggested through an unclear or impartial image; think of Germanicus' and Scarlett's dreams, the quick jump to "dangers and rewards" for Sejanus, or the brief juxtaposition inherent in name substitution. In all of these instances, the future (and its import) is shown in a short burst, its full meaning left unexplained for the reader to unpack and decipher. In backshadowing, however, the episode from the past which is being mobilized for additional meaning has, by the time of its importance as an image, been fully viewed and explained. The moment has already occurred in the narrative, and in most cases the audience has had an opportunity to understand and interpret its meaning in the first instance. When the image is again activated through backshadowing, the viewer is aware of the full import of the recurrence, having seen the first instance played out in detail earlier in the account. Thus, backshadowing can be an incredibly powerful device, as the reader is drawn into the same horror as the characters, realizing only too late that history has repeated itself.

Victor Fleming's *Gone with the Wind* (1939) here again provides an illustrative example of this technique. In the first half of the film, Gerald O'Hara (Thomas Mitchell) falls from his horse and is killed while jumping a fence on his property. His death had been heavily foreshadowed, creating pathos for the event and imbuing the scene with meaning. Although warned by his daughter, Gerald insisted that he had a right to decide what to do. Thus, his stubbornness and willful determination are both his defining characteristics and his fatal flaws.

Later in the narrative, Scarlett and Rhett's young daughter Bonnie (Cammie King) decides that she wants to jump her new pony over a bar-rack. Scarlett and Rhett tell her not to try, but Bonnie, unheeding, rides off to jump. An exasperated Scarlett remarks, as an aside, "... just like Pa." Her expression changes at the awful purport of her words and, in a close-up, she whispers, "Just like Pa!" With Scarlett, the audience recalls Gerald O'Hara's death, and the scene suddenly becomes nightmarish. Fearing for her daughter, Scarlett calls to Rhett, and the pacing becomes frantic as he attempts to stop Bonnie. As Scarlett (and the audience) fears, Bonnie falls, and dies "just like Pa." This scene is pivotal in the film, since Bonnie's death drives Scarlett and Rhett apart and foreshadows their final separation.

The horror of this scene comes from the impact of backshadowing. As soon as Scarlett likens her daughter to her father, the scene changes in tone. History threatens to repeat, with the characters powerless to prevent it. Scarlett, and the audience, must witness Bonnie's death in the same way that both witnessed Gerald's. What is particularly interesting about backshadowing is the way in which the event is experienced. Since the occurrence is already known, the moment of re-engagement is experienced as *enargeia*. Even in written narrative, the reader's own mental image of the earlier event "comes alive" before the mind's eye and signals, seconds ahead of the text, what danger is in store. The old image superimposes itself on the new, making this a highly visual technique regardless of the medium in which it is presented.

Tacitus was well aware of the power of this rhetorical (and later, cinematic) device, and he uses it to great effect in the *Annales*. In this portion of the chapter, we will be looking at examples of backshadowing, in which the nightmarish quality of inescapable fate brings the reader into temporal sympathy with the historical characters.

Teutoburg Forest[64]

One of Rome's greatest defeats was the destruction of Quinctilius Varus and his legions in the Teutoburg forest. In AD 9, Quinctilius Varus, governor of Germania, led his three legions through a swamp in the Teutoburg forest, unaware that a Roman turncoat was lying in wait with an army of hostile German warriors. This misstep resulted in the annihilation of the governor and nearly all of his men at the hands of Arminius, a Germanic chieftain. So important was this historical moment that Tacitus routinely alludes to it throughout the first book.[65] Thus, there has been a great deal of build-up and anticipation, and the reader is likely to share Germanicus' desire to pay proper respects. In a dramatically visual passage, Germanicus tours the battlefield and buries the Roman dead (1.60.3–61).

Caecina's Nightmare

Following this scene, the specter of the past casts its shadow, when one of Germanicus' commanders, Caecina, becomes surrounded by Arminius' German forces during his march through the forests. Both armies then pass a restless night, during which Caecina has a dream.

> ducemque terruit dira quies: nam Quinctilium Varum sanguine oblitum et paludibus emersum cernere et audire visus est velut vocantem, non tamen obsecutus et manum intendentis reppulisse.
>
> 1.65.2

> The General was terrified by a ghastly dream: Varus, blood-smeared and risen from the marsh. He seemed to see and hear him beckoning, but did not follow and pushed away the outstretched hand.

The image of Varus' ghost, calling out an unheeded warning to his future counterpart, is both horrible and tragic; locked in the cycle of the past, he is powerless to prevent another Roman conflict.[66] Caecina, even in his dream, must fight to avoid the fate of Quinctilius Varus. He ignores Varus' summons, which he seems to hear as Varus calls to him (*audire visus est velut vocantem, non tamen obescutus*), and pushes away Varus' beckoning hand (*manum intendentis reppulisse*). The reader feels the palpable suspense of this charged drama, knowing what has come before and fearing for the fate of Caecina and his men. Caecina seems marked for death by the appearance of this specter calling to him from the other side of the grave.[67]

Behold Varus Again!

The unsettling dream of Varus' ghost draws a parallel between Caecina and Varus, which Tacitus expands upon and makes explicit during the battle narrative of the following day.

> neque tamen Arminius, quamquam libero incursu, statim prorupit: sed ut haesere caeno fossisque impedimenta, turbati circum milites, incertus signorum ordo, utque tali in tempore, sibi quisque properus et lentae adversum imperia aures, inrumpere Germanos iubet, clamitans "en Varus [et] eodemque iterum fato vinctae legiones!"
>
> 1.65.4

> Arminius, though free to attack, did not make an immediate sally. But when the baggage was stuck in the mud, with the soldiers in confusion around it, the standards in disarray and, as happens at such moments, everyone quick for himself with ears slow to orders, then he ordered the Germans to go in, shouting "It's Varus and his legions again, caught by the same fate!"

This passage maintains the nightmare-like quality of Caecina's Varian vision; images are piled one on another in a vivid montage. We see the muck-laden baggage train, confused soldiers, and the dream-like disruption of visual and auditory sensory input.[68] The reader has the awful feeling of *déjà vu*, even though the coming battle is still unseen,[69] and expects that an identical fate awaits Caecina. Arminius himself notes that history is repeating itself (*eodem iterum fato*). This statement, in which Arminius equates Varus and Caecina echoes Tacitus' use of name-driven foreshadowing seen elsewhere in the *Annales*,[70] and links the two episodes in the mind of the viewer.

Pagán, in looking at this episode, has expressed frustration at Caecina's foolhardy ignorance of the Varian example.[71] Certainly it seems ill-advised for Caecina to put his troops into the same risky situation. I contend, however, that Tacitus' purpose was not simply to portray Caecina as a fool, instantly forgetful of both the horrors of Teutoburg and of Varus' ghost (1.64.3).[72] Instead, through the use of Caecina's dream-image and Arminius' oddly cyclical interpretation of the battle, both commanders are "viewing" the moment through the lens of the past. The face of Varus looms before them both. Arminius, mistakenly, equates the two Roman combatants, and expects to replay his prior glory. Caecina, doubly mindful of the dead commander, has already experienced a mini-drama of this battle in his dream, and by refusing Varus' summons to join him in ignominious death he has pre-figured the change in history.

Both Arminius and Caecina thus read the Varian disaster onto the current situation, but Arminius underestimates the Romans' ability to learn from their mistakes. Caecina escapes the fate of Quinctilius Varus by defeating not only the Cherusci, but Arminius (1.68.2–5), and it is his soldiers who taunt the enemy (1.68.3, *exprobantes non hic silvas nec paludes, sed aequis locis aequos deos*).

Through victory in this battle, Caecina breaks the spell of the Varian disaster. Caecina, unlike Bonnie Butler, is sufficiently aware of the past to escape the fate that he seems doomed to follow. Tacitus employs backshadowing in the story of Caecina in order to achieve suspense and dread in his reader, then subverts his own tension through Caecina's escape. Clearly the past can only be escaped with knowledge and bravery, but the reader retains the unsettling feeling that the past can alter the present.

Livia and Agrippina

Tacitus is equally able to mobilize meaning through the use of names in the context of backshadowing. Just as Tacitus' descriptions of Tiberius were made terrible through the name of Nero, in the latter portion of the *Annales* Nero's character is darkened through the preceding examples of Tiberius.[73] Similarly, Tacitus raises the specter of early imperial rumors to remind his readers of the similarities between the politically powerful Livia and Agrippina the Younger, as well as reviving his insinuations concerning Livia's complicity in Augustus' death.

In the first book of the *Annales*, Tacitus merely hinted that Livia may have had a role in Augustus' death. Instead of making direct allegations, Tacitus relayed the rumor that, at the time, some thought her guilty (1.5.1, *quidam scelus uxoris suspectabant*). Following this statement, Tacitus records that it was uncertain whether Augustus was still alive when Tiberius returned to Nola (1.5.3). Throughout this time, Livia was in control of the news emanating from the palace.

> acribus namque custodiis domum et vias saepserat Livia, laetique interdum nuntii vulgabantur, donec provisis quae tempus monebat simul excessisse Augustum et rerum potiri Neronem fama eadem tulit.
>
> 1.5.4[74]

> For a strict cordon was placed around the house and its approaches by Livia and happy news was occasionally broadcast. Once provision was made for the occasion's demands, word went out simultaneously that Augustus was gone and Tiberius in control.

It is important to note that Tacitus only reported a rumor suggesting Livia's involvement, and merely hinted that Livia may have had ulterior motives for delaying the news of Augustus' death until Tiberius could reach his adoptive father's bedside. The phrase "once provision was made for the occasion's demands" is curious, and this is the only direct statement that Tacitus makes concerning Livia's motivation in withholding the truth and issuing false favorable news. Livia's behavior is suspect, but there is nothing overt to link her to the death of her husband. This appearance of innocence lasts only until the reader reaches the end of book 12, however, and reads the account concerning the death of Claudius. In the telling of his death, the past again comes crashing into the present, as Augustus melds with Claudius and Livia melds with Agrippina:

> et cunctos aditos custodiis clauserat, crebroque vulgabat ire in melius valitudinem principis, quo miles bona in spe ageret tempusque prosperum ex monitis Chaldaeorum adventaret.
>
> 12.68.3

> After closing and manning all approaches, [Agrippina] circulated frequent notices that Claudius' condition was improving, intending that the soldiers remain hopeful and the moment pronounced advantageous by astrologers arrive.

The propitious moment which had been prophesied by the Chaldaeans was Nero's ascension. Agrippina, who had murdered her husband with the help of his own doctor, now put her son on the throne. These passages are remarkably similar, and by this parallel construction Tacitus not only casts a spotlight on Agrippina's guilt, but also re-activates the previous rumors concerning Livia. By juxtaposing the two women in this way Tacitus is able to add weight to the suggestion of Livia's culpability, and to reintroduce the theme of familial murder.

In order to see these comparisons, it is helpful take a close look at the verbal similarities in these two passages. Both of the women station guards to block the entrances to the palace (*acribus namque custodiis domum et vias saepserat / cunctos aditos custodiis clauserat*). Both issued positive news about the ailing or deceased emperor (*laetique interdum nuntii vulgabantur / crebroque vulgabat ire in melius valitudinem principis*).[75] Though these verbal echoes, Tacitus is able to call forth the vivid passages from earlier in the *Annales*, raising in the mind of the viewer the image of Livia and her associated misdeeds. The mental conception of Livia is thus twinned to the image of Agrippina, and both women come to mind when these murderous deeds are discussed. Further connecting them, both women are imperial stepmothers (*novercae*) promoting their own sons over those of the emperor's family: Agrippa Postumus and Britannicus.[76]

Strengthening their connection on these grounds, Agrippina specifically emulates Livia in regard to Claudius' funeral preparations in a following passage.[77]

caelestesque honores Claudio decernuntur et funeris sollemne perinde ac divo Augusto celebratur, aemulante Agrippina proaviae Liviae magnificentiam.

12.69.3

Divine honors were voted for Claudius and his funeral was celebrated like the deified Augustus', since Agrippina rivalled her great-grandmother Livia's magnificence.

By implication, then, Agrippina plans Claudius' murder with not only Augustus, but also with Livia in mind. The current imperial-mother must outdo her predecessor (*aemulante Agrippina proaviae Liviae magnificentiam*). Already the reader can see the coming shadow of Nero's penchant for competitive spectacle in place of, and as a mask for, reality as Agrippina considers the funeral, thinking of it in terms of a show for the populace. The mechanism is the same as in *Gone with the Wind*, but in this instance the viewer is not experiencing tension and pathos alongside a sympathetic character. Here, the viewer, mindful of the example of Livia, is helpless to prevent the murder of another emperor, and must look on as the cycle not only repeats but struggles to surpass the past in treachery.

With the two accounts so rich in echoes between each other and across the *Annales*, the Tacitean inference must be that both women murdered their husbands. Agrippina's narrative encourages a reinterpretation of Livia's actions and a belated confirmation of guilt. The reader, at this point in the *Annales*, has connected the deeds and characters of Agrippina the Younger and Livia, but there is an important difference between them. Just as Tacitus is more explicit about the murder of Claudius than he was concerning Augustus' end, Tacitus also depicts Agrippina as more overt and daring than Livia.

First of the New Principate

Another remarkable example of backshadowing occurs at the start of Nero's reign, and harkens back to the ascension of Tiberius.[78] The attentive reader may remember that the first deed (*primum facinus*) of Tiberius' principate was the slaughter (*caedes*) of Agrippa Postumus, of which Tiberius claimed to be unaware (*neque imperasse sese ... respondit*) (1.6.1, 3).[79] Tacitus expects his reader to remember this striking beginning at the dawn of Nero's reign, when, after the soldiers had been paid and Claudius had been deified, Nero assumes the throne.[80]

prima novo principatu mors Iunii Silani proconsulis Asiae ignaro Nerone per dolum Agrippina paratur.

13.1.1

> The new regime's first death—Junius Silanus, Asia's governor; Nero was unaware—was set up by Agrippina's plotting.

In both locations in the text, the passages concerning these "first murders" occur immediately after the sections in which the imperial mothers (Livia and Agrippina the Younger, respectively), took an active role in orchestrating the funereal announcements of the former emperor. Tacitus makes use of backshadowing here, at the start of Nero's reign, to let the reader know what to expect in the coming narrative. The difference is the bold openness of the crime. No longer the ambiguous "deed" (*facinus*) of *Annales* 1, Agrippina's regime has achieved its "first death" (*prima mors*) with Nero consigned to a parenthical ablative absolute—nominal emperor and ignorant beneficiary reduced to an afterthought by Agrippina's plans.

The tenor and tone of the Neronian narrative is broader, bolder, and more overtly showy than the Tiberian books. Unlike the taciturn, impassive Tiberius, Nero is unconcerned about discovery. Nero's actions are explicit; he craves publicity for his authorship, even of unsavory or illegal deeds. Thus, from this beginning of Nero's reign, the reader expects variations on Tiberian themes, played at much higher volume and with the constant emphasis on spectacular effect: from the subtle darkness of Hitchcock to the screaming technicolor of Fellini. As seen in the Vatican sarcophagus, Tacitus has shown us the end of the *Annales* right from the start of the narrative, and as we reach the end of the work the parallels are pronounced. We have known what to expect from the beginning, with Tiberius foreshadowed by the name of Nero. And with Nero, we see all the flaws and foibles of the Julio-Claudians parading unchecked upon the stage.

Although I can certainly see Pagán's argument, that backshadowing can be a frustrating technique for readers, in that it can be difficult to understand how a character in full possession of the facts of the past can make the same mistakes over again, I believe that Tacitus employed this device not to portray his characters as fools but is instead playing with the reader's expectations.[81] Backshadowing is a useful tool, allowing the author to connect scenes from prior history with the mistakes (or triumphs) of the current moment, providing context and a powerful connection to history. Whether history repeats itself or tragedy is narrowly averted, backshadowing provides an excellent vehicle for reader engagement, thematic connection, and the creation of suspense. In Tacitus, the shadows of the past are never truly dormant, shaping the coming events of history with unseen hands.

Final Thoughts

Temporal shadowing, whether operating forward or backward through the narrative, has as its end goal the coloring or manipulation of the present account. Foreshadowing creates the illusion, briefly, of a fatalistic world wherein every event is preordained. Tiberius seems to serve as a precursor to Nero, Agrippina's faults are horribly magnified in her daughter, originally minor characters such as Sejanus grow in importance to overshadow the entire narrative, and retroactive connections solidify the guilt of Livia.

The mechanisms behind foreshadowing and backshadowing are critical components of a meaningful history; that events can be foreseen and crises either met or averted, and that the cycles of history repeat. In this, a knowledge of the past can help us to understand the present and better prepare ourselves for the future. What is noteworthy about the way in which they are used in the *Annales* is the additional level of meaning mobilized by their use. Tacitus is able not only to meet reader expectation, but also to build additional layers of political and narrative subtext. Through innuendo, inter-character connection, and repetition of visual language, Tacitus is able to provide stories-within-stories, providing his reader with a rich and highly nuanced image of the early empire. By employing these techniques, Tacitus is able to tell an accurate and visceral history unbounded by considerations of time.

5

Eloquent Collisions: The Quick-Cut[1]

Although many recent Tacitean scholars have addressed the use of rhetoric and innuendo in the *Annales*, there has been very little attention devoted to his unusual use of abrupt transitions.[2] Far from being appreciated as a technical device, some notable scholars have accepted these instances as examples of poor draftsmanship or structural construction on the part of the historian.[3] Tacitus, however, was not negligent in crafting these scenes. The mechanism is not readily apparent due to its inherently visual nature, which requires us as readers to think differently about these scenes. In this section, we will be looking at Tacitus' abrupt transitions through the lens of classical Hollywood film, where the technique is known more generally to modern readers as "the quick-cut," as well as the application of the device in visual media during Tacitus' own time period in the narrative construction of the Column of Trajan.[4]

The quick-cut is a concept most modern readers will be familiar with, but it is still important to discuss the ways in which the technique works and to discuss the types of quick-cut that are at play in the narrative accounts we will be comparing. As a transitional mechanism, the quick-cut has been with the film industry almost from its inception. Sergei Eisenstein, one of the most influential early filmmakers, spent considerable time investigating and testing the limits of this device.[5] Conceptually, the quick-cut works by engaging the inherently narrative-driven nature of the human mind. When two images are presented, the brain will naturally attempt to make a connection between them.[6] In most cases, both in film and in literature, the story itself leaves some clue or suggestion as to how the two scenes are to be connected. Thus, the context guides the viewer in many instances, although some forms of quick-cut intentionally place disconnected images together in order to achieve a sense of discomfort in the viewer, or to involve the audience in the creation of narrative. Tacitus employs this latter device to great effect, enabling him to forge narrative on multiple levels simultaneously.

The idea that transitions themselves play a critical role in the creation of meaning did not originate with film, nor did the use of abrupt changes in images or theme. Film is, however, uniquely effective as an illustrative tool, as its effects are made vivid and clear in visual format. Moreover, film has the additional benefit of being widely accessible to a modern audience and, unlike the stage-play of earlier eras, can be counted on to provide an identical "performance" each time it is viewed. Although some visual techniques noted by Classics scholars in the context of ancient literature can be likened to the action of plays or stage dramas, the quick-cut does not readily lend itself to that form of expression. Quick-cutting is effective in film, literature, and some forms of the static arts, but it cannot be showcased well on stage.

According to film theorist Jean Mitry, there are four classes of quick-cut: narrative, intellectual, lyrical, and the "montage of ideas."[7] The narrative and intellectual cuts are of the most interest to us in this regard, and where we will be focusing our attention. Narrative cuts, as the name implies, serve to connect scenes in a way that directly drives the story. Intellectual cuts are somewhat more complicated, and the term serves to cover a fairly wide range of visual movement. To better focus our discussion, we will be looking at two specific sub-types, drawing on Mitry's terminology, which I will refer to as "collision" and "attraction."

The Column of Trajan provides a helpful illustration of these techniques, as it uses a number of different transitions to move through the battle narrative of the Dacian wars. As has been noted, the Column is a difficult monument to read. This is due in part to simple physical reality; the spiraling narrative, which comprises the bulk of the story contained in the monument, stretches to a height of 100 Roman feet (c. 30 m).[8] Even though the Column was initially painted with vivid pigments, few ancient Romans would have been able to make out the scenes near the top. The existence of a multi-level marketplace and libraries flanking two sides of the Column may have made the higher portions more accessible, but this still does not fully address the issue, as it is unlikely that the highest panels would have been easy to read even from these structures. Nor is it only a matter of altitude, but also of narrative flow. The story of the Column is told, much like a comic-strip wrapped around a cylinder, from bottom to top in a sweeping curve.[9] Thus, in order to properly read the monument, Roman viewers would have had to walk all the way around the Column as it rises upward.

Even if we set aside for the moment questions of perspective, there remain a number of considerations regarding the correct "read" on the Column even when we are able to view it comprehensively. Some scholars have argued that it was not necessary for ancient viewers to see each panel of the monument in order to understand its story, instead intuiting its meaning.[10] It has been noted that the figures of the emperor Trajan align in an almost-vertical band on the southeast side, which may have assisted Roman viewers in locating the elements of the story, as well as having served as a reminder of the glory of the Column's hero.[11] The Trajan figures appear to have been painted in a different color from that of any of the other figures, further marking out his importance and highlighting these locations.[12] Similarly, the scenes in which the Roman army leaves its fortifications in order to cross the Danube river are arranged in an almost vertical line.[13] It has also been observed that the panels form discrete *tableaux*, in which the participants in a given scene face one another across an open space. Panels are separated from one another through differing types of methods including the use of scenery, edges of buildings or walls, and differently facing armies. Moreover, there are recognizable changes in perspective, scene depth (including a form of close-up), and shifts between static scenes and those depicting motion.[14]

One suggested reading of the monument incorporates three separate paths of interpretation, all of which serve complementary purposes.[15] Scholars have pointed to the cinematic qualities of the Column, pointing to the realistic use of detail, focus on important individuals, the largely temporal nature of the events, and the use of discrete scenes joined together to form a logical sequence.[16] Additionally, it has been suggested that the Column's cinematic parallels extend to point of view, camera angle, and, as we will be discussing in this section, the use of cutting between subject matter.[17] Thus, the Column of Trajan employs many techniques that we, as modern readers, associate with film and which serve to direct the gaze of the viewer.

Especially important in the context of this chapter, the Column of Trajan relies heavily on temporal juxtaposition for the creation of meaning. As discussed above in the context of montage, the placing of two disparate scenes next to one another forces the viewer to forge the connection between them. Thus, the placing of a scene showing the Dacian camp next to one in which the Roman army is arrayed for battle brings to mind specific potential meanings. This use of cutting, to heighten suspense, contrast, and dramatic appeal, is used throughout the Column. To date, however, this aspect of its construction has gone largely unexamined. Often, individual panels are considered out of their contexts, while the importance of transitions (and the meaning they create) remains unaddressed. These connections are of great interest from a narratological perspective, as they help to shape and create the deep narrative of the frieze. While the images tell the surface story, the mechanics of transition provide additional meaning.

From the inclusion of a wide array of visual narrative transitional techniques in the Column of Trajan, we can infer that second-century Romans were familiar with, and able to read, complex visual images. Since the designers and builders of the Column wanted it to serve as a narrative monument, it would be logical for them to select a mechanism readily understandable to their intended audience. Just as a Roman viewer would have been able to understand these visual cues and devices in artwork, Tacitus' contemporaries would have been attuned to similar techniques employed in literature.

The connection between the visual descriptions shown on the Column of Trajan and the works of Tacitus is one that has been recognized by other scholars. Not only are the two narratives roughly contemporary, scholars have noted the similarity in the Column's battle scenes and those of Tacitus' *Agricola*.[18] Tacitus employs many parallel techniques, and may certainly have drawn some of his inspiration from the Column, but, regardless, both works were designed to be read by Romans of the second century and they employ many of the same visual techniques.

We will look at the quick-cut technique in conjunction with both Tacitus and Roman art (in this case, the Column of Trajan). Since there are three different types of film comparanda, however, I will break the material on that basis, considering the narrative, collision, and attractive quick-cuts as they apply to Tacitean visual narrative.

The Narrative Quick-Cut and *Strangers on a Train*

Narrative quick-cuts are primarily concerned with advancing the storyline and help the viewer to form a connection between two related, or soon-to-be related, images, ideas, or individuals. As Mitry stated, the purpose of the narrative cut "is to ensure the continuity of the action—whatever the ideas expressed or suggested by the scenes described."[19]

An illustrative example is found in Hitchcock's *Strangers on a Train* (1951), where a series of narrative quick-cuts are used to draw a parallel between the two main characters, thus connecting their actions and movements. The camera shows two distinctive pairs of feet, walking in opposite directions. First the bi-colored spats, then a pair of dark loafers, back to the spats, and so on. In all, the viewer is shown nine cuts of these shoes, walking in opposite directions and, finally, the pair of loafers bumps into the spats once the two men have boarded their train. As the story continues, the audience learns that Bruno (Robert Walker) and Guy (Farley Granger) are parallel characters who will shortly become involved in a murderous intrigue, but long before the plot itself unfolds (in fact, even before a single word of dialogue is spoken) the audience knows that these men are connected.[20] Moreover, we know that the motion is contemporaneous; these men are arriving at the train station, walking inside, and boarding their train during the same space of time. We are only shown the faces of the men, and the dialogue of the movie begins, once the feet have connected. The narrative juxtaposition itself has been used to create meaning. Turning then to the Column of Trajan, the transition between scenes 67 and 68 employs a similar use of the narrative quick-cut.[21]

As you can see in Fig. 5.1, from the portion of the column concerning the first Dacian War, a small stand of trees is used as a divider between the two scenes. The first of these shows the camp of the Dacian army, while the second depicts the Roman camp. The trees serve to separate these two images in space, while also suggesting that our view of the two camps is contemporaneous. While the

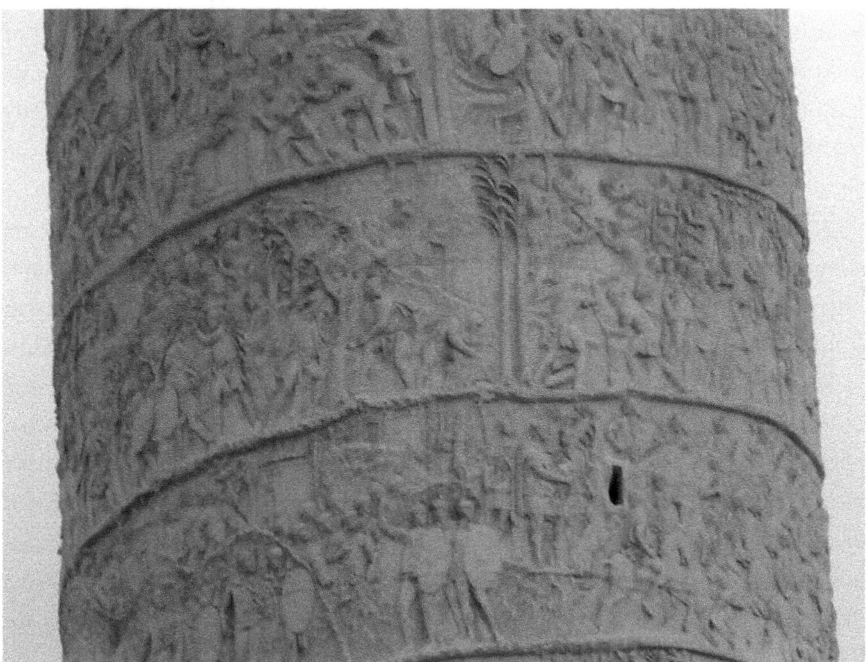

Figure 5.1 Trajan's Column, scenes 67–68, image © Philip Waddell, 2013.

Dacians make camp and prepare for battle, the Romans are doing likewise. The trees in this instance not only suggest the physical distance that separates them, but also indicate a parallel relationship between the two images. We do not take away the impression of a continuous linear flow from panels 67 to 68, but instead view them as contemporaneous realities. Viewers are thus offered a look at each army's preparations, and a Roman audience would likely note the professional and orderly nature of their own fighters in contrast with the haphazard camp of their enemies.

By using the trees to separate, and thus equate, the two camps the designer of the Column has provided an excellent foil for the audience, giving the viewer an opportunity to compare the relative merits of each camp (and by extension, its army), thus signaling the eventual success (or failure) that the audience will expect. Thus, the outcome of the first Dacian war can be predicted via this comparison.

Tiberius and Germanicus

Tacitus uses the narrative quick-cut in a very similar manner to that employed in *Strangers on a Train* and panels 67–68 of the Column of Trajan at various points in the *Annales*,[22] often switching between scenes using a short connective word such as *at*.[23] Although the use of *at* to transition between images is not unique to Tacitus, only Sallust uses the technique to similar effect.[24] Moreover, as has been noted, Tacitus employs this device in the *Annales* far more commonly than any other ancient historian.[25] This single-word cue often turns not only the vision, but the tone of the scene.

A striking example of the quick-cut to show this alteration in tone occurs when Tacitus contrasts the popular Germanicus with the suspicious and introverted Tiberius, when Germanicus is holding funerary rites for the Roman soldiers fallen during the Varian disaster in the Teutoburg forest. At this time, Germanicus is the commander of the Roman forces on the German frontier, one of the most contested borders in the Empire and, subsequently, one of the most heavily garrisoned. Thus, as Tacitus leads his reader to suspect, Tiberius may have viewed Germanicus as posing a substantial threat to the empire with the armies of the Rhine at his back. At the site of the Teutoburg massacre Germanicus is shown placing the first portion of earth over the resting place of the deceased, and Tacitus records that Germanicus shares in the pain that all of his soldiers are feeling (1.62.1). The mood of the passage is emotional and sympathetic as the virtuous deed is undertaken.[26]

This patriotic remembrance is cut short, however, as Tacitus cuts abruptly away to the fears and machinations of the jealous Tiberius:

> quod Tiberio haud probatum, seu cuncta Germanici in deterius trahenti, sive exercitum imagine caesorum insepultorumque tardatum ad proelia et formidolosiorem hostium credebat; neque imperatorem auguratu et vetustissimis caerimoniis praeditum adtrectare feralia debuisse.
>
> 1.62.2
>
> Tiberius did not approve, either interpreting everything of Germanicus' for the worse, or else he believed that the sight of unburied casualties made an army slower for battle and more cowardly toward enemies. *A commander responsible for augury and our most ancient rites should not have handled dead remains.*

With just four short words (*quod Tiberio haud probatum*), Tacitus discards the sympathetic scene of the loyal commander, and instead provides a laundry list of objections forwarded by the suspicious and devious emperor. The language used after the cut mirrors the ominous tenor of much of the *Annales*, in which rumor and distrust fuel imperial politics. By employing this adversative cut, Tacitus takes us from an objective scene of virtuous Roman behavior, and directly supplants it with the inner thoughts of Tiberius, which the emperor may (or may not) have ever actually expressed. Readers are placed into a subjective and uncomfortable position; during the prior episode, they may have felt sympathy for the Romans who died or enjoyed a sense of pride along with the right-acting army of Germanicus. The abrupt substitution of Tiberius and his anger, castigating the behavior of Germanicus, leaves the reader in a degree of turmoil, unsure whether to credit the noble thoughts of the prior passage and unsure which "read" is correct.

By using the quick-cut in this manner, Tacitus gains another useful narrative tool. In reality, Tiberius would not have been immediately aware of Germanicus' actions, and would have learned only weeks later that his nephew and adoptive son had elected to bury the dead in the German forest.[27] But, via the quick-cut, Tacitus is able to immediately connect action and reaction, and to represent the full force of the emperor's disapproval in a meaningful and dramatic way. This is akin to the use of the technique in the Column of Trajan, where the small grouping of trees serves to elide the space between the two camps, and allows the viewer to see them side-by-side. Viewers are left to draw their own conclusions from the comparison, and in both instances the author of the work is able to color and modify those impressions.

Additionally, by using this device, Tacitus is able to create the impression of an all-knowing, all-seeing emperor, and to transmit to his readers the oppression and foreboding experienced by Tiberius' subjects.[28] In this way, the emperor appears constantly aware of the actions of his officials and generals, ready to condemn or judge their actions anywhere in the empire. It has been noted that Tiberius' sudden appearance in this way casts a pall of fear over the narrative of the first hexad, creating a sense of his malicious and subtle power.[29]

After this interjection and judgment by the displeased emperor, Tacitus then returns to Germanicus, discussing the progress of his campaign against the forces of Arminius. Arminius was a defector from the Roman army who assisted the German forces during the Varian disaster, and thus Germanicus' actions against him would be viewed positively by Tacitus' readers. The surface narrative continues, and the looming and brooding Tiberius fades as the reader follows the new action of the story. The disruption to the temporal flow goes unnoticed, yet the suggestion it leaves, of Tiberius' omniscience, remains on the edge of the mind.

From an historiographical perspective, the insertion of Tiberius' immediate disapproval has the added narrative benefit of bringing into stark contrast the temperament of the two characters, and prefigures the eventual (and now seemingly inevitable) conflict between them. Therefore, in this instance the narrative quick-cut serves not only to forward the direct motion of the story, but also to power the deep narrative of deception and discord which underlies Tacitus' portrayal of the empire.

Empty Arches

Another example of Tacitus' use of the narrative quick-cut occurs in book 15, and is illustrative of the breadth of Tacitus' employment of the technique. The passage, which occurs at 15.18.1, comes after a relatively lengthy account of the action of the Parthian campaign. For reference, this portion of the *Annales* occurs during the reign of Nero, at a time when Caesennius Paetus, a sycophantic and ineffective proconsul was put in charge of the province of Armenia while the experienced general Corbulo managed the war against Parthia. Paetus attempted to win the war by himself, undertaking military action that was poorly planned and executed. Eventually, the war was ended through diplomacy, as Corbulo was able to negotiate a peace with Vologaeses, the king of Parthia. This peace, however, was simply a reinstitution of the pre-existing boundaries between Armenia and Parthia, and did not represent the conquering of new territory.

Vologaeses required the Romans to dismantle their fortifications across the Euphrates river, and Corbulo was able to force the Parthian troops to leave Armenian territory (15.17.3).

At this point in the history, having gone through all of the complicated twists and turns of the two armies in the conflict, Tacitus returns the attention of the reader to what was happening at Rome.

> at Romae tropaea de Parthis arcusque medio Capitolini montis sistebantur, decreta ab senatu integro adhuc bello neque tum omissa, dum adspectui consulitur spreta conscientia.
>
> 15.18.1

> In Rome, victory monuments 'Over the Parthians' were set up, including an arch halfway up the Capitoline hill. They were decreed by the senate with the war still undecided and work continued while appearances were being maintained, common knowledge notwithstanding.

With "*at Romae*," Tacitus abruptly moves from the far reaches of the empire back to the city, and places the story squarely within the shadow of the imperial gaze. The reader is presented with a senate more concerned with appearances than honor; having decreed a victory monument with the war not yet won, they were more interested in the appearance of triumph than with the historical facts of the war.[30] This is deeply upsetting, as the reader naturally wants to see a senate that cares about reality. That the leading citizens of Rome are more concerned with empty appearances, rather than dealing with the reality of the Roman conflict in the east, suggests that the dissolution inherent in the empire has spread to the senate. The sham and play-acting of the emperor Nero have become the voice of the Roman state. Through the use of the quick-cut the viewer is immediately shown both the inglorious end of the war and the erection of false victory monuments. In this way, Tacitus highlights the irony of false memorialization, pointing out that the Romans are celebrating a near fabrication, rather than either giving thanks for the preservation of their armies in the east or offering propitiations for an unsuccessful campaign.

This use of the quick-cut places the reality of the Parthian war, and the illogical Roman reaction to it, in stark contrast. The transitional technique allows Tacitus to create, and thus stress, simultaneous action, and also to connect the anticlimactic ending of the war with the "empty arches," the false signs of conquest that were erected to memorialize this sham victory.[31] Additionally, Tacitus is able to highlight the theatrics and duplicity that were the hallmarks of Nero's reign.[32] Everything had become form without substance.

These two passages serve to illustrate Tacitus' use of the narrative quick-cut, which parallels the use of the technique in both the Column of Trajan and *Strangers on a Train*. In all of these cases, the narrative cut's primary goal is the forwarding of the surface narrative of the story in question via a change of scene, and may be used both to imply simultaneous action and to provide illustrative contrast between the interposed images.

Collision Quick-Cut and *The Godfather*

The second type of quick-cut that we will be discussing, the intellectual cut, was pioneered by Eisenstein, and he used it to great and memorable effect in both *The Battleship Potemkin* (1925) and *October* (1928). According to Mitry, the intellectual cut is "less concerned with ensuring the continuity of the narrative than with constructing it, and less with expressing ideas through this narrative than with determining them dialectically."[33] In other words, the intellectual cut may be used to juxtapose two images that have little connection within the current line of story, and thus by their ordering urge the viewer to forge meaning between them. Tacitus uses this device extremely efficiently in the *Annales*, and in this chapter we will examine several examples. In order to further differentiate the techniques used by the historian, I will subdivide the discussion of this intellectual quick-cut into two types on the basis of Mitry's montage categories, specifically those of "collision"[34] and "attraction."

The first of these, the collision quick-cut, is the more dramatic of the two forms of intellectual cuts, and draws its strength from opposition. Unlike narrative cuts, which serve to reinforce connections, parallelism, and contemporaneous action in the storyline and characters, the collision cut places before the viewer two unconnected (and often jarring) images, forcing him or her to make sense out of the juxtaposition. The viewer must attempt to forge meaning between the two, often wholly unrelated, scenes and to create a connection where none had previously existed. The collision cut is extremely powerful, as it draws the viewer into the narrative as a secondary story-teller, and the viewer must take an active role in creating sense and meaning of the images.[35]

A memorable example of this technique's use in film is found in Coppola's *The Godfather* (1972). Near the end of the film, Michael Corleone (Al Pacino) holds his infant nephew Michael Rizzi (Sofia Coppola) at his christening, at a time in the story when he takes over the family's mafia business after the death of his father Don Vito Corleone (Marlon Brando). Thus, at this moment, he is standing godfather to his nephew, and also taking on the role of Godfather to the Corleone family. As he stands with the white-swaddled baby and, in the course of the ritual, swears on his nephew's behalf "to renounce Satan and all his works," the film cuts away to reveal what else is happening in order to bring this moment about. As the ritual builds with organ music and the Latin liturgy, the film cuts to the preparations of the Corleone assassins as they ready themselves for the upcoming murders. Often, this cutting is highlighted with thematic connections between the scenes. For example, the chrism that the priest is going to use to anoint the infant is paired with the shaving foam which is about to be used on Moe Greene (Alex Rocco). These thematic connections thus also serve to rhythmically interlock the sets of images.

The tension increases as the scenes cut back and forth from the christening to the several scenes of preparation for murder. To further unite these cuttings, the organ music and Latin liturgy are the dominant sounds across all of the scenes, with the only exception being the eventual gunfire as the Corleone hitmen kill their targets. At the height of the ritual, the language changes to English as the priest asks Michael the-call-and-response questions of whether he, speaking for the child, renounces Satan. Interspersed with Michael's answers are some of the most violent images in the film, depicting the murders of mafia dons and people who have betrayed the Corleone family, including Moe Greene and the person who ultimately attempted to destroy the Corleone family, Don Barzini (Richard Conte).

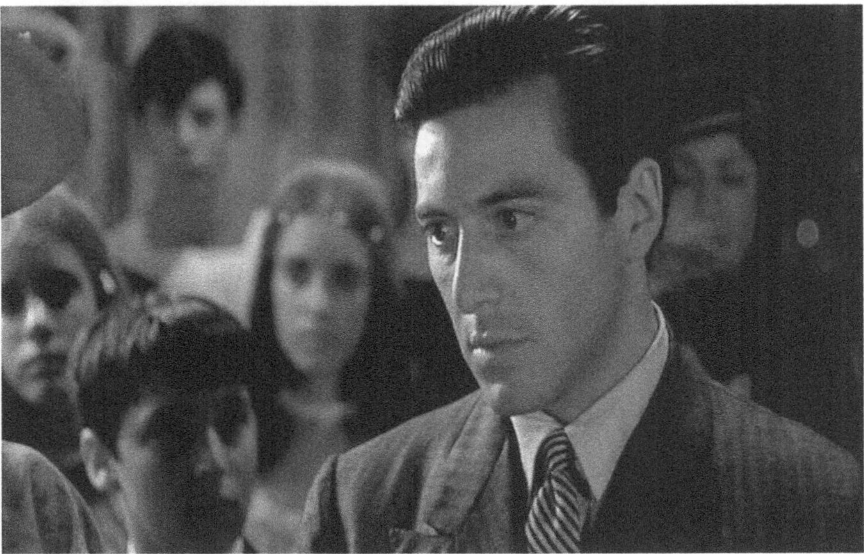

Figures 5.2–5.6 *The Godfather*, directed by Francis Ford Coppola © Paramount Pictures 1972. All rights reserved.

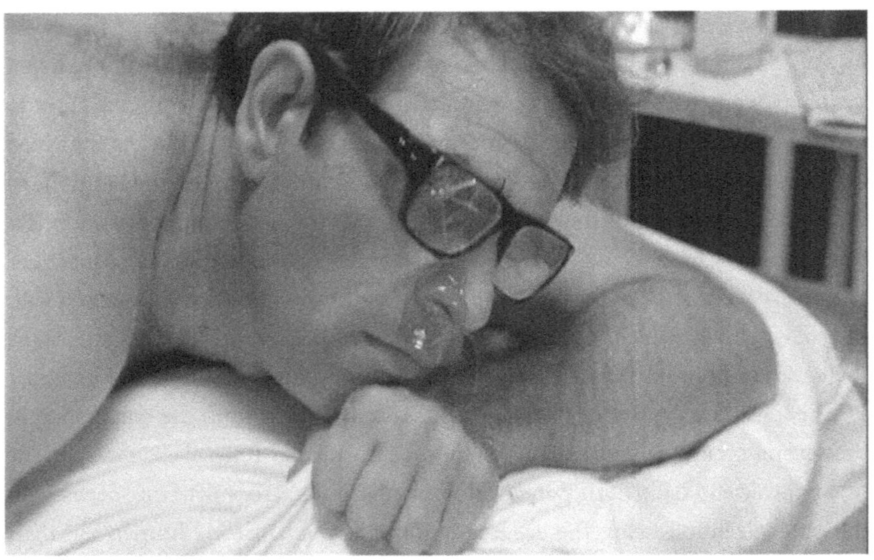

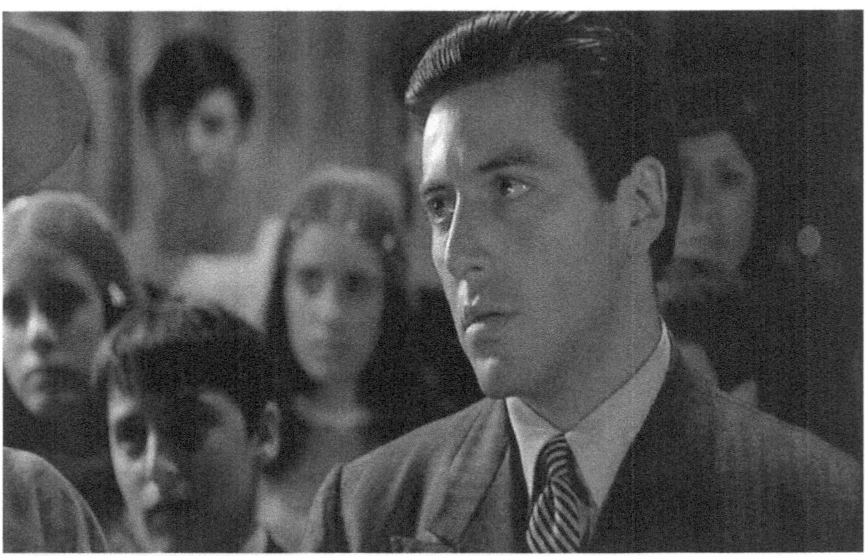

Figures 5.2–5.6 *Continued.*

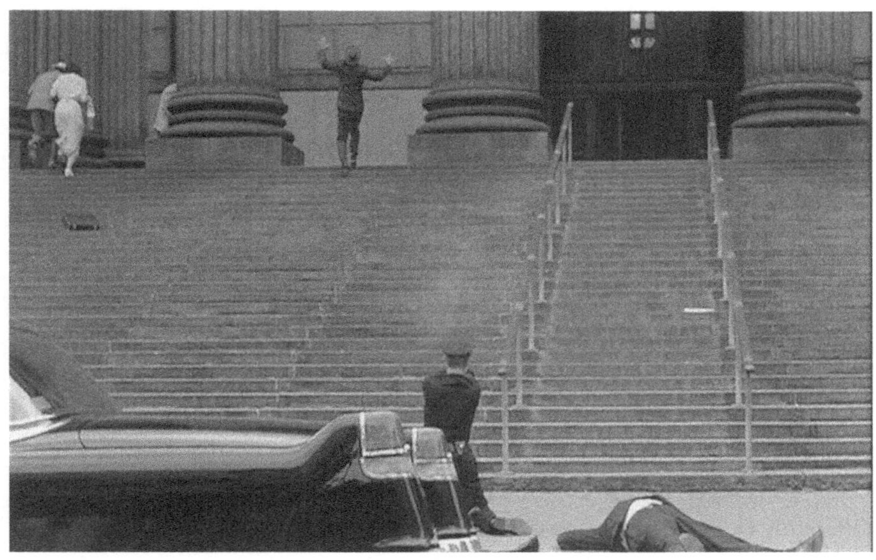

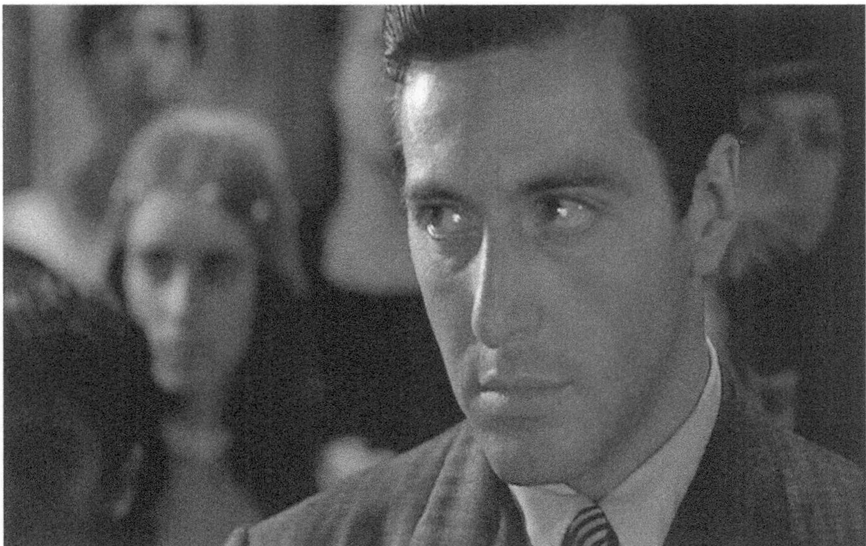

Figures 5.2–5.6 *Continued.*

After each short action sequence of resulting carnage, we are returned to the christening, alternately watching the sleepy infant or the inscrutable face of Michael as he responds in accordance with the baptismal liturgy. Thus Coppola suggests, through the use of apposite images and effective collision cuts, that the baby is hereby baptized in the blood of the Corleone family's enemies.[36]

In order to see how this same concept was employed in Roman art, we will again turn to the Column of Trajan, where the same type of transition is used to connect scenes 44 and 45.

In panel 44, also in the portion of the Column that deals with the first Dacian war, we see a Dacian chieftain surrendering to the victorious Trajan. On the next panel, however, we see a Dacian city, in which the native women are beating and torturing naked Roman captives. The transition between these two scenes is made even more dramatic as there is no clear delineation marker, only the differently facing figures serve to indicate the separation. In panel 44, the Roman army faces left (as though looking at Trajan) while the Dacians are turned to the right, as though looking toward the Dacian city depicted in panel 45. At the

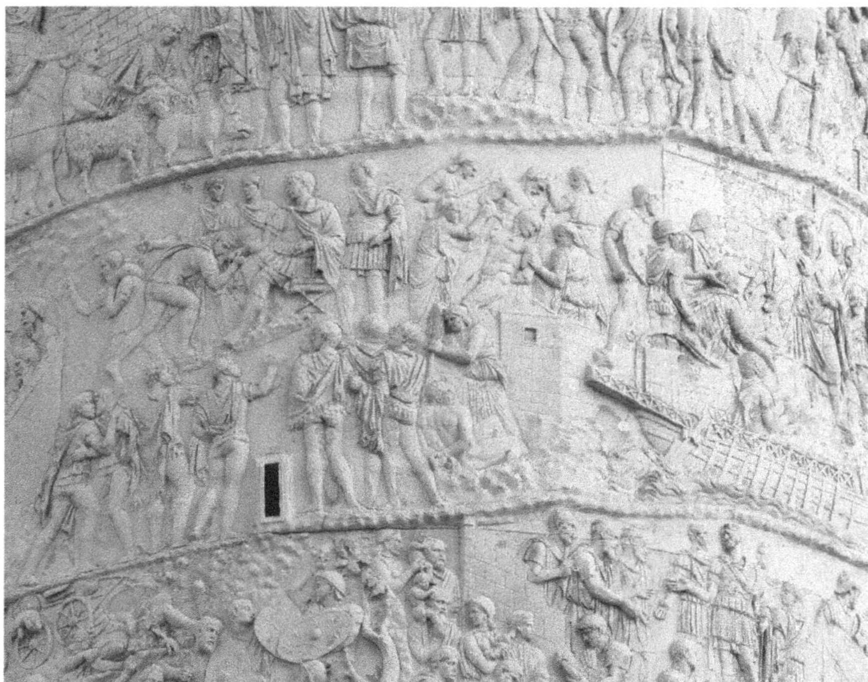

Figure 5.7 Trajan's Column, scenes 44–45; image used by permission, Roger B. Ulrich.

conjunction of the panels, a member of the Roman army stands with his back nearly touching that of a Dacian woman.

This "collision" conjunction provides a layer of meaning impossible to convey effectively in any other manner; the viewer must make sense of these almost overlapping images, and forge meaning between them.[37] The reader knows that, despite the appearance of victory, there is still much fighting to come and the need for resolution is critical. This juxtaposition allows the designer of the Column to show the progress of the Romans without losing the suspense and immediacy of the battle narrative. It also serves to signal to the viewer that the war is not over simply because one chieftain has surrendered. Rome has many enemies, and the army cannot afford to rest on its laurels even for a moment of celebration.

The importance of this transition is further underscored by the vertical arrangement of the panels on the Column. Directly above panels 44 and 45 are the Victory scenes shown on 74–75.

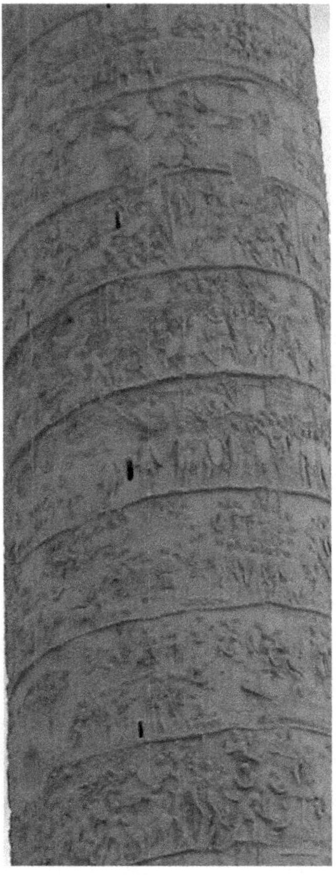

Figure 5.8 Trajan's Column, lower NW side, image © Philip Waddell, 2013.

This conflict, the torture of Romans following a surrender, constitutes an important moment in the war, and a key moment on the journey to Trajan's eventual success. Romans of the second century would have had the additional ability to interpret the Column vertically, and would be able to see that this moment, though pivotal, eventually results in Roman glory, as symbolized by Trajan's gilded statue at the top of the monument.

Tacitus makes notable use of the collision quick-cut at numerous points in the *Annales*. In some instances he juxtaposes scenes across time and space for rhetorical effect, and in some cases he confines the collision to the use of specific language and grammar within sentences. With regard to the latter, I am referring to Tacitus' expert and subtle use of the ablative absolute, which is one of the hallmarks of his authorial technique.[38] For readers less familiar with Latin, the ablative absolute can be a difficult construction to translate into English because of its inherent ambiguity. For example, the ablative absolute can be taken causally (=because), temporally (=when), or adversatively (=although).[39] The reader of the Latin must parse out how the material in the ablative absolute relates to the main sentence. One example that has received a great deal of attention is Tacitus' use of the absolute near the beginning of the *Annales*:

> postquam Bruto et Cassio caesis nulla iam publica arma, Pompeius apud Siciliam oppressus exutoque Lepido interfecto Antonio ne Iulianis quidem partibus nisi Caesar dux reliquus.
>
> 1.2.1

> After Brutus and Cassius were killed, the state was no longer armed. Sextus Pompey was crushed in Sicily and, with Lepidus discarded and Antony dead, the only Julian faction-leader was Octavian.

Many scholars have noted that a judgment call must be made here in order to properly understand Tacitus' meaning.[40] Moreover, Tacitus often relies on this ambiguity to force the reader to make constant decisions about cause and effect and even the basic meaning of his histories.

Thus, Tacitus' use of the collision cut can be extremely subtle, as most readers (particularly those coming to his work initially in translation) will not be aware on first reading of the power he is mobilizing at this level. Rather, the unease generated by these constructions is more felt than noticed, leaving the reader unsettled on a deep level but unsure as to what aspect of the account has caused the sensation. More obvious are the direct visual juxtapositions he creates by the jarring placement of material, which we will look at now.[41]

Triumph and Trial

The first example of the collision quick-cut we will be examining comes from Book 3 of the *Annales*, at which point Tacitus is wrapping up a discussion of the Roman army's fight against Numidia (3.21.4). As readers of Tacitus are aware, the historian rarely recounts clear victories, preferring to populate his history with near misses, close escapes, mutinies, and successes overshadowed by politics, impending danger, or the greedy ambitions of the powerful. In this instance, however, Tacitus provides the reader with a clear, uncomplicated statement of triumph:

> missu patris Apronius Caesianus cum equite et cohortibus auxiliariis, quis velocissimos legionum addiderat, prosperam adversum Numidas pugnam facit pellitque in deserta.
>
> 3.21.4

> Apronius Caesianus, sent by his father with cavalry and auxiliary cohorts plus the legions' swiftest, successfully fought the Numidians and drove them into the desert.

The *tableaux* created here is something that we might expect to see in Livy (or on the wall of a victory monument); an attractive, uncomplicated scene in which the Roman army is depicted vanquishing its foes. But Tacitus does not let this image stand unchallenged. After this brief description, and with no warning to suggest the impending shift, Tacitus changes not only subject but also continent, and moves from the glory of the army to the state of debased political machinations taking place at Rome. As we have seen previously, Tacitus here employs the *at Romae* construction, further denying the reader any warning or context for the dramatic shift.[42]

> at Romae Lepida, cui super Aemiliorum decus L. Sulla et Cn. Pompeius proavi erant, defertur simulavisse partum ex P. Quirinio divite atque orbo; adiciebantur adulteria venena quaesitumque per Chaldaeos in domum Caesaris
>
> 3.22.1

> In Rome Lepida, who had, in addition to her Aemilian lustre, Sulla and Pompey as forebears, was reported for simulating a birth to the wealthy and childless Publius Quirinius. Additional charges: adulteries, poisonings, consulting astrologers about the imperial household.

This second scene, into which the reader is abruptly thrown, shows the almost farcical trial of a noblewoman. The charges against her are, if not trumped up entirely, certainly embellished to an excessive degree, and the manner in which Tacitus records them seems to cast doubt on their merits or sincerity. The primary cause of action appears to be the falsification of the birth of a child to a wealthy man. To this, the increasingly predictable charges of poisoning and adultery have been added, as though tossed in as afterthoughts in order to round out the complaint.[43] All three of these charges were state crimes, and could incur the penalties of either execution or banishment. Finally, she is accused of consulting with the Chaldeans, notable fortune-tellers, which Tacitus seems to imply was at least potentially treasonable under the *lex maiestatis*, since she was apparently attempting to learn the date of the emperor's death.[44] That the woman in question is related to some of the most powerful families of the Roman Republic serves as an additional layer of commentary about the inappropriate actions of the emperor, and the state of moral rectitude during the reign of Tiberius.

The juxtaposition of these two scenes is extremely striking and surprising, since they have absolutely nothing to do with one another, and Tacitus makes no attempt to forge a transition between them. This is upsetting for the reader of Roman historiographical accounts, since under the normal convention for successful battle the narrative the account would progress to some celebration of victory, the joyous receipt of the news back at home, or a digression into how the good morals of the civilization (or a particular commander) led to the inevitable and triumphant conclusion. Here, there is nothing to indicate that the Roman people have any interest in the victory of their soldiers, no suggestion of pride or anticipation of a homecoming. Instead, the reader is abruptly thrown into a visceral description of the debased morals of Tiberius' city. There is nothing to suggest that Roman valor played a role in winning Numidia, nor is there any other basis for drawing a parallel between the two events. The reader is left unsure whether the victory means anything, and whether anyone at Rome cares that it has happened.

Thus, the collision cut is used here to highlight discord, and to pair honor with immorality, working to build the deep narrative of the *Annales* through a sense of unease and discomfort. The scene is made all the more striking because Tacitus so rarely provides an uncomplicated and unambiguous statement of martial valor as that of the Numidian campaign, and yet it seems the purpose of this telling is at least in part to provide a background for the horrors of the empire. The viewer needs no other suggestion or statement from Tacitus to know that something is deeply wrong here, and to see the hints that the empire is on unstable ground.

Marriage and Flames

The second passage that we will be looking at in the context of the collision cut is one of the most discussed and most famous juxtapositions of unrelated material in the *Annales* (15.38.1).[45] The first scene in question takes place in the summer of the year 64, during the reign of Nero, during one of the emperor's elaborate and theatrical parties. Tacitus goes into minute detail concerning the types of debaucheries and outrages committed against the Roman sense of decency, using exact terminology to heighten the sense of horror. Unlike the sections which deal with the secretive and suspicious Tiberius, Nero's moral offenses are open and flagrant. The party, as Tacitus describes it, incorporates many forms of inversion, a troubling and culturally charged concept for the Roman people. Marriageable Roman women are confused for prostitutes and, rather than exercising decorum and restraint, the guests and host make effusive displays of their extravagant wealth.[46] The greatest horror, as Tacitus shows us, is the emperor's participation in a form of marriage ceremony in the female role.[47] This image, extremely offensive to Roman sensibilities, is described in precise and lengthy detail by the historian, in order to ensure that the full horror of the situation is understood by his readers.[48] Tacitus presents this scene as the inversion of all things Roman and traditional, with Nero as circus leader to a band of unruly and dangerous revelers.

The collision cut occurs at the beginning of the next passage, which abruptly changes from this image-parade of horror and delight to one of utter calamity, the Great Fire of Rome.

> sequitur clades, forte an dolo principis incertum (nam utrumque auctores prodidere), sed omnibus, quae huic urbi per violentiam ignium acciderunt, gravior atque atrocior.
>
> 15.38.1

> Next came a calamity. Whether by accident or by the Emperor's plotting is uncertain—authorities give both accounts—but it was more harmful and fearful than any others that have befallen the city through fire's violence.

Tacitus goes on to describe the effects of the fire, which burned most of downtown Rome and destroyed the vast majority of the city. Without confirming his own suspicions, and indeed claiming that it would be impossible to know the truth of the matter since the various sources do not agree, he puts forward the rumor that Nero himself started the blaze.[49] The further portion of text gives rise to one of the most famous quotations from the Roman world, which is still in common parlance today: that Nero "fiddled while Rome burned."

> quae quamquam popularia in inritum cadebant, quia pervaserat rumor ipso tempore flagrantis urbis inisse eum domesticam scaenam et cecinisse Troianum excidium, praesentia mala vetustis cladibus adsimulantem.
>
> 15.39.3
>
> These were popular measures, but fruitless, since rumour spread. *With the city aflame, Nero mounted his domestic stage and performed a "Sack of Troy," likening present ills to ancient calamities.*

Tacitus gives his readers some time to accept this information, and to take in the rumors and innuendo presented, before then unequivocally stating that Nero could not have been directly involved in the conflagration, since he was out of town in Antium at the time (15.39.1).

Tacitus wants his reader to accept the rumor, rather than the information provided as absolute fact, as the driving narrative. By giving the reader such vivid descriptions of the fire, and of Nero's involvement, as opposed to the bare statement of Nero's actual absence, the more involved and detailed account must be intended to supplant the banal, yet true, alternative account. Additionally, by providing the rumor, with all of its color and life, as the first account and the initial explanation, Tacitus is attempting to subvert what he knows to be true. He wishes his readers, like the populace of Rome at the time, to always have in mind Nero's guilt. This is an elegant trick, which enables Tacitus to remain faithful to the historical record, while still painting the picture he wishes, which he is able to do by citing to the presence of a rumor in his sources. The suggestion of Nero's guilt is made all the more forceful by Tacitus' use of the collision cut; showing the fire right on the heels of Nero's misdeeds naturally suggests a connection between them.[50] Nero is guilty of immorality and, by extension, his guilt here is also suspected.[51] Since the mind looks for a connection where none is immediately apparent (coupled here with Tacitus' provision of the rumors of Nero's involvement), the collision cut is an ideal way to guide readers to the assumption that Nero's wrongdoing is the key link between the two passages. Moreover, Tacitus' Roman audience would, due to normal literary convention, expect divine retribution to follow images of immoral deeds and the profanation of sacred ceremonies. Thus, the connection of guilt between the two passages is additionally strengthened.

In this instance, Tacitus is able to employ structure, coupled with the helpful device of reporting innuendo, to force his reader to create meaning that differs from the actual historical facts. This is a striking example of Tacitus' creation of deep narrative through visual technique, which strikes below the conscious level of reason, leading the reader to intuitively accept this subtext of secret history as truth. Although often not so readily accessible, these mechanical devices serve to provide much of the disquieting, brooding atmosphere of the *Annales*, and give much of the force and emphasis to his descriptions. In the next section, we will look at a third example of quick-cut techniques, which offers yet another helpful option to the author of visual history.

Attractive Quick-Cut and *Lawrence of Arabia*

While the narrative quick-cut serves to forward the storyline of a work, and the collision cut is used to force meaning between unrelated scenes, the attractive quick-cut is concerned with the thematic or representational aspects of the narrative. This cut is used to create a meaningful parallel between a specific character or story component and an external image or object. This bonding of the two elements, in the mind of the viewer, enhances understanding of the motivations, fears, or thoughts of the character involved in the match, and works directly on the level of deep narrative.[52]

To see the attractive cut illustrated in film, consider its memorable use in *Lawrence of Arabia* (David Lean, 1962). In one of the most distinctive moments in the film, the character T. E. Lawrence (Peter O'Toole) lights a match, watching the flame as it burns for a few seconds, and then blows it out. The attractive cut then occurs, as the scene jumps to an image of the blazing sun rising on the edge of the Arabian Desert. The match, representing themes of heat and light, is thus connected to and linked with the much more powerful sun. The viewer is reminded at this moment in the film of an earlier moment, in which T. E. Lawrence had toyed with a match, allowing it to burn him as a form of sport or amusement. The character's comments about not minding the heat, coupled with his own apparent lack of self-regard and desire to punish himself, are mirrored in this attractive cut, as the heat and light of the desert—where Lawrence has elected to go—are infinitely more terrible and difficult than those of his matches.[53]

In this instance, the attractive cut has been used not only to link the images with T. E. Lawrence's character, but also to elide time in the narrative. Lawrence is thus transported, as we skip over his traveling to Cairo, and the story continues seamlessly from this new point in space and time. Thus, this cut is able, through the linking of initially disparate-seeming images into a meaningful thematic bond, to provide deep insight into elements of the story as well as to make critical, theme-based jumps through the narrative timeline.[54]

Having seen how the attractive quick-cut works in film, we will turn again to our Roman source—the Column of Trajan. The panel we will be focusing on is located at 74–75, in which a goddess representing Victory is writing or carving the history of great deeds onto a large shield. She is depicted winged, facing toward the right, as though showing the viewer what she is recording. The image of great deeds inscribed on shields is a common motif in Roman art and literature, including of course the famous shield of Achilles in the *Iliad*.

In this instance, Victory's historical efforts follow closely on the heels of another surrendering Dacian chieftain and the heroic Trajan.[55] Therefore, the viewer understands that another page in the story of this war is written, and Victory is recording the winner and recounting Roman glory. The shield, then, becomes an important object that is not part of the story itself (it plays no role in

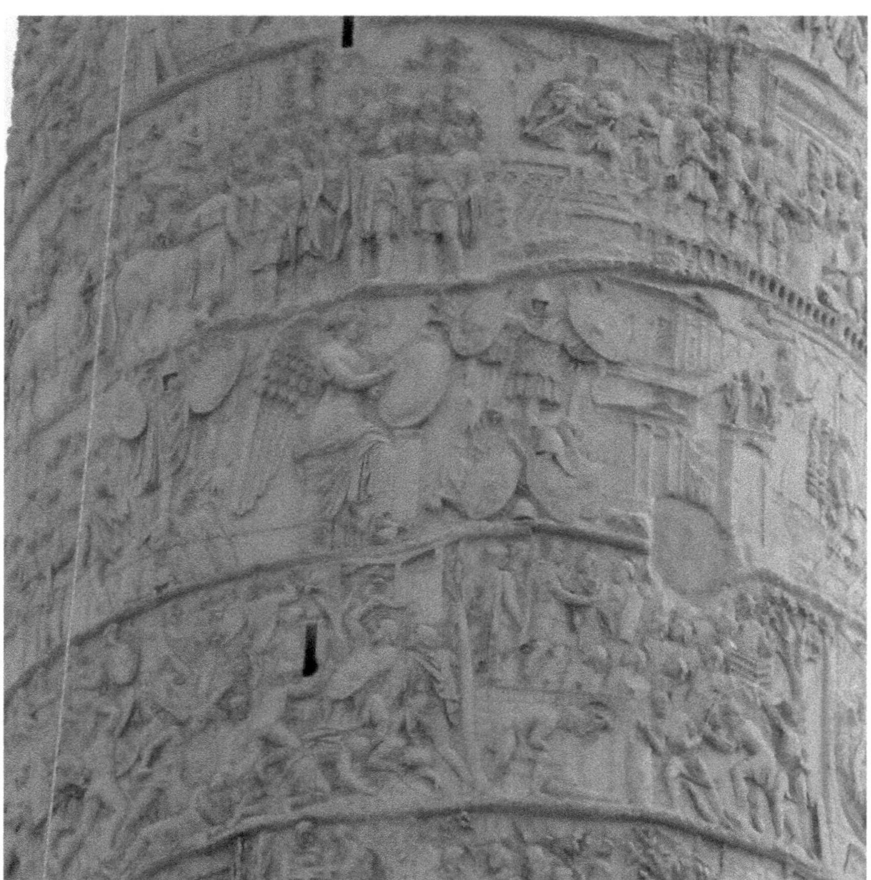

Figure 5.9 Trajan's Column, scenes 74–75, image © Philip Waddell, 2013.

the Dacian wars), and is an outside, symbolic image. Through this panel, it is made representative of the war and its battle honors, and becomes emblematic of those aspects of the narrative. In this panel, the regular flow of the story is interrupted for a moment for Victory's external comment, and to thereby connect the shield with these concepts. Moreover, the fact that Victory is at this time ready to record her history, and to set down for all times the Roman conquest on a great shield, signals to the viewer that this is a final victory, and that Trajan's armies have been successful in quelling their foes. Panels 74–75 denote the end of the first Dacian war, which would be readily understood by the Column's audience. The goddess is ready to award the spoils, and so the war must be truly ended. Even if the reader were unable to determine the identity of the chieftain in panel 73, he or she would know it to be the Dacian king after the image-connection of the following scene.

A Dead Tree Grows in Rome

The final scene of Book 13 has long puzzled Classics scholars, since it seems a strange ending to a book of historical prose, and leaves the narrative without a sense of closure. Over time, scholars have posited a wide array of theories as to why Tacitus ended the book in this apparently haphazard or offhand manner, and some have suggested that an additional section of text (with, presumably, a more suitable book-ending) has been lost. Others have suggested that it represents a poor or lackadaisical selection on the part of the historian,[56] or that Tacitus was bound to mention the episode at that point due to his annalistic framework. I disagree with these arguments, and would instead posit that this section must be read as a transitional piece, rather than as an isolated scene in itself.

The text itself concerns the Ruminal Fig, which was considered a sacred object and historical monument in Roman times. It was believed that the tree had played a role in protecting Romulus and Remus, the orphaned twin boys who founded the city in legendary times. The tree had, it was believed, either become ill or died, which the Roman people took as an omen, until it began to show signs of life:

> eodem anno Ruminalem arborem in comitio, quae octingentos et triginta ante annos Remi Romulique infantiam texerat, mortuis ramalibus et arescente trunco deminutam prodigii loco habitum est, donec in novos fetus revivisceret.
>
> 13.58

> That same year the "Ruminal" tree in the assembly place, which 830 years earlier shaded Remus and Romulus as infants, was reduced to dead brush and drying trunk. This was considered a portent, until it revived with new growth.

The initial description of the tree, which has withered and twisted, and appears to be dying or dead, appears to align with the narrative Tacitus is recounting. This portion of text appears in the Neronian books, and in the previous sections Tacitus has painted an ever-darkening picture of the state of political and moral decline in Rome under Nero's reign. Thus, the picture of the Ruminal Fig, a symbol of the founding of the city and its shining destiny, now shriveled and dried out, serves as an imagistic parallel for Tacitus' account. The last portion of the text, however, which tells us that the tree revived and began to grow anew, seems highly out of place, particularly since Nero will remain in power for ten more years.

Generally speaking, the Romans relied (at least in part) on omens and portents to guide their important decisions, and augury was an integral component of Roman religious life. Omens were thought to be direct messages from the gods, which had to be recognized and correctly interpreted in order to avoid disaster. It has been argued that Tacitus disregards or dismisses omens,[57] but a more careful reading suggests otherwise.[58] Tacitus' scorn and concern are directed not at the omens themselves, or those who take them into account, but is instead reserved for individuals who misread them.[59] As Liebeschuetz notes, most of the omens mentioned in the *Annales* are eventually fulfilled.[60] Although the Fig is reborn while Nero is in power, we should not assume Tacitus is casting aspersion on the portent.[61] A longer view of this omen is, in my view, more appropriate. As has been suggested by McCulloch, the withering of the tree may represent the coming additional ten years of rule by Nero (as well as the following disastrous year of four emperors). The regrowth, then, is an omen of the coming of Vespasian at the end of 69 and the relative peace and prosperity that his rule brought to Rome.[62]

While this is an interesting puzzle, and one that has occupied scholars for many years, understanding the meaning of the omen itself is only one portion of the question. The placement of the Ruminal Fig episode at the end of Book 13 where, at least from a surface narrative perspective, it seems to serve little purpose is still unclear. Tacitus is one of the most highly technical, and highly skilled, writers of ancient history that we have extant. His brilliance and literary skill have been attested to for, quite literally, centuries, and it is unlikely that he simply "forgot" to pay attention to the ending of Book 13. It has been long recognized that book endings play an important role in the narrative of the *Annales* and indeed, Book 13 is no exception.[63] In parsing the meaning of this passage, however, we should consider that its potential importance may not be contained within the scene itself as an isolated phenomenon, but in its function as a transitional component in an attractive quick-cut.

Accordingly, we must look to the preceding events to help ground the meaning of the Ruminal Fig, specifically at section 13.57.3, where Tacitus discusses a significant fire in one of the Roman colonies. Tacitus does not name the colony, merely indicating that it was recently founded and located in the territory of the Ubii. The name of colony he is referring to is highly relevant, however, as it is the *Colonia Agrippinensis* (modern-day Cologne), where Agrippina the Younger (the mother of the emperor Nero) was born and which was named in her honor. It is significant that the fire occurs in her city, as shortly after Book 14 begins Tacitus recounts her death at the hands of her son.[64] In this penultimate section of Book 13, Tacitus spends some time describing the fire and the desperate attempts of the citizens to quell it, before moving on to the episode of the Ruminal Fig.

With this context in mind, the function of the Fig tree becomes more apparent. Like the shield of Victory on the Column of Trajan, and the burning match as a cipher for the sun in *Lawrence of Arabia*, the Ruminal Fig is a symbolic image that serves to bind and connect the narrative of Books 13 and 14. The fire ravaging Agrippina's colony and Nero's wicked reign in Rome are represented thematically by the withering of the tree, which is in itself a powerful and charged symbol of Rome's history and honorable traditions. The deaths of Agrippina and Nero, and the eventual coming of Vespasian, are heralded by the image of new growth. Thus, the theme of slow degradation and decay, as well as the new dawn of Roman glory, are made thematic and encapsulated by the image of the Ruminal Fig.[65] Although the Ruminal Fig, and its horticulturally surprising behavior, are likely to be historical facts, Tacitus mobilizes this image to great narrative effect in his placement of the event. Far from being an afterthought or accidental addition, this scene is replete with deep narrative and connective meaning. In this way, the Fig also serves as a bridge to the action of the *Historiae*, where the reign of Vespasian is discussed.[66]

Just as David Lean and the designer of the Column of Trajan carefully selected their thematic images, and used them in calculated ways to deepen the meaning of their works, so too did Tacitus craft and organize the account of the Ruminal Fig. The use of the attractive quick-cut allows for a quick and highly effective bonding of relevant story elements and a representational image, which both bring home the importance of theme and create an important touch-point for readers or viewers. Although these moments do serve to connect the narrative, in that they join one scene to the next, they are in many ways outside the narrative and operate as an encapsulated summary of the story itself.

Final Thoughts

The use of the quick-cut is now so ubiquitous and commonplace that we, as modern readers, may not even notice the technique when used in literature. As scholars, however, it is important for us to slow down and pay careful attention to the material, and to keep in mind the context in which these historical accounts were written. Unlike a modern author, who might unconsciously borrow from the methods of current film-makers, Tacitus was not daily exposed to the kinds of quick-cut digital advertisements of our current era. His decision to employ this technique was deliberate and considered, and it was used in each instance to create deep narrative meaning below and appurtenant to the main story.

Similarly, the designer of the Column of Trajan selected these transitions with their additional capabilities in mind. Both texts, though inscribed in different media, are accounts which require both deep and surface understanding. In the Column, the primary narrative of the Roman conquest of Dacia is moved forward through the use of the narrative cut, made vivid and poignant through the interposition of collision cuts, and inspired with deep patriotic meaning with the attractive cut.

Throughout the *Annales*, we see the same kinds of transitions used to motivate the forward motion of the story, highlight important differences, to provide a fair and balanced reading while at the same time instilling the suggestions of nefarious intent,[67] and to mobilize Roman symbols that encapsulate the meaning of the narrative. Transitional techniques are a subtle and effective way of building deep narrative in the mind of the reader, enabling Tacitus to not only write, but to show history, pulling his reader into the lived experience of the past. Like the great directors of film, Tacitus' work is hard to look away from, and leaves intense images that have remained with his audience for generations.

Notes

Introduction

1 Throughout the text, any unattributed citations are to Tacitus' *Annales*. I use Heinz Heubner's 1983 Teubner text for the *Annales*, and Cynthia Damon's 2012 Penguin translation. Damon's translation is extremely helpful due to its nuanced interpretation, and careful marking of focalization and indirect discourse through italics. Thus, the italics in translations are all original to Damon's work. Further, all unattributed citations are to Tacitus' *Annales*.

2 Ronald Syme, *Tacitus* (Oxford: Oxford University Press, 1958), 193.

3 Monica Cyrino, ed., *Rome, Season One: History Makes Television* (Oxford: Blackwell, 2008), *Rome, Season Two: Trial and Triumph* (Edinburgh: University of Edinburgh Press, 2015), and, co-editing with Antony Augoustakis, *STARZ Spartacus: Reimagining an Icon on Screen* (Edinburgh: University of Edinburgh Press, 2017).

4 Jon Solomon, *The Ancient World in Cinema* (rev. ed. orig. publ. 1978; New Haven: Yale University Press, 2001), xvi.

5 Martin Winkler, ed., *Classics and Cinema* (Lewisburg: Bucknell University Press, 1991).

6 Kristina Passman, "The Classical Amazon in Contemporary Cinema," in ibid. at 81–105.

7 Mary-Kay Gamel, "An American Tragedy: *Chinatown*," in ibid. at 209–31.

8 James Baron, "*9 to 5* as Aristophanic Comedy," in ibid. at 232–50.

9 Kirsten Day, ed., *Celluloid Classics: New Perspectives on Classical Antiquity in Modern Cinema = Arethusa* 41.1 (2008).

10 Geoff Bakewell, "The One-Eyed Man is King: Oedipal Vision in *Minority Report*," *Arethusa* 41.1 (2008): 95–112.

11 Jane O'Sullivan, "Virtual Metamorphoses: Cosmetic and Cybernetic Revisions of Pygmalion's 'Living Doll,'" *Arethusa* 41.1 (2008): 133–56.

12 Day, *Cowboy Classics*, 4.

13 Rather than attempt an in-depth analysis of each of these disparate areas, all of which are complex and rich fields of study in their own right, this introduction is designed to provide the specific tools the reader will need to engage with the text of the *Annales*.

14 Jaś Elsner, *Roman Eyes: Visuality and Subjectivity in Art and Text* (Princeton, Princeton University Press, 2007), xvi–xvii. The following discussion is greatly indebted to Elsner's work.

15 Elsner, *Roman Eyes*, xi–xvii.

16 Andrew Feldherr, *Spectacle and Society in Livy's History* (Berkeley: University of California Press, 1998).

17 Feldherr, *Spectacle*, 37–39.

18 For the monumentality of Pompey's building program, see Mary Beard, *The Roman Triumph* (Cambridge: Harvard University Press, 2007), 21–29.

19 Feldherr, *Spectacle*, 3. Much of Feldherr's discussion of *enargeia* draws on Graham Zanker's "Enargeia in the Ancient Criticism of Poetry," *RhM* 124 (1981), Frank Walbank's "History and Tragedy," *Historia* 9 (1960), 216–34, and Ann Vasaly, *Representations: Images of the World in Ciceronian Oratory* (Berkeley: University of California Press, 1993).

20 Feldherr, *Spectacle*, 9. The Romans also employed a number of additional terms to identify the technique, including *demonstratio*, *illustratio*, *evidentia*, and *sub oculos subiectio*. Feldherr, *Spectacle*, 4, and see also Zanker, "*Enargeia*," 297–311.

21 Elizabeth Keitel, "'No vivid writing, please': *Evidentia* in the *Agricola* and *Annals*," in *Les* opera minora *et le développement de l'historiographie tacitéenne*, ed. Olivier Devillers (Bordeaux: Ausonius Scripta Antiqua, 2014): 59–70.

22 Feldherr, *Spectacle*, 17–18, citing Vasaly's *Representations*, 88–104.

23 Feldherr, *Spectacle*, 218–19.

24 Ibid., 224–25.

25 E.g., Edmond Courbaud's *Les Procédés d'art de Tacite dans les Histoires* (Paris: 1918): 121–66; and Hildebrecht Hommel's "Die Bildkunst des Tacitus," *Würzburger Studien zur Altertumswissenschaft* 9 (1936): 116–48.

26 Elizabeth Walker, *The Annals of Tacitus: A Study in the Writing of History* (Manchester: Manchester University Press, 1952), esp. 82–137.

27 Syme, *Tacitus*, 304–21.

28 Ibid., 316. "[N]ot content with the bare recital, but evoking the men of the time, whether their sentiments happen to stand on record or have to be surmised."

29 Ibid., 317, also 374–75.

30 Ibid., 396.

31 Francis Goodyear, *Tacitus, Greece and Rome: New Surveys in the Classics* 4 (1970), 22–23.

32 Ibid., 23.

33 Anthony Woodman, *Rhetoric in Classical Historiography: Four Studies* (London: Croom Helm, 1988), 91–95 on verisimilitude; and Woodman, *Rhetoric*, 25–28 (of *enargeia* in Thucydides), 90 (on Cicero's concept of *enargeia*).

34 Woodman, *Rhetoric*, 197. Woodman goes on to explain that this difference arises from the ability of ancient historiography to include what was factually plausible rather than true.

35 Ibid., 207–12. Tacitus and Thucydides are explicitly mentioned as analogous to modern visual media.

36 Ibid., 208.
37 Ronald Mellor, *Tacitus* (London: Routledge, 1993), 122.
38 Ibid., 124.
39 Ibid., 125–26.
40 Ronald Mellor, *Tacitus' Annals* (Oxford: Oxford University Press, 2011), 63–77.
41 Ibid., 65. Mellor notes that Pompeian wall art included not just depictions of mythology, but specifically Ovidian readings of those myths. Further, Mellor draws attention to the historical and visual rendering of the Column of Trajan (see Chapter 5) and Nero's extremely visual *domus aurea.*
42 Ibid., 77.
43 Ibid., 71.
44 Ibid., 72.
45 Zangara discusses the process whereby *enargeia* allows and compels the reader to "see" the events described by the ancient historians, basing her discussion on ancient and modern critical theory. Adrianna Zangara, *Voir l'histoire: Théories anciennes du récit historique* (Paris: Éd. de l'EHESS, 2007), esp. 233–300.
46 Mieke Bal, *Narratology: Introduction to the Theory of Narrative, 3rd edn* (Toronto: University of Toronto Press Incorporated, 2009), 3–4.
47 For discussions of the antecedents and scholastic debts of narratology, see Bal's *Narratology*, 13–14, 71–74, 175–80, 222–24; and Irene de Jong's *Narratology and Classics: A Practical Guide* (Oxford: Oxford University Press, 2014), 3–6.
48 Roland Barthes and Lionel Duisit, "Introduction to the Structural Analysis of Narratives," *New Literary History* 6 (1975): 237–272; Gérard Genette, *Narrative Discourse*, transl. Jane Lewin (Ithaca: Cornell University Press, 1980); Gerald Prince, *Narratology: The Form and Function of Narrative* (Berlin: Mouton, 1983); and David Bordwell, *Narration in the Fiction Film* (Madison: University of Wisconsin Press, 1985).
49 Bal, *Narratology*, 5–9.
50 Ibid., 10.
51 Ibid., 5, 10.
52 Ibid., 9.
53 Ibid., 15–17.
54 For the metaphor of facts as the cake and rhetorical effects as icing, see John Moles' "Truth and Untruth in Herodotus and Thucydides" in *Lies and Fiction in the Ancient World*, Christopher Gil, T.P. Wiseman, eds. (Austin: University of Texas Press, 1993), 114.
55 Bal, *Narratology*, 10.
56 Ibid., 20.
57 Ibid., 24–29.
58 Ibid., 48–58.
59 Ibid., 160–63.

60 Ibid., 4–5; Prince, *Narratology*, 1–2.
61 Dorrit Cohn, "Signposts of Fictionality: A Narratological Perspective," *Poetics Today* 11.4 (1990): 775–804.
62 Ibid., 780–81.
63 Ibid., 778–79.
64 Ibid., 781.
65 Ibid.
66 Ibid., 782.
67 Ibid., 783.
68 Ibid., 785, 789.
69 Ibid., 786.
70 Ibid.
71 Ibid., 792.
72 De Jong, *Narratology*, 6; Genevieve Liveley, *Narratology* (Oxford: Oxford University Press, 2019), 203–204. For de Jong's work on narratology, see, e.g., *A Narratological Commentary on the* Odyssey (Cambridge: Cambridge University Press, 2001), "Homer" and "Herodotus" in *Studies in Ancient Greek Narrative. 1, Narrators, Narratees, and Narratives in Ancient Greek Literature*, Irene de Jong, René Nünlist, and Angus Bowie, eds. (Leiden: Brill, 2004): 13–24 and 101–14, respectively.
73 De Jong, *Narratology*, 167–70.
74 Ibid., 170–71.
75 Ibid., 172–73.
76 Ibid., 171–72. On the topic of the ancient historians' creation of a narrator within their historical works, see John Marincola's *Authority and Tradition in Ancient Historiography* (Cambridge: Cambridge University Press, 1997), 5–12, 246–57.
77 Noted by de Jong, *Narratology*, 6–9.
78 Example taken from Bal, *Narratology*, 25–26.
79 Bal, *Narratology*, 19–20.
80 Ibid., 20.
81 Ibid., 165–75.
82 Ibid., 170–73. Bal expands her discussion of the visuality of Proust following the metaphor of still art and photography in her *The Mottled Screen: Reading Proust Visually*, Anna-Louise Milne, transl. (Stanford: Stanford University Press, 1997).
83 Bal, *Narratology*, 173–75.
84 Character Narrator identified with the character Joe.
85 Bal, *Narratology*, 174–75.
86 Ibid., 166.
87 In the context of film studies, there is great debate about the author, ranging from directorial *auteurism* to various collaborative understandings. Questions of internal narrator, however, closely map the questions asked in traditional narratology,

including to what degree the author assumes a narratorial pose, or engages in focalizing and other voice-altering techniques. See David Bordwell, *Making Meaning: Inference and Rhetoric in the Interpretation of Cinema* (Cambridge: Harvard University Press, 1989), 161–65. I will speak about film as though the director were the author, in line with the majority of film scholarship.

88 I will use the terms "film" and "movie" interchangeably in this book, making no connotative separations between the two terms. For this general trend in film scholarship, and possible other indications, see Richard Maltby, *Hollywood Cinema* 2nd ed. (Oxford: Blackwell Publishing, 2003), 585, s.v. "movie."

89 David Bordwell, Janet Staiger, and Kristin Thompson, *The Classical Hollywood Cinema: Film Style and Mode of Production to 1960* (New York: Columbia University Press, 1985) 1–84, 339–64. Although this work has three listed authors, they are individually credited with authorship for portions of it. Thus, I credit Bordwell for the material in pp. 1–84, although all three share authorship for the book; see also Bordwell, *Narration*, 156–204.

90 David Bordwell and Kristin Thompson, *Film Art: An Introduction* 8th ed. (New York: McGraw-Hill, 2008), 94–96.

91 During the course of this book, I present a number of films as comparanda to illustrate visual narrative techniques parallel to those seen in Tacitus. These films, all examples of classical Hollywood cinema, have been chosen with an eye toward their clarity and often simplicity in showcasing the relevant effect. That said, these films are products of the times in which they were created, and can contain cultural artifacts now distasteful to a modern audience. Some of these aspects include elements of racism, sexism, homophobia, and imperialism. I do not endorse these themes in the films, nor do I seek to glorify their depictions. Similarly, as students of Ancient Greece and Rome, we must always be mindful of the problematic elements of the cultures that we study, rather than attempt to disavow or destroy the troubling realities of antiquity.

92 While Bordwell did not invent the term "classical Hollywood cinema," nor is his the only model or method of discussing it, I will be following his theories concerning the films in this category.

93 Bordwell et al., *Classical Hollywood Cinema*, 3. For more on the Aristotelean unities, see also Bordwell, *Narration*, 162–63.

94 Bordwell et al., *Classical Hollywood Cinema*, 3.

95 Maltby, *Hollywood Cinema*, 16–18. While Maltby asserts that these areas should be taken into consideration, he generally follows Bordwell, Staiger, and Thompson's ideas about stylistics, even adopting their periodization of 1920–*c.* 1960 and their terminology of "classical Hollywood." Robert Lapsky and Michael Westlake, *Film Theory: An Introduction* (Manchester, Manchester University Press, 1988), 130–31, while agreeing with Bordwell et al. concerning periodization and general style, see an evolution toward classical Hollywood films rather than a set and defined aesthetic from the first.

96 Kristin Thompson, *Storytelling in the New Hollywood: Understanding the Classical Narrative Technique* (Cambridge: Harvard University Press, 1999), 336.
97 Bordwell and Thompson, *Film Art*, 94.
98 Bordwell, *Narration*, 162–63.
99 Bordwell and Thompson, *Film Art*, 90–92, 95.
100 A notable exception from this general rule is the detective film, where information is often limited to that of the investigator. Ibid., 95.
101 Bordwell et al., *Classical Hollywood Cinema*, 5.
102 Ibid., 7.
103 Elsner, *Roman Eyes*, xvi–xvii.
104 Jocelyn Small, *Wax Tablets of the Mind: Cognitive studies of memory and literacy in classical antiquity* (London: Routledge, 1997), 100.
105 Bordwell, *Narration*, 18–20.

Chapter 1

1 Alignment is the subject of Chapter 2, and will be discussed in more detail there.
2 Don Fowler, *Roman Constructions: Readings in Postmodern Latin* (Oxford: Oxford University Press, 2000), 41.
3 See the section "Focalization and Visual Control," below.
4 For a thorough discussion of focalization as it applies to antiquity, see De Jong's *Narratology*, 47–72, and Bal's *Narratology*, esp. 165–67, for focalization within visual narratives.
5 Susan Smith, *Hitchcock: Suspense, Humour and Tone* (London: The British Film Institute, 2000), 82.
6 Fowler, *Roman Constructions*, 41.
7 The use of focalization for a villain can be seen as early as Aeschylus's *Agamemnon* and Euripides' *Medea*. The effectiveness of this technique is demonstrated by its continued use in such works as Shakespeare's *Richard III* and Milton's *Paradise Lost*.
8 In writing about Tacitean historiography, I often take Tacitus at his intention while discussing the impressions that his narrative technique is conveying. The historical Sejanus may have been a savvy political player and wonderful person, but Tacitus does not characterize and present him in this way. I am more interested in Tacitus' representation of Sejanus rather than his real and historical base. When I use charged terms, it is to mirror the impression that Tacitus' style and narrative creates in the reader. Thus, I describe complex historical figures such as Tiberius, Sejanus, and Agrippina the Younger as "villains" since it is with this literary coloring that Tacitus presents them.

9 John Fawell, *Hitchcock's Rear Window: The Well-Made Film* (Carbondale: Southern Illinois University Press, 2001), 46.
10 "The refusal to intervene is testimony not just to a generalized apathy, but actually to a culpable complicity with the politics of the regime that Lucan detests." Matthew Leigh, *Lucan: Spectacle and Engagement* (Oxford: Oxford University Press, 1997), 110. At p. 157, Leigh also states that "to watch is to be complicit."
11 Daniel Shaw, "The Mastery of Hannibal Lecter," in *Dark Thoughts: Philosophic Reflections on Cinematic Horror*, ed. Steven Schneider and Daniel Shaw (Oxford: Scarecrow Press Ltd., 2003), 10–24.
12 Bordwell notes, in his discussion of Hitchcock's narrative technique, that "there is thus a tension between what a character knows and what the narrative tells." Bordwell, *Classical Hollywood Cinema*, 79.
13 As with most films in this work, *The Third Man* contains period notions of sexuality and gender roles, as well as an overall neo-imperialist viewpoint of Holly, framed according to Anna Cooper as the image of the "sublime" (*An American Abroad: Imperialist Aesthetics in Postwar Hollywood Cinema*, New York, Bloomsbury Press, forthcoming, pp. 41–56, esp. 53). For a recent discussion of *The Third Man*, see Ulrike Schwab's "Authenticity and Ethics in the Film *The Third Man*," *Literature/Film Quarterly* 28 (2000), 2–6, and, for a comparison of the film and the novel upon which it is based, see Jim Gribble's "*The Third Man*: Graham Greene and Carol Reed," *Literature/Film Quarterly* 26 (1998), 235–39.
14 Much of this section is greatly indebted to Jaś Elsner's chapter "Ekphrasis and the Gaze: From Roman Poetry to Domestic Wall Painting" in his *Roman Eyes*, 67–112.
15 For the myth, see, e.g., Ovid, *Heroides*, 10.
16 Elsner notes that the image of a crying or sorrowful Ariadne "shifts the weight of the pictorial interpretation away from the gaze as such and toward the misery that is its result." Elsner, *Roman Eyes*, 94–95.
17 Ample evidence of the senate's dependence on a *princeps* is found in the panicked fawning at 1.11.3. See Woodman's chapter "Tacitus on Tiberius' Accession" in his *Tacitus Reviewed* (Oxford: Oxford University Press, 1998), 40–69. Woodman interprets Tacitus' Tiberius as being intelligently cautious, rather than duplicitous.
18 Kurt von Fritz remarks that Tiberius, in effect, was forced to take control of the armies in order to avoid a civil war. Tacitus, then, does not depict Tiberius as falsely hesitating, but as hesitating through genuine ambiguity on taking the office. Kurt von Fritz, "Tacitus, Agricola, Domitian, and the Problem of the Principate" *CP* 52 (1957), 88–89.
19 The reader should recall that the narrative proper began only a few chapters prior to this section, and that, in the summary of events under Augustus, the pace had been exceptionally rapid. See, e.g., 1.2.1 where Tacitus takes the reader from Philippi to the Augustan settlement, covering decades in a single sentence.

20 For this visual back-and-forth, in film known as the shot-reverse shot, see the section "The Murder of Agrippina: The Ideal Spectator and the Shot-Reverse Shot," below.

21 Koestermann notes that Gallus was not playing by the established rules of the game (*Spielregeln*), by provoking Tiberius. Erich Koestermann, *Annalen* (Heidelberg: Carl Winter Universitätsverlag, 1963), v.1, 108.

22 Tacitus records that Gallus reminded Tiberius of most of his previous accomplishments. This allows the historian to omit notice of them (thus coloring the narrative while remaining technically true to the events of history), and to further undercut their importance by putting them in the mouth of a courtier trying desperately to placate Tiberius.

23 Robin Seager, *Tiberius* (Berkeley: University of California Press, 1972), 82.

24 For a discussion of Tacitus' foreshadowing of Sejanus through his character assassination of Agrippina in this scene, see the section "Sejanus" in Chapter 4.

25 Goodyear notes that the "particulars [Tacitus] relates about Agrippina allow him to switch smoothly to the recurrent theme of Tiberius' malice." Francis Goodyear, *The Annals of Tacitus Volume II (Annals 1.55–81 and Annals 2)* (Cambridge: Cambridge University Press, 1981), 124.

26 Adam points out the additional narrative power of the opposing points-of-view of Agrippina and Tiberius as a method of building their characters within the *Annales*. Adeline Adam, "Agrippine l'Aînée ou le paradoxe. Les femmes de la domus Augusta et le pouvior dans les *Annales* de Tacite (livres 1 à 4)." *Pallas* 99: *Femmes et actes de mémoire: La temporalité dans les échanges 2015* (2015), 116.

27 It is a natural propensity of the mind to attempt to forge meaning between disparate pieces of information and, where missing or incomplete information is supplied, readers will work to create plausible or possible connections. For more on the creation of narrative meaning, see chapter 5.

28 This is not the only occasion in the *Annales* when Tiberius expresses concerns about how he will be remembered by future generations. See, for example, Tiberius' speech replying to the Spanish legates concerning the building of a temple to himself and Livia at 4.37.1–38.3.

29 Sejanus is mentioned prior to book 4, but only in order to foreshadow his later role in the *Annales*. For Tacitus' use of foreshadowing in the *Annales*, see chapter 4.

30 For a discussion on how Tacitus uses Sallust's Catiline as a model for the biography of Sejanus, especially at 4.1.3, see Syme, *Tacitus*, 353–56, esp. 353; Ronald Martin and Anthony Woodman, *Tacitus Annals Book IV* (Cambridge: Cambridge University Press, 1989), 84; and Ronald Martin's "Structure and Interpretation in the *Annals* of Tacitus," *ANRW II*, 33, 1501–81, esp. 1514–16.

31 Martin explains that Sejanus' presence in the *Annales* must be more restrained than that of Germanicus. "We do not have the long, self-contained sections dominated by

Sejanus: his role, at least in the extant portions, is, rather, insidious and pervasive." Martin, "Structure and Interpretation," 1541.

32 Koestermann, vol. 2, 39. Here, and at select other points of discussion in this chapter, Tacitus uses the narrative technique known as free indirect discourse (hereafter, FID) to allow the audience to see a character's thoughts. There is no indication that these thoughts are spoken, even within the mind of the character in question. Andrew Laird, in his *Powers of Expression, Expressions of Power: Speech Presentation and Latin Literature* (Oxford: Oxford University Press, 1999), 140–41, brings up Genette's distinction between FID and focalization, on the grounds that FID records speech, even if unspoken, while focalization implies only emotional coloring and the feelings of the character. This feelings/thoughts distinction seems arbitrary, as Laird points out, citing *Ann.* 14.8.3, "free indirect discourse and focalization can be conflated. Both represent an equivalent level of intrusion in the narrator's discourse" (Laird, 1999, 141). In the present chapter, I am more concerned with Tacitus' use of embedded focalization than I am with the levels of narrative subordination, although the latter is certainly present.

33 Tacitus' penchant for changing scenes thematically, rather than temporally, has often been noted. For example, see Goodyear, v. 1, 43 n. 1. "Occasionally, I suspect, T.'s arrangement of material is determined by the merest chance: one topic happens in some way to suggest another." While Tacitus' thematic scene changes certainly make fixing exact chronology for the events narrated very difficult, this in no way makes Tacitus a poor historian. Rather, Tacitus sacrifices constant chronology for a fluid and coherent narrative.

34 Note especially such moments as at 1.69.3–4, in the section above, "Agrippina at the Bridge."

35 O'Gorman notes that the character of Sejanus presents problems to Tacitus' reader "since her sense of privileged insight into the characters of the *Annals* invites her to consider her own possible parallels with Sejanus," implying the complicity in viewing these events through Sejanus as focalizer. Ellen O'Gorman, *Irony and Misreading in the Annals of Tacitus* (Cambridge: Cambridge University Press, 2000), 91.

36 See the section above, "Plotting against Drusus."

37 The use of *ferox scelerum* has been noted to parallel Sallust's *Jugurtha* at 14.21, in Adherbal's description of Jugurtha (*sceleribus . . . ferox*). See Koestermann, *vol. 2*, 69, and Martin and Woodman, *Book IV*, 132.

38 Martin and Woodman, *Book IV*, 132, on the unusual occurrence of a historical infinitive in a main clause following a historical present in a temporal clause.

39 Koestermann notes that the *secum* is used as an "Intensivum" with *volutare*. Koestermann, v. 2, 69. Tacitus' use of an unnecessary intensifier further enhances the vividness of the passage.

40 See the section above, "Agrippina at the Bridge."

41 Martin and Woodman, *Book IV*, 199, note that this section "is Sejanus' private interpretation of the *quies et solitudo* he will urge on Tib[erius] at [4.41.]3."

42 Ibid., 199.

43 E.g., at 12.3.2.

44 Ryberg notes that "in the last six books of the *Annals* Tacitus' technique of creating an impression for which he declines to accept responsibility appears only rarely." Inez Ryberg, "Tacitus' Art of Innuendo" *TAPA* 73 (1942), 398.

45 Martin notes that "the ambiguities in Tiberius' character and the ensuing uncertainty of senators how to respond provided material that was peculiarly congenial to Tacitus' own cast of thought." Martin, "Structure and Interpretation," 1551.

46 Sallitt notes the lack of disruption on the viewer in four of Hitchcock's films which include shot-reverse-shot. Daniel Sallitt, "Point of View and 'Intrarealism' in Hitchcock," *Wide Angle* 4 (1980): 40–43, esp. 39. While Sallitt's main thesis is the introduction of the idea of the camera as eyes moving within the film universe, his introduction grants the basic powers of point of view scenes which I have explained earlier in this chapter.

47 Kristin Thompson, "The Formation of the Classical Style: 1909–1928" in Bordwell's *Classical Hollywood Cinema*, 208.

48 Wood notes the suspense created in this scene, especially as the viewer is in doubt as to Guy's motivations. Robin Wood, *Hitchcock's Films Revisited* (New York: Columbia University Press, 1989), 95.

49 See the section above, "Agrippina the Younger."

50 Syme notes that the technique of "the ideal spectator is available, with pertinent or insidious reflections." Syme, *Tacitus*, 315.

51 The use of point of view/focalization "effaces the very operations and mechanisms by which such effects were achieved." Smith, *Hitchcock*, 82.

52 See 12.66.1, with the full text given in the section "Agrippina the Younger," above. (*sceleris olim certa* = *usu scelerum*); (*consultavit* = *consultans*); ([*sc. venenum*] *exquisitum aliquid placebat* = *placuit primo venenum*).

53 Agrippina, unlike Nero, had only to decide on the type of poison. *de genere veneni cosultavit.* 12.66.1.

54 Again, there are verbal echoes here with *epulas principis* mirroring, at 13.16.1, *principum . . . epulante Britannico*. These echoes are increased, as Nero gives Britannicus' murder as a reason not to kill Agrippina in the same way.

55 Seeking safety through feigned ignorance is a common theme in the *Annales*. See, e.g., the senators' behavior with Tiberius (*at patres, quibus unus metus si intellegere viderentur*, 1.11.3), and the banqueters at Britannicus' death (*at quibus altior intellectus, resistunt defixi et Neronem intuentes*, 13.16.3).

56 Koestermann, vol. 4, 37, notes the telegram-esque brevity in this passage as a cipher for Nero's mental excitement.

57 In Hitchcock's *Rebecca* (1940), the character Mrs. Danvers does not make entrances, instead simply appearing next to one of the other characters. Hitchcock played up the unnerving quality of this effect in order to create a suitably frightening aspect for the character. Fawell, *Rear Window*, 60.

58 Galtier notes the dramatic changes in focalization throughout this passage. Fabrice Galtier, "Le motif du rivage dans l'épisode de la mort d'Agrippine (Tac., *Ann.*, 14.1–10)," in *Neronia IX: La villégiature dans le monde romain de Tibère à Hadrien*, ed. Olivier Devillers, 309–16 (Paris: Bordeaux, 2014), esp. 311.

59 "Hitchcock emphasized repeatedly in interviews that point of view shots were successful only in proportion to how carefully they are integrated into the film, how carefully they are laid into the other shots." Fawell, *Rear Window*, 41.

Chapter 2

1 For this view of Claudius, see Simon Malloch's *The Annals of Tacitus Book 11* (Cambridge: Cambridge University Press, 2013), 73–74, and 417–18.

2 Throughout this chapter, I use the terms "excursus" and "digression" interchangeably. Also, to avoid confusion, I use the non-Latin plural "excurses" for excursus.

3 Herodotus Book 2.

4 Cicero, *Brutus*, 322. For the Latin in the *Brutus*, I have used A. E. Douglas' 1996 Oxford Classical Text.

5 Livy 9.17–19.

6 Livy 9.17.1.

7 For a discussion of the excurses in the *Annales*, see Eleonore Hahn, *Die Exkurse in den Annalen des Tacitus*, diss. München (Borna-Leipzig: Universitätsverlag von Robert Noske, 1933).

8 For Tacitus' *apologia* for his grim and repetitive subject matter, see 4.32–33 and 16.16.

9 Elizabeth Keitel, "The Non-Appearance of the Phoenix at Tacitus 'Annals' 6.28," *AJP* 120 (1999), 439–40.

10 These digressions occur at 6.28.1–6 and 16.1.1–3.2, respectively.

11 For the use of sudden transitions within the *Annales*, see chapter 5.

12 Gerald Prince, *A Dictionary of Narratology* (Lincoln: University of Nebraska, 1987), 102–103.

13 For a discussion on the creation of authority in ancient historiography, see Marincola's *Authority and Tradition*, 3–12.

14 Christopher Pelling in his "Tacitus' Personal Voice," in *The Cambridge Companion to Tacitus*, ed. Anthony Woodman, 147–67 (Cambridge: Cambridge University Press,

2009), notes the several different registers with which Tacitus manipulates his narrative voice, moving from the first-person "I" to the corporate first-person (including the rest of the senate) "we"/"our," to another register wherein Tacitus leaves his "voiceprint" through third-person opinion. Cynthia Damon further discusses the impression of Tacitean presence and his use of *enargeia* in her "The Historian's Presence, or, There and Back Again," in *Ancient Historiography and its Contexts: Studies in Honour of A.J. Woodman*, ed. Christina Kraus, John Marincola, and Christopher Pelling, 353–63 (Oxford: Oxford University Press, 2010). The following discussion seeks to build on these two studies by examining the narrative effect created by Tacitus' deliberate assimilation of his voice to those of the emperors.

15 See, for example, Martin and Woodman, *Book IV*, 177.

16 Prince, *Dictionary*, 101.

17 The following discussion owes much to Jaś Elsner's chapter "Viewer as Image: Intimations of Narcissus," in his *Roman Eyes*, 132–76.

18 For the story of Narcissus, see Ovid's *Metamorphoses* 3.337ff.

19 Elsner, *Roman Eyes*, 153.

20 Ibid, 161.

21 Elsner discusses the conjunction of these two images as a possible reference to Ovid's *Metamorphoses*, and the possibility that the images are thematically and stylistically paired. Ibid., 160.

22 Prince, *Dictionary*, 102–103.

23 Telotte notes that this scene lets "us see as Marlowe does," and how this combination of objective and subjective filming in *Murder, My Sweet* is purposely disorienting to the viewer. J. P. Telotte, "Effacement and Subjectivity: *Murder My Sweet's* Problematic Vision," *Literature/Film Quarterly* 15 (1987): 230.

24 See Bordwell, *Narration*, 68–69.

25 Modern scholars accept this view of Tiberius, stressing that he began his reign as a fair ruler concerned with justice and the example of his adoptive father, Augustus. In her *Tiberius the Politician*, Barbara Levick states that Tiberius "sought a reputation for knowledge of the law, both religious and secular. His knowledge he displayed on more than one occasion in the Senate, and he extended it by consorting with a least one distinguished jurisconsult." Barbara Levick, *Tiberius the Politician* (rev. ed., London: Routledge, 1999), 89. Levick comments on Tiberius' legal interests at 27, 85, 89, and 180. See also Seager's *Tiberius*, 125–26. Ducos has noted the legal focus of the Tiberian books, although he ascribes this to Tacitus' interests, rather than Tiberius'. Michèle Ducos, "La justice et les procès dans les livres I et II des *Annales* de Tacite," *Vita Latina* 187–88 (2013): 248–66, esp. 264.

26 See, e.g., 1.14.4; 1.77.4; and 4.37.3. Syme notes that Tiberius was "compelled to honour the precedents set by Augustus everywhere" and that, as a consequence, he was burdened "by the oppressive memory of Augustus," a "victim" of his imperial

predecessor. Syme, *Tacitus*, 427–28. For a discussion of the further implications and complications of Tiberius' use, adaptation, and reliance on Augustus as a model or precedent, see Eleanor Cowan's "Tacitus, Tiberius and Augustus," *CA* 28.2 (2009): 179–210, esp. 199, 207–208.

27 Syme, *Tacitus*, 421.

28 For Suetonius, I use Robert Kaster's Oxford Classical Text (2016) edition for the Latin, and J. Rolfe's Loeb (1960) for the translation.

29 Velleius Paterculus was a historian and legionary commander who wrote a history of Rome in two books during the reign of Tiberius, and his work bears a strong pro-Tiberian slant.

30 For Velleius, I use Joseph Hellegouarc'h's Budé (1982) edition, and the translation is my own.

31 See also Velleius 1.126.2: *sepultaeque ac situ obsitae iustitia, aequitas, industria civitati redditae* (justice, fairness, and hard work, buried and covered over in place, have been returned to the state).

32 See also ILS 3783 = CIL 6.3673 for another usage of the adjective *iustissimus* in Tiberius' titulature. The translation of the Latin epigraphy here is my own.

33 Tiberius Caesar Augustus, son of the Deified Augustus, Pontifex Maximus, holder of the Tribunicia Potestas for the twenty-fourth year.

34 See the British Museum and Harold Mattingly's *Coins of the Roman Empire in the British Museum* (London: Trustees of the British Museum, 1923) vol. I, p. 131, n 79–80. For Tiberius' use of coinage to present his virtues to the empire, see Humphrey Sutherland's *Coinage in Roman Imperial Policy: 31 B.C.–A.D. 68* (London: Methuen & Co., 1951), 96–98, plate 8.1. Anthony Woodman's *The Annals of Tacitus Book 4* (Cambridge: Cambridge University Press, 2018), 92, notes that Tiberius is the only Julio-Claudian emperor to use "*iustitia*" in his coinage.

35 Martin also notes that the purpose of this section is to foreshadow themes and individuals who will become important later in Tiberius' reign. Ronald Martin, *Tacitus* (Berkeley: University of California Press, 1981), 119.

36 O'Gorman views the *maiestas* trials as a re-definition of law in conjunction with a (mis)reading of "the significance of individuals' acts, to determine whether they are meaningful symbolic gestures against the state, or meaningless in relation to the public affairs of Rome." O'Gorman, *Irony*, 84–85.

37 Seager, *Tiberius*, 151.

38 Ibid., 152.

39 On Tiberius' respect for Augustan precedent, see 1.14.4; 1.77.4; 4.37.3.

40 Seager takes umbrage at Tacitus' use of *reduxerat* in this passage, as Tiberius merely allowed the law to remain on the books. Seager, *Tiberius*, 152.

41 Goodyear doubts the validity of Tacitus' suggested motive for Tiberius, citing *Annales* 2.50.2 and Suetonius, *Tiberius*, 28 as proof of Tiberius' patience for personal

slander at this point in his reign. F.R.D. Goodyear, *The Annals of Tacitus vol II: Annals 1.55–81 and Annals 2* (Cambridge: Cambridge University Press, 1981), 153.

42 Anthony Woodman and Ronald Martin, *The Annals of Tacitus Book 3* (Cambridge: Cambridge University Press, 1996), 235.

43 This excursus borrows heavily from Sallustian themes (Hahn, *Exkurse*, 11; Syme, *Tacitus*, 729; and Woodman and Martin, *Book 3*, 237–39, who also note that the language may borrow from Cicero's *de Legibus*).

44 See 1.1.1, in which the Regal Period, the *decemviri*, the military tribunes, the succession of Sulla and Cinna, the Triumvirates, and the reign of Augustus are mentioned in succession.

45 Woodman and Martin note the ancient truism that society worsened in proportion to the sheer volume of laws needed to control it. Woodman and Martin, *Book 3*, 237.

46 The Roman legal system differed in many key ways from those of the United States or modern Britain. Public prosecutors did not exist in Rome, and thus all charges were brought either by the parties affected (as in the case of murder, torts, etc.), or by informers. These informers, or *delatores*, made a profession (or lucrative sideline) out of bringing claims against law-breakers, thus serving as an unofficial judicial police force. In return for their services, they received a portion of the guilty party's property if the charges were proven.

47 Woodman and Martin note that the verbiage changes to that of disease and surgery at *laborabatur*, continuing through to *excisi*. For the general metaphor, see Woodman and Martin, *Book 3*, 236; on *laboro*, 236, for *penetrabant*, *corripuerant* and *excisi*, 260.

48 Ibid., 260–61.

49 Suetonius, *Tiberius*, 33. See the section above, "Tiberius: the (Mis)Rule of Law."

50 Martin and Woodman note that, while the praise of Drusus has dramatic importance, the vital portion of this passage is the double excursus on the state of the empire with regard to both the military and politics. Martin and Woodman, *Book IV*, 95–96.

51 Since Tiberius made it a point not to alter imperial policy after the death of Augustus, this would presumably be very similar to the situation as it stood at the time of Augustus' death. Martin and Woodman suggest that, rather than list the legions in book 1 (1.11.4), Tacitus placed this disposition of the legions at the start of book 4 in order to stress a new beginning with the second half of the Tiberian narrative. Ibid., 96.

52 Remember, for example, Tacitus' casting of aspersion on Tiberius' allegedly noble desire to maintain Augustus' expansion of the *maiestas* laws with the suggestion that Tiberius merely wanted personal revenge (at 1.74.2), and later Tacitus' open accusation that Tiberius committed judicial murder in more than one case through the abuse of this law (1.73.1).

53 OLD, s.v., *cohibeo*.
54 See Anthony Woodman, "Tacitus' Obituary of Tiberius," *CQ* 39 (1989), 203–204.
55 See the section above, "Lex Maiestatis."
56 OLD, s.v. "quidem," def. 4.
57 Martin and Woodman note that the comparison to be drawn is doubtless between Tiberius and Claudius, whose freedmen Narcissus and Pallas were infamous. Martin and Woodman, *Book IV*, 112.
58 Martin and Woodman comment here on Tacitus' propensity to depreciate Tiberius after describing some of his good qualities or actions. Ibid., 113.
59 For this view of Claudius, see, e.g., 11.28.2: *hebetem Claudium et uxori devinctum* (Claudius was doltish and attached to his wife).
60 Syme notes that Tacitus includes digressions with "peculiar erudition" and "manifestations of the Claudian idiosyncrasy" in the *Annales*, but Syme links these similarities with Tacitus' use of Claudian source material, mainly from the *acta*. Syme, *Tacitus*, 708.
61 Suetonius, *Divus Claudius*, 3.1.
62 Suetonius, *Divus Claudius*, 41–42. Suetonius gives the following totals for the books in each work: two, then forty-one books of Roman history, eight books of autobiography, twenty books of Etruscan history, and eight books of Carthaginian history. Seneca snidely alludes to Claudius' historical works at *Apocolocyntosis* 5, when Claudius meets Hercules in heaven and thinks that he might find a market for his histories: *Claudius . . . sperat futuram aliquem historiis suis locum*.
63 Seneca, *De Brevitate Vitae*, 14.1. *soli omnium otiosi sunt qui sapientiae vacant, soli vivunt.* (Of all people, only those who make time for philosophy are at leisure, only they live.)
64 For Seneca, I use G. Williams' Cambridge (2003) text for the Latin, and John Basore's Loeb (1958) for the translation.
65 We will be looking in detail at Tacitus' coverage of Claudius' extension of the *pomerium* in the section "Expanding the Pomerium," below.
66 For Seneca's jokes at Claudius' physical ailments, see *Apocolocyntosis* 1, 3–5, and 8. For jokes at the expense of Claudius' judicial pronouncements, see sections 7 and 10–14.
67 ILS 212 = CIL 13.1668. For the translation, I use E. Smallwood's from his *Documents Illustrating the Principates of Gaius Claudius and Nero* (Cambridge: Cambridge University Press, 1967), which is collected in Barbara Levick's *The Government of the Roman Empire: A Sourcebook* (London: Routledge, 1985), 178–80.
68 For a discussion of Tacitus' alterations to the speech and his possible motivations for doing so, see Miriam Griffin, "The Lyons Tablet and Tacitean Hindsight," *CQ* 32 (1982), 404–18. For Tacitus' use of Claudian sources in general, see Syme, *Tacitus*, 317–19, 703–10 and Miriam Griffin, "Claudius in Tacitus," *CQ* 40 (1990), 482–501.

69 For ease of reference, when quoting from the *Tabula Lugdunensis*, I will use the ILS line numbers.

70 *deprecor, ne quasi novam istam rem introduci exhorrescatis, sed illa potius cogitetis, quam multa in hac civitate novata sint et quidem statim ob origine urbis nostrae in quod formas statusque res publica nostra diducta sit.* ILS 212, 4–7.

71 ILS 212, 9–27.

72 Syme refers to Claudius' discussion here as "trivial, inept, and wantonly impairing the validity of his own argumentation." Syme, *Tacitus*, 319.

73 Syme notes that Tacitus, in his version of this speech at 11.24, mercifully discards the Etruscan antiquities. Ibid., 704, 707.

74 Books 7–10 are missing entirely, along with the first portion of book 11.

75 O'Gorman notes that Claudius "is more like the anti-historian, embodying none of the qualities of insight, skepticism and vigilance for the truth." O'Gorman, *Irony*, 109.

76 For a thorough discussion of the historical and textual issues at play during the excursus, see Malloch, *Book 11*, 216–31. According to Suetonius, Claudius had written a book on the Latin alphabet before he became emperor. Suetonius, *Divus Claudius*, 41.

77 O'Gorman states that "what Claudius has learned about the history of the alphabet could be seen to be the substance of most of the ensuing digression, so that it seems at first as if the narrative voice has been temporarily taken over by the emperor." O'Gorman, *Irony*, 110.

78 Martin notes Claudius' pedantry, describing the emperor as having a "tendency to digress." Martin, *Tacitus*, 149.

79 Hahn postulates that Tacitus may be drawing the Claudian reforms from the *acta*, or from a vanished Claudian history. Hahn, *Exkurse*, 65–66.

80 For examples of Tacitus' introduction of these excurses, see 1.73.1. *haud pigebit referre . . .*; 3.25.2. *ea res admonet ut de principiis iuris . . . disseram*; 3.55.1. *causas eius mutationis quaerere libet . . .*; 4.4.3. *quod mihi quoque exequendum reor . . .*

81 O'Gorman notes that both Claudius' letters and the Egyptian ones exist in Tacitus' own day "as indelible traces of past memory" which are "presented in the text stripped of their appearance and context, with only their 'real' meaning conveyed." O'Gorman, *Irony*, 110–11. I would argue that even this "real" meaning is irrelevant without Tacitus to bear witness to these empty signs.

82 For more on this adjectival use of *atrox odii* as it relates to foreshadowing between Agrippina the Elder and Agrippina the Younger, see the section in chapter 4, "Like Mother Like Daughter: The Two Agrippinas."

83 Tacitus clearly states that Agrippina's motive was simple jealousy toward a competitor, which is also the driving force behind Agrippina's destruction of Calpurnia, whose appearance Claudius praised. 12.22.3.

84 Syme asserts that this section is drawn from the senatorial *acta*, and therefore derives ultimately from Claudius himself. Syme, *Tacitus*, 705.

85 Syme takes Claudius' authorship of the information in this passage for granted, noting that the passage is "clearly from Claudius." Ibid., 378 n. 5.

86 Alternatively, and more likely, the bull illustrates the purpose of the cattle market.

87 Filipo Coarelli, *Rome and Environs: An Archaeological Guide*, translated by James Clauss and Daniel Harmon (Berkeley: University of California Press, 2007), 57.

88 *quidam Cecropem Atheniensem vel Linum Thebanum et temporibus Troianis Palamedem Argivum memorant sedecim litterarum formas, mox alios ac praecipuum Simoniden ceteras repperisse.*

89 Specifically, Messalina's marriage to Gaius Silius and Agrippina's control over the empire.

Chapter 3

1 Both Racine and Napoleon Bonaparte referred to Tacitus as a painter, Jefferson and Adams both noted the historian as a moralist, and Justus Lipsius referred to Tacitus' theater of everyday life. Mellor, *Tacitus*, 1, 47, 118, 122, 184 n. 43.

2 E.g., at *Hamlet* III.ii. 252–62.

3 Elsner, *Roman Eyes*, 67–109; 136–37.

4 Shadi Bartsch, *The Mirror of the Self: Sexuality, Self-Knowledge, and the Gaze in the Early Roman Empire* (Chicago: University of Chicago Press, 2006), 115–52.

5 Laura Mulvey, "Visual Pleasure and Narrative Cinema," in her *Visual and Other Pleasures*, 2nd ed. (New York: Palgrave Macmillan, 2009), 16–21.

6 Mulvey, "Visual Pleasure," 27.

7 Mary Ann Doane, *The Desire to Desire: The Woman's Film of the 1940s* (Bloomington: Indiana University Press, 1987), and "The Woman's Film: Possession and Address," in *Home Is Where the Heart Is: Studies in Melodrama and the Woman's Film*, ed. Christine Gledhill (London: British Film Institute, 1987), 283–98; Tania Modleski, *The Women Who Knew Too Much: Hitchcock and Feminist Theory*, 3rd ed. (New York: Routledge, 2016).

8 Doane, "The Woman's Film," 287–88.

9 Bordwell, *Film Art*, 191; David Bordwell, *Poetics of Cinema* (New York: Routledge, 2008), 63.

10 See Bordwell, *Film Art*, 227–28 for a through discussion of the "Kuleshov effect."

11 Welles' *Touch of Evil*, as is the case with many of the film selections in this work, must be understood as a product of its time, and contains troubling aspects, especially elements of sexism and racism (including the casting of Charlton Heston as a Mexican police officer, portrayed in dark stereotypical makeup). While I do not

endorse this film's biases, I feel that it serves as the best example of the ambiguous close-up and challenged gaze to illustrate these techniques in Tacitus. Further, the film problematizes the viewer's ability to construct truth, either from evidence or experience, and it has been extensively studied as an iconic film.

12 Terry Comito, "Touch of Evil," *Film Comment* 7.2 (1971): 51–53., esp 52: "Quinlan's very face, like a mask or an icon" and 53: "[Quinlan's] rotting face still cunning, as used up and inscrutable as the debris around him."

13 *Touch of Evil*'s most discussed aspect is the long opening shot, wherein the camera roves through a crowded street scene showing us a bomb being planted, then pans to the Vargases as they walk down the street until the car explodes. This constant change in camera focus highlights the film's ambiguous nature—we don't know where or at whom to look for the majority of the film. James Naremore, *The Magic of Orson Welles*, 3rd ed. (Urbana: University of Illinois Press, 2015), 161, 175.

14 Béla Balázs describes power of the "silent soliloquy" of the close-up: "In this silent monologue the solitary human soul can find a tongue more candid and uninhibited than in any spoken soliloquy, for it speaks instinctively, subconsciously . . . in the enlarging close-up we see even that it is concealing something, that is looking a lie." Béla Balázs, "The Close-Up" collected in Leo Braudy and Marshall Cohen, eds., *Film Theory and Criticism: Introductory Readings* (Oxford: Oxford University Press, 2016): 202.

15 For more on the layers involved in (mis)reading Tiberius, see O'Gorman, *Irony*, 78–105.

16 E.g., 2.43.4. "Some believed that [Piso] had secret instructions from Tiberius. Plancina was certainly advised by Livia—female rivalry!—to harass Agrippina." *credidere quidam data et a Tiberio occulta mandata; et Plancinam haud dubie Augusta monuit aemulatione muliebri Agrippinam insectandi.*

17 For a brief discussion of Piso's guilt, see Syme, *Tacitus*, 429 and 492.

18 Martin and Woodman note that this scene begins with "an appeal to the reader's visual sense." Martin and Woodman, *Book IV*, 229.

19 Ibid., 229.

20 See GL 647 for the syntax of this usage.

21 Martin and Woodman, *Book IV*, 229–30.

22 Ibid., 230, for the "graphic writing" in this passage.

23 For more on Nero's theatricality, see Anthony Woodman's "Amateur Dramatics at the Court of Nero (*Annals* 15.48–74)" in *Tacitus Reviewed*, 190–217; and Shadi Bartsch's *Actors in the Audience: Theatricality and Doublespeak from Nero to Hadrian* (Cambridge: Harvard University Press, 1994), 36–62.

24 A. Gerber and A. Greef, *Lexicon Taciteum* (Hildesheim: Georg Olms Verlagsbuchhandlung, 1962), vol. 1, 563.

25 OLD, s.v. "imaginor," definition 1: "To form a mental picture of, imagine." Ash notes that the unusual verb "captures Nero's strange inner world . . . vividly constructed by Tacitus and others." Rhiannon Ash, *Tacitus Annals Book XV* (Cambridge: Cambridge University Press, 2015), 306.

26 Huston's *Maltese Falcon* contains problematic elements, such as misogyny and an almost pathological homophobia, but is worthy of study in this work for the effectiveness of this particular scene, which is the more powerful as its sudden cutting and multiple close-ups are used to great effect at only this point in the film.

27 For a discussion of this scene, see James Naremore, "John Huston and *The Maltese Falcon*," *Literature/Film Quarterly* 1 (1973), 248.

28 Bordwell sums up this effect of exchanged glances well: "The direction of the glance would function as a seesaw trigger, informing us of the object of the person's attention. It stands as another cross-cultural regularity of human activity that can elicit effects in beholders." Bordwell, *Poetics*, 67.

29 The term "gunsel" that Spade uses of Wilmer throughout the film implies that he is both a hired gun and a homosexual. Philippa Gates, "The Three Sam Spades: The Shifting Model of American Masculinity in the Three Films of *The Maltese Falcon*," *Framework* 49.1 (2008): 7–26, esp. 17–18.

30 Thomas Leitch, *Crime Films* (Cambridge: Cambridge University Press, 2002), 198.

31 Bartsch, *Actors*, 1.

32 Michel Poirier notes the cinematic qualities here, especially the dramatic use of the close-up (*gros plan*) to highlight each character. Michel Poirier, "L'organisation de l'espace dans trois textes latines célèbres, entre géométrie et découpage cinématographique (Hor., O., 2.3; Liv., 5.41; Tac., An., 13.16)," in *Nouveaux horizons sur l'espace antique et moderne: actes du symposium "Invitation au voyage" juin 2013, Lycée Henri IV*, ed. Marie-Ange Julia, *Scripta Receptoria* 2, 81–88 (Bordeaux: Ausonius, 2015), 86–87.

33 Bartsch notes that "as [Britannicus] falls, he sets into play an elaborate drama of fear and concealment among the other diners." Bartsch, *Actors*, 15.

34 Syme, *Tacitus*, 262.

35 Indeed, Agrippina notes when threatening Nero that Britannicus is, in effect, her only safeguard against her son (*id solum diis et sibi provisum, quod viveret privignus.*, 13.14.3).

36 Bartsch notes that the spectators must play their parts as actors for Nero. Bartsch, *Actors*, 15.

37 Ibid., 15–16.

38 Koestermann, vol. 3, 265. See also Gerber and Greef's *Lexicon Taciteum* vol. 1, 292. OLD, s.v. *diffugio*: "to run away or flee in several directions, scatter."

39 Bartsch sums up much of Tacitus' historical and visual power in the following: "Tacitus' version of the past, in unveiling the distortions worked by power, offers

apparent access to the reality underlying the surface of a given situation: granted admission into the thoughts and fears of Nero's victims as they hastily slip on their masks before the emperor, we are led time and again to accept Tacitus' version of such interactions as an accurate representation of the theatricalized overlay on truth, so persuasive is Tacitus' cynical and apparently clear-eyed vision of the workings of power, so intuitively familiar his co-optation of theatricality as a paradigm for human behavior under an absolutist régime." Bartsch, *Actors*, 22.

40 This seems to be a telling of these events from Tacitus' point of view through the device of *prudentes*. Syme, *Tacitus*, 315.

41 Andrew Walker notes that "The *enargeia* of a text is contingent upon the reader's experience of *pathê* like those suffered by the spectators of the original event." Walker, "*Enargeia* and the Spectator in Greek Historiography," *TAPA* 123 (1993), 360.

42 Walker points out that "the distinction between past and present events is collapsed into the moment of reading as a kind of visual perception." Ibid., 360.

43 Quotations from Tacitus' *Agricola* are taken from the OCT edited by R. M. Ogilvie (Oxford: Oxford University Press, 1975) and Henry Furneaux's English translation, revised by J. G. C. Anderson (London: Penguin Books, 1970).

44 Nero's passion for entertaining in public becomes increasingly more pronounced throughout his reign. His exhibitionism increases along with his other vices and crimes at, e.g., 13.3.3; 14.15.4–16.2; 15.33.1; 16.4.1–4.

45 Francesca Santoro L'Hoir, *Tragedy, Rhetoric, and the Historiography of Tacitus' Annales* (Ann Arbor: University of Michigan Press, 2006), 190.

46 "The point is not that anyone is deceived by the charade, but that everyone is forced either to participate in it or watch it silently." Bartsch, *Actors*, 16.

47 The expressive verb "*emicare*" is only found here in Tacitus. Gerber and Greef, vol. 1, 345.

48 OLD, s.v. "parricidium," def. 1a.

49 For a discussion of Agrippina and poisoning in both the Britannicus and Claudius murders, see Santoro L'Hoir, *Tragedy*, 190.

50 For the necessary differences between Livy's visual *exempla* and Tacitus', especially in the *Historiae*, see Feldherr, *Spectacle*, 218–21.

51 According to Santoro L'Hoir, Tacitus foreshadows Agrippina and Octavia as future victims of Nero by the very fact of their ignorance. Santoro L'Hoir, *Tragedy*, 190.

52 Octavia is killed while in exile in 62, seven years after the death of Britannicus. 14.64.1–2.

53 Wuilleumier notes on this line: "le récit se termine par un trait sarcastique." Pierre Wuilleumier, *Tacite: Annales Livre XIII* (Paris: Presses Universitaires de France, 1964), 41.

54 For a thorough discussion of *damnatio memoriae* and memory sanctions, see Harriet Flower's *The Art of Forgetting: Disgrace and Oblivion in Roman Political*

Culture (Chapel Hill: The University of North Carolina Press, 2006), to which this discussion is indebted.

55 Because of the high cost of sculpture, imperial statuary was often refashioned to represent another emperor. While this removed the likeness of the condemned from public view, the altered countenance of a statue did not summon the same reaction as an epigraphic erasure. For more on this, see Eric Varner, *Mutilation and Transformation: Damnatio Memoriae and Roman Imperial Portraiture* (Leiden: Brill, 2004), 4.

56 CIL 3.13580.

57 For a more in-depth discussion of this monument, see Flower's *Art of Forgetting*, 237.

58 Flower argues that the lost name here is that of the *Praefectus Aegyptus*, M. Mettius Rufus. Ibid., 237.

59 Ibid., 237.

60 Charles Hedrick uses the Freudian terminology of repression to understand the imposed forgetfulness of *damnatio memoriae*. Charles Hedrick, Jr., *History and Silence: Purge and Rehabilitation of Memory in Late Antiquity* (Austin: University of Texas Press, 2000), 113–14.

61 Hitchcock's *Rebecca* has been discussed by such film scholars as Doane and Modleski for its interplay between the feminine spectator and the patriarchal world in which it must function, even fictionally. This scene, wherein the deceased Rebecca is filmed as absence, is the most visually striking sequence in the picture.

62 Doane, *Desire to Desire*, 170. Tania Modleski, in her *Women Who Knew* (50–51 and 188 n. 20), appraises the scene differently, stressing the potency of the absent Rebecca and the feminine spectatorship that it enables, rather than the supplanting and co-opting of the feminine gaze of the second Mrs. de Winter by Maxim, and Hitchcock.

63 Doane, "The Woman's Film," 287–88.

64 Doane, Ibid., 290, notes that the challenges to the feminine gaze include the instability of the voice-over and point-of-view shot, which are rarely retained by the women in the film, but are usually co-opted by male characters. On this scene and a similar example in Hitchcock's *Rope*, see Bordwell, *Poetics*, 39.

65 Modleski, *Women Who Knew*, 50.

66 Diane Waldman, "At Last I Can Tell It to Someone!: Feminine Point of View and Subjectivity in the Gothic Romance Film of the 1940s" *Cinema Journal* 23.2 (1984), 31.

67 Modleski, *Women Who Knew*, 51–52.

68 This film technique of blocking for and showing the invisible can be seen in a comic sense in Henry Koster's *Harvey* (1950) in which Elwood Dowd (James Stewart) is helped and aided by an invisible 6'3.5" tall rabbit. The illusion of Harvey's presence in certain scenes is achieved by Koster's inclusion of extra space in the frame, implying another character is present, though invisible. Fowkes notes that Harvey's

presence in the film is shown through "a function of camera framing that routinely leaves space for a character that we cannot perceive." Katherine Fowkes, *The Fantasy Film* (Chichester: Wiley-Blackwell, 2010), 69.

69 Norma Miller, "Style and Content in Tacitus," in Thomas Dorey's *Tacitus* (London: Routledge, 1969), 103–105; Woodman, *Tacitus Reviewed*, 27–33.

70 Marie Gingras, "Annalistic Format, Tacitean Themes and the Obituaries of *Annals* 3," *CJ* 87 (1992), 245.

71 His grandfather was a centurion under Sulla. 3.75.1.

72 Gingras, "Obituaries," 254–55.

73 Syme, however, points out that Tacitus "goes too far" in claiming an imperial acceleration of Capito's tenure of office as he only became suffect consul in 5 CE. Syme, *Tacitus*, 761. For Labeo's possible refusal of the offer of a consulship, see Nicholas Horsfall, "Labeo and Capito," *Historia* 23 (1974), 253–54.

74 Woodman and Martin, *Book 3*, 491.

75 Gingras, "Obituaries," 255 n. 33.

76 This section owes much to Dylan Sailor's *Writing and Empire in Tacitus* (Cambridge: Cambridge University Press, 2008), especially to his illuminating discussion of this passage at 24–33.

77 Ibid., 24.

78 Ibid., 25. Sailor terms this "a sort of spectral sequence of offices *not* held that proves noncompliance and therefore a species of merit."

79 Ibid., 25 n. 56.

80 See Thomas Strunk, "Collaborators Among the Opposition?: Deconstructing the Imperial *Cursus Honorum*," *Arethusa* 48 (2015), 47–58.

81 The inversion of Roman religious practice had already been foreshadowed by the death of Agrippina, when, under Seneca's advice, Nero concocted a story of his own near escape from his mother's treachery. The senate voted thanks for saving their emperor and lined Nero's route back to Rome, as though triumphing over his mother. 14.11–14. For more on this, see Beard, *Triumph*, 277–80.

82 On the structure of book 14, see Martin, "Structure," 1557.

83 Concerning Tacitus' avoidance of gory details, see Woodman, tranls., *The Annals*, 177 n. 73.

84 O'Gorman notes that Tacitus here implies that even the meaning of words and language have changed with the coming of the principate. O'Gorman, *Irony*, 143–45.

85 For a discussion of the Republican meaning(s) and overtones in this passage, from the dating (from the battle of Philippi) and relations (Cato, Brutus, and Cassius), see Woodman and Martin, *Book 3*, 495–98.

86 The funeral ends the year 22, the third book, and the first half of the first hexad of the *Annales*. For the now general consensus that Tacitus' first hexad is divided into two halves of three books each, see Syme, *Tacitus*, 253.

87 For a full description of a Roman elite funeral, see Polybius 6.53–54.
88 Koestermann, vol 1, 567, notes that the surprise last sentence is striking.
89 Gingras notes that Junia's funeral is one of the last vestiges of *libertas* in the *Annales*. Gingras, "Obituaries," 248–49.
90 Martin notes that the ending of *Annales* 3 ties in very well with the Cremutius Cordus episode. Ronald Martin, "Tacitus and His Predecessors," in T. A. Dorey's *Tacitus* (London: Routledge, 1969), 146 n. 86.
91 Woodman notes that Cordus' speech uses *enargeia* in order to argue that what is in his history is real, rather than described. Martin and Woodman, *Book IV*, 183. See also O'Gorman, *Irony*, 60 n. 25.

Chapter 4

1 Later in the chapter, we will also consider Victor Fleming's *Gone with the Wind* (1939), with regard to both foreshadowing and backshadowing effects.
2 For a detailed discussion of this technique in classical Hollywood cinema, see David Bordwell's *Reinventing Hollywood* (Chicago: University of Chicago Press, 2017), 68–72.
3 My inclusion of *Gone with the Wind*, as with all other films under discussion, does not imply my acceptance of the film's values and *mores*. This discussion is included to elucidate the specific film technique of temporal shadowing through parallels in theme and shot composition. As noted in the Introduction, we must be circumspect in dealing with material from times and cultures whose values we do not share.
4 For an analysis of the art of Roman sarcophagi, see Michael Koortbojian's *Myth, Meaning, and Memory on Roman Sarcophagi* (Berkeley: University of California Press, 1995), to which my discussion here is greatly indebted.
5 Koortbojian refers to these temporal shifts as alterations in the "scansion" of the visual narrative. Ibid., 43f.
6 See, e.g., Ryberg's "Innuendo," 383–404 and Donald Sullivan "Innuendo and the Weighted Alternative" *CJ* 71 (1976), 312–26.
7 For a discussion of Tacitean *variatio*, see Gunnar Sörbom's *Variatio Sermonis Tacitei Aliaeque Apud Eundem Quaestiones Selectae* (Upsalia: Almquist and Wiksell Soc., 1935). Specifically, Sörbom notes the tendency of ancient historians to employ elision with regard to ancient names, not only to create *variatio* but also to briefly disorient the reader until all the components of the tria-nomena are supplied.
8 Ibid., 3.
9 Ibid., 4. There is even one instance of *praenomen* following *cognomen* at *Annales* 6.9.3, when Tacitus records the name as Scaurus Mamercus.

10 For Tiberius' name at birth, see Suetonius, *Tiberius*, 4.3.

11 Sörbom, *Variatio*, 13. "Tiberius" is interchangeable with "Caesar," "princeps," and "imperator" (2.35–37). These are the same titles that Tacitus later uses for Nero (14.51–52).

12 Tacitus refers to Tiberius as "Nero" at the following places 1.3.1; 1.3.3.; 1.4.3; 1.5.4; 2.3.2; and 3.56.2.

13 Ronald Martin, citing Syme (*Roman Papers III*, 1023) and Goodyear (ad. loc. 1.5.4) notes the "anachronistic and probably malicious use of *Neronem*." Ronald Martin, "Structure," 1508 n. 28. For more on this, see also Ronald Martin, "Tacitus and the Death of Augustus," *CQ* 5 (1955), 123 n. 1.

14 This device also provides Tacitus with an elegant ring structure for the *Annales*, able to begin and end the work with references to Nero. On the whole, however, I believe that the desire to parallel, and thus connect, the characters of Tiberius and Nero was the primary intent of this technique.

15 Martin, "Structure," 1508 n. 28, and Norma Miller, *Tacitus Annals Book I* (London: Bristol Classical Press, 1992), 114–15.

16 Tacitus is extremely careful with his naming. In the Claudian books, Nero is never referred to as "Ahenobarbus," but always as "Domitius." In fact, the name "Ahenobarbus" only occurs once in the extant *Annales*, when Tacitus refers to Nero's father, at 12.3.2. Nero is referred to as "Domitius" in the *Annales* at 11.11.2; 12.3.2; 12.8.2; 12.9.1; 12.25.1; and 12.26.1, when Tacitus relates his adoption into the imperial family. The use of "Domitius" for Nero is definitely a *figura etymologica* with Nero's dominion, and could possibly be a foreshadowing of Domitian, who, as Tacitus' readers would recall from the *Historiae*, ended his reign in similar circumstances to Nero.

17 Martin, "Death of Augustus," 123.

18 For Nero's name at birth, see Suetonius, *Nero*, 1, 6, and also Richard Holland, *Nero: The Man Behind the Myth* (Thrupp: Sutton Publishing, 2000), 14. For his imperial titulature see, e.g., *IGRR* 1124.

19 Sörbom, *Variatio*, 13.

20 This intentional misnaming incident is also recorded by Suetonius in *Nero*, 7.

21 Miller also notes that "in 4.3 and 5.4 the reference is to AD 14 and the use of the name [Nero] must be deliberate and malicious." Miller, *Book I*, 114–15.

22 We will be looking at this passage again, in light of Tacitus' use of name-driven foreshadowing between the two Agrippinas, in the next section.

23 O'Gorman notes this parallelism and ring-structure in naming Tiberius "Nero." O'Gorman, *Irony*, 127.

24 As noted in the section "Nero: Tiberius by Another Name," above, there are realities to Roman naming that Tacitus could not entirely avoid. Although he uses the same form of the name (rather than the diminuitives, used by, e.g., Suetonius), I hope to

show that the connections between the two Agrippinas are much more than fortuitous naming.

25 Pelling notes that Agrippina the Younger is "often a darker counterpart to her mother." Christopher Pelling, "Tacitus and Germanicus," in *Tacitus and the Tacitean Tradition*, T. J. Luce and Anthony Woodman, eds., 59–85 (Princeton: Princeton University Press, 1993), 71 n. 29.

26 O'Gorman, *Irony*, 131. O'Gorman also notes that Agrippina the Elder is the *imago* of Augustus and that her daughter, Agrippina the Younger, is the continuation of her mother's example of the designing imperial wife and mother. O'Gorman, *Irony*, 69.

27 Suetonius, *Tiberius*, 1–2.

28 Martin and Woodman note the use of *atrox* for both of the Agrippinas, positing a shared characteristic trait, but without comment as to potential foreshadowing. Martin and Woodman, *Book IV*, 216.

29 Tacitus tells us (at 4.53.2.) that this exchange between Agrippina the Elder and Tiberius was recorded in her memoirs, which were published posthumously by her daughter. O'Gorman notes that in this way it is Agrippina the Younger who gives voice to her outspoken mother. See O'Gorman, *Irony*, 123.

30 TLL, s.v. *atrox*.

31 Caligula's reign is mentioned at 4.71.1 and 5.1.4. Tacitus recalls his nickname pointedly at 1.41.2 and at 1.69.4, which may, in itself, be a form of foreshadowing.

32 Claudius would likely have been mentioned in the Caligulan narrative far more than under Tiberius, but with the loss of books 7 through the first portion of 11, this discussion is, of necessity, limited to the Tiberian books.

33 Before book 11, Tacitus mentions Claudius at 1.1.2; 1.54.1; 3.2.3; 3.3.2; 3.18.3–4; 3.29.4; 4.31.3; 6.32.4; 6.46.1. In most of these instances, Tacitus mentions Claudius only as a part of his introductory list of emperors (1.1.2), in asides (1.54.1; 3.3.2; 4.31.3; 6.32.4), or to show relation (3.29.4).

34 Intriguingly, this delay in the placement of Claudius' name also occurs in the *senatus consultum de Cn. Pisone Patre* (CIL II.2.5.900). Claudius is mentioned after Germanicus' female relations and his infant son, at line 148. For the text and translation, see D. S. Potter and Cynthia Damon's "Senatus Consultum de Cn. Pisone Patre," *AJP* 120 (1999): 13–42.

35 On the viability of the choice of Claudius for emperor, see Timothy Wiseman's "Calpurnius Siculus and the Claudian Civil War," *JRS* 72 (1987): 57–67, esp. 62.

36 For more on Tacitus' characterization of emperors through excurses, see chapter 2.

37 For a discussion of this passage as Tiberian focalization, see the section in chapter 1, "Choosing a Successor."

38 As has been pointed out, both Claudius and Gaius Caligula, as future emperors, have a large part to play in the *Annales* following book 6. The loss of all but the last book and a half of this hexad makes the reader wonder how Tacitus would have related

these two reigns in their entirety. The mere mention of their names, however, summons up before the reader the idea of each of these rulers as they would be revealed in books 7 through 12 and, for the *Annales*' original audience, public opinion of these imperial figures.

39 *nam iuveni civile ingenium, mira comitas et diversa a Tiberii sermone vultu, adrogantibus et obscuris.* 1.33.2.

40 See Pelling, "Tacitus and Germanicus," 78.

41 In this discussion, I am greatly indebted to Christopher Pelling's "Tragical Dreamer: Some Dreams in the Roman Historians," *G&R* 44 (1997), 197–213.

42 Livia has not been mentioned since 1.33.3, which is suggestive as she was then plotting with Plancina for the ruin of Agrippina. For Livia's behavior at Germanicus' funeral, see 3.3.3; and at Piso's trial, 3.15.1 and 3.17.2. Interestingly, when introducing Germanicus to the narrative of the *Annales*, Tacitus specifically outlines Germanicus' reasons for fear and mistrust of both Livia and Tiberius, thus providing an early signal as to how Germanicus *should* have interpreted his dream. 1.33.1.

43 As Pelling noted, the appearance of Livia in this context is enough to "make the reader wonder whether there is not more to it, whether any goodwill from this sinister figure can be any more than transient." Pelling, "Tragical Dreamer," 208.

44 For Tacitus' implication that Tiberius had cut short a successful campaign, see 2.26.1, 4.

45 Goodyear merely notes that "for T[acitus] spectacle in itself holds little interest" and that Tacitus "tends to concentrate on particular details and above all on the thoughts and emotions of those involved. So it is here with the gloomy forebodings he imputes to the spectators." Goodyear, vol 2, 316–17.

46 E.g., the Delphic oracle's response to Croesus' question about attacking Persia, that if he attacked, a great empire would fall. Croesus misinterpreted the oracle as meaning the Persian Empire, but it meant his own. Herodotus 1.53.3.

47 Woodman notes that the two meanings of the Oracle are impossible to translate into English simultaneously. He also points out that, although the MS has *exitium*, he prefers Karl Heraeus' emendation *exitum*, which can mean either departure or death. Anthony Woodman, transl., *Tacitus: The Annals*, 67 n. 3.

48 2.55.1–6. Pelling notes Tacitus' rhetorical pairing of the two couples, Germanicus and Agrippina with Piso and Plancina, in order to highlight the best and worst of Republican tendencies. Pelling, "Tacitus and Germanicus," 82–84.

49 For Germanicus' blame of Piso, see 2.71.1, 4.

50 Woodman and Martin note that the passage is "heavily ironical: in two years' time his 'dearest wife' would conspire with Sejanus to murder him." Woodman and Martin, *Book 3*, 308.

51 4.3.3–5; 4.7.3–8.1. The wife of Drusus the Younger is referred to by Suetonius as "Livilla" rather than Livia. This convention is very convenient, and is generally used

by modern scholars. Tacitus, however, expressly avoids any use of a diminutive, preferring the ambiguity in order to trade on the parallels between the two women. This is similar to his use of "Agrippina" for both mother and daughter, as discussed in the section "Like Mother Like Daughter: The Two Agrippinas" of this chapter.

52 Tacitus only uses the superlative of *carus* three other times in the extant *Annales* (at 14.23.2, 15.54.2, and 15.57.2). The last of these also seems ironic, as it occurs in the context of Roman *nobiles* betraying their dearest friends, although untouched by torture, while Epicharis, a freedwoman, endures tortures and protects the names of strangers.

53 L'Hoir notes that the mention of Livia and Livilla by Drusus brings Caecina's speech "into thematic perspective: by recalling Agrippina the Elder and Plancina . . . and also by foreshadowing Agrippina the Younger." Francesca Santoro L'Hoir, "Tacitus and Women's Usurpation of Power," *CW* 88 (1994), 17.

54 Pliny the Elder, *Naturalis Historia*, 29.20. *iam vero et adulteria etiam in principum domibus, ut Eudemi in Livia Drusi Caesaris, item Valentis in qua dictum est regina.* For Pliny's text, I use Karl Mayhoff's Teubner edition (Stuttgart: B.G. Teubner, 1967).

55 Other accounts independent of the *Annales* also allude to Livilla's involvement in Drusus' murder. Suetonius, *Tiberius*, 62.1, and Cassius Dio at 57.22.1–2 and 58.11.6–7.

56 E.g., Pliny the Elder, *NH*, 29.20; Suetonius, *Tiberius*, 62.1; and Cassius Dio 57.22.1–2 and 58.11.6–7.

57 Unfortunately, the section of the *Annales* that deals with the fall of Sejanus is lost, but something of the dramatic possibilities of the story can be gathered from Juvenal's *Saturae*, 10.56–77, 90–107.

58 See Martin and Woodman, *Book IV*, 80.

59 In addition to the present example and the previous, at 1.24.2, Sejanus is mentioned at: 3.16.1; 3.29.4; 3.66.3; 3.72.3; and 3.72.4.

60 For a much fuller treatment of this section, especially as it applies to Tacitus' use of focalization, see the section "Agrippina at the Bridge" in chapter 1.

61 Goodyear notes the effectiveness and development of this metaphor. Goodyear, vol. 2, 129.

62 Martin and Woodman, *Book IV*, 262.

63 Morson refers to backshadowing as "foreshadowing after the fact," and notes that the device cannot occur in situations where the later event could not have been in some way predicted by the prior narrative. Gary Morson, *Narrative and Freedom: The Shadows of Time* (New Haven, Yale University Press, 1994), 234–38.

64 Victoria Pagán first applied the term "backshadowing" to Tacitus' *Annales* in her "Actium and Teutoburg: Augustan Victory and Defeat in Vergil and Tacitus" in *Clio and the Poets*, ed. David Levene, 45–59 (Leiden: Brill, 2002), esp. 50–54. Pagán lays primary stress on the ekphrastic nature of Germanicus' tour of the battlefield,

whereas I here stress backshadowing as exemplified in the Caecina episode. Regardless, I am deeply indebted to Pagán's work on this topic, and encourage any reader interested in this aspect of temporal suggestion to seek out her publications.

65 Tacitus makes reference to the Varian disaster at 1.3.6; 1.43.1; 1.55.2–3; and at 1.60.3–62.2. After the section under discussion at 1.65.2 and 4, Tacitus continues to remind the reader of the Teutoburg forest at 1.71.1; 2.25.1; and 2.45.3.

66 Victoria Pagán notes that the appearance of Varus' ghost is "a fitting coda," as the ghost transgresses the boundaries between the living and the dead in parallel to the acts of Germanicus in her "Beyond Teutoburg: Transgression and Transformation in Tacitus *Annales* 1.61–62," *CP* 94 (1999), 315.

67 Woodman notes the reader's emotional involvement at this tense point in the narrative, stating that "[t]he reader's fear returns, and not without reason." Woodman, *Tacitus Reviewed*, 122–23.

68 Modern scholars here will note the connection between Tacitus' narrative and the battle filming common to recent movies, in which sounds are disrupted or suppressed and camera tracking becomes intentionally confused. For example, see Ridley Scott's *Gladiator* (2000) and Oliver Stone's *Alexander* (2004), amongst others.

69 Goodyear notes that Tacitus' description of Caecina's return to the Rhine "is literary rather than historical. Since disaster was averted, albeit narrowly, the episode possesses meagre historical interest." Goodyear, vol. 2, 67.

70 For the discussion on Tacitus' use of names in the context of foreshadowing, see the section "What's in a Name" of this chapter.

71 Pagán, "Actium and Teutoburg," 57.

72 Pagán, in her "Shadows and Assassinations: Forms of Time in Tacitus and Appian," *Arethusa* 39 (2006): 193–218, esp. 197–98, takes as a model Michael Bernstein's *Foregone Conclusions: Against Apocalyptic History* (Berkeley: University of California Press, 1994): 16 on the concept of backshadowing as inherently involving the judgment of the characters by the narrator and reader "as though they should have known what was to come." While this judging of the characters is definitely one use of backshadowing, the technique can be employed for a range of audience reactions, including the evocation of horror or pity, especially when the character is not directly responsible for the engagement with the past pattern of events. With Caecina's recognition of Varus' fate, Tacitus does not use backshadowing to castigate his lack of forethought, but rather to dramatically threaten the present with the past.

73 Martin discusses the famous parallels between 1.5 and 12.68, including the idea of backshadowing, noting that "the borrowing of language is in the reverse direction, i.e., Tacitus' Nero passage depends upon what he had already written of Tiberius." Martin, "Death of Augustus," 124.

74 For a discussion of this passage as it relates to the pointed use of "Nero" for Tiberius, see the section above, "Nero: Tiberius by Another Name."

75 Martin makes a convincing argument for verbal parallels in these passages. I have only taken the more obvious parallels as examples, but I think Martin is correct in his analysis. Martin, "Death of Augustus," 123–24.

76 Elizabeth Keitel, "Tacitus on the Deaths of Tiberius and Claudius," *Hermes* 109 (1981), 207, notes that Claudius' adoption of Nero is parallel to Augustus' adoption of Tiberius.

77 Santoro L'Hoir notes that Tacitus, in book 12, depicts Agrippina the Younger as "a mother and *noverca* as unnatural as Livia," in her "Women's Usurpation," 18.

78 Morford notes that there is a parallel between 13.1.1 and 1.6.1, but he simply notes that these words "give the historian's rhetorical *color* for his account of the reign of Nero," later defining this further as "irony and foreboding." Mark Morford, "Tacitus' Historical Methods in the Neronian Books of the *Annals*." *ANRW* II 33.2 (1990), 1582, 1601. Morford again notes the "ominous parallel" between Nero and Tiberius concerning the *maiestas* trials under Nero. Morford, 1610.

79 Woodman notes that 1.5 foreshadows the end of book 12, but surely it must read the other way, with book 12 reading back onto and reinforcing book 1. Woodman, *Tacitus Reviewed*, 35.

80 Friedrich Klingner, "Beobachtungen über Sprache und Stil des Tacitus am Anfang des 13. Annalenbuches," *Hermes* 83 (1955), 189–90.

81 Pagán, "Actium and Teutoburg," 57.

Chapter 5

1 An earlier version of this chapter appeared in *Arethusa* in 2013: Philip Waddell, "Eloquent Collisions: The *Annales* of Tacitus, the Column of Trajan and the Cinematic Quick-Cut," *Arethusa* 46 (2013): 471–97. I am grateful to Martha Malamud for her kind permission to reuse this material in its revised form.

2 For some of the commentary on this point, see Syme's *Tacitus*, 310; Koestermann vol. 4, 234; Woodman and Martin *Book 3*, 210; O'Gorman's *Irony*, 171; and Rhiannon Ash's *Tacitus* (London: Bristol Classical Press, 2006), 93. Only the latter three discuss quick-cuts, and this examination is often limited to single sentences.

3 For example, a number of notable scholars have suggested that the episode of the Ruminal Fig, which ends Book 13, is merely a truncated or added-on omen placed there solely due to annalistic structure and without additional meaning. See, e.g. Frank Moore, "Annalistic Method as Related to the Book Divisions in Tacitus," *TAPA* 54 (1923): 5–20; Syme's *Tacitus*, 266, 269, and 745; Wuilleumier, *Livre XIII*, 104; Charles Segal, "Tacitus and Poetic History: the End of *Annals XIII*," *Ramus* 11 (1973): 109–15; and Morford, "Tacitus' Historical Methods," 1582–627. The Ruminal Fig is discussed in more detail in the section below, "A Dead Tree Grows in Rome."

4 Tacitus uses the quick-cut device fairly regularly, and given the space limitations for this chapter I cannot go into detail on each instance. I have selected some of the most striking examples, but those covered here are by no means an exhaustive list.
5 See below, especially the section "Collision Quick-Cut and *The Godfather*."
6 André Bazin tells us that "the meaning is not in the image, it is in the shadow of the image projected by montage on the field of consciousness of the spectator." André Bazin, "The Evolutions of the Language of Cinema." In *Film Theory and Criticism*, 6th edn., ed. Leo Braudy and Marshall Cohen, 41–53 (Oxford: Oxford University Press, 2004): 44.
7 Jean Mitry, *The Aesthetics and Psychology of the Cinema*. C. King, transl. (Bloomington: Indiana University Press, 1997), 129–30. We will not be discussing lyrical cuts, which are concerned with the flow or pacing of an individual scene, nor the "montage of ideas," which is generally reserved for use in newsreels.
8 Valérie Huet, "Stories One Might tell of Roman Art: Reading Trajan's Column and the Tiberius Cup." In *Art and Text in Roman Culture*, ed. Jaś Elsner, 8–31 (Cambridge: Cambridge University Press, 1996), 10.
9 Ibid., 21–22.
10 Ibid., 22–24.
11 Richard Brilliant, *Visual Narratives: Storytelling in Etruscan and Roman Art* (Ithaca: Cornell University Press, 1984), 98–99.
12 Ibid., 106.
13 Werner Gauer, *Untersuchungen zur Trajanssäule* (Berlin: Gebr. Mann Verlag, 1977), 9–12.
14 Brilliant, *Visual Narratives*, 100.
15 Ibid., 97 and 115.
16 See, e.g., Brilliant, *Visual Narratives*, 100; and Lino Rossi, *Trajan's Column and the Dacian Wars*, translated by Jocelyn Toynbee (London: Thames & Hudson, 1971), 16–19.
17 Alain Malissard, "Une nouvelle approche de la Colonne Trajanne," *ANRW II* 12.1 (1982): 579–606.
18 Ronald Tanner, "The Development of Thought and Style in Tacitus." *ANRW II* 33.4 (1991): 2706–709.
19 Mitry, *Aesthetics*, 129.
20 For a discussion of the film's themes of doubling, especially of Bruno as the "dark underside of Guy," linked to the film's dualistic opening, see Donald Spoto's *The Art of Alfred Hitchcock: Fifty Years of his Motion Pictures* (Garden City, NY: Doubleday, 1976), 208–19, esp. 210–12 and Robin Wood's "*Strangers on a Train*," in *A Hitchcock Reader*, 2nd ed., ed. Marshall Deutelbaum and Leland Poague (Oxford: Blackwell Publishing, 2009): 172–81, esp. 172–73.

21 Following standard convention, I am using Cichorius' numbering of the panels in Trajan's Column. See Conrad Cichorius, *Die Reliefs der Trajanssäule* (Berlin: G. Reimer, 1896).
22 Although I will only be covering in detail two examples, for more instances of the narrative quick-cut in the *Annales* see 1.38.1, 1.77.1, 2.56.4, 3.72.2, 4.56.1, 6.33.1, 12.31.1, 12.62.1, and 14.34.2.
23 23 OLD, s.v. at, def. 3a, 194.
24 For example, see BC 31.4: *at Catilinae* and 34.2: *at Catilina*. Also, in the BJ, Sallust uses "*at Iugurtha*" at several instances, including 28.1, 35.8, 38.1, 50.3, and 97.1.
25 Woodman and Martin have observed the relative rarity of the phrase *at Romae* in the *Historiae* (found in three examples), in Sallust (only at C. 43.1), and Livy (none), as opposed to frequency with which Tacitus uses it in the *Annales*. Woodman and Martin, *Book 3*, 210.
26 As Goodyear has noted, the scene recalls the imagery of the disaster in a vivid manner, stating "the disaster is almost relived." Goodyear, vol. 2, 67.
27 Pagán has noted this elision and posits that Tacitus modifies time in order to enable Tiberius' immediate disapproval of Germanicus' actions. Pagán, "Actium and Teutoburg," 56.
28 Tacitus deploys sudden cuts to the emperor Tiberius at several points in the *Annales*, including: 1.52.1, 1.62.2, 1.69.3, 2.5.1, 2.43.2, 3.41.3, 4.8.2, 4.13.1, 4.67.1, 4.75.1, and 5.2.1.
29 Walker notes that "[Tiberius'] influence is traced in events which seem quite independent of him (this is due to the supposition of '*ars Tiberii*' as something almost inhuman)." Walker, *Annals*, 18.
30 See Ash, *Book XV*, 113.
31 Syme notes here that "the homage paid to appearances was a cynical defiance of what all men knew to be the truth." Syme, *Tacitus*, 411.
32 For further discussion of the "theatrical paradigm" under Nero, see Bartsch, *Actors*, 1–35.
33 Mitry, *Aesthetics*, 130.
34 Mitry's work on montage follows Eisenstein, who discussed the technique in terms of the collision of two physical bodies in nature. The elasticity of said bodies will determine the type of their collision, and from their physical composition it will be possible to predict the outcome, in this case the resulting effect on the viewer. For Eisenstein, there is always an element of collision involved in montage. Sergei Eisenstein, *Film Form: Essays in Film Theory*, ed. and transl. J. Leyda (New York: Harcourt, Brace, 1949): 37–38.
35 Eisenstein particularly favored this form of transitional shot, and saw it as a stark contrast to the "brick and mortar" theory of connection through montage: "By what, then, is montage characterized and, consequently, its cell—the shot? By collision. By

the conflict of two pieces in opposition to each other. By conflict. By collision," and that "from the collision of two given factors arises a concept." Eisenstein, *Film Form*, 37.

36 For a discussion of the uses of Christian iconography within the *Godfather* trilogy, see Naomi Greene's "Family Ceremonies: or, Opera in *The Godfather Trilogy*," in *Francis Ford Coppola's* The Godfather *Trilogy*, ed. Nick Browne, 133–55 (Cambridge: Cambridge University Press, 2000).

37 Malissard has noted that this type of juxtaposition appears at four points in the Column, stating that it is "une liaison par forte opposition," and further that it is "proche du 'cut' de cinéma." Malissard, "Nouvelle Approche," 597.

38 Some particularly instructive uses of the ablative absolute occur at 1.15.1, 1.70.5, 1.77.1, 1.77.3, 2.35.2, 3.7.1, 4.2.3, 4.11.2, 4.29.2, 4.74.1, 6.30.4, 13.1.1, and 14.49.3. For an excellent analysis of Tacitus' use of the construction as an "appendix" of sorts to the primary clause, see Martin and Woodman *Book IV*, 23–24, and Martin, *Tacitus*, 221–23.

39 See, e.g., G&L 409–10.

40 Many scholars have noted the unusual and disjointed transition here, including: Miller, *Book I*, 14: "there is no clearly marked connection between clauses, either organically or chronologically—the impression is almost of contrast rather than connection"; and Goodyear, vol. 1, 101: "the articulation [in this sentence] is disjointed, constructions change abruptly or are left unfinished, and thought crowds upon thought suddenly and tangentially."

41 For some additional instances where Tacitus employs the collision cut, see 1.7.1, 1.46.1, 2.82.1, 4.28.3, 4.52.1, 6.2.1, 14.33.1, and 15.73.3. Many of these examples begin with the transition "*at Romae*," which is especially jarring because through this usage Tacitus is expressly denying any causal relationship between the two passages.

42 It has been noted the use of *at Romae* in this instance serves additionally to highlight the stark difference between the conditions in the desert of Numidia and in the city of Rome, and to compare the latter's domestic tribulations with the glory of the successful battle. See Woodman and Martin, *Book 3*, 210.

43 Romans generally thought of adultery and poisoning as related charges. See e.g., Woodman and Martin, *Book 3*, 212 and Santoro L'Hoir, *Tragedy*, 178.

44 For more on the *maiestas* trials, and their increasing use under the empire as a mechanism for the disposal of political enemies, see Santoro L'Hoir, *Tragedy*, 177.

45 For an in-depth discussion of this passage, see Ash, *Book XV*, 177–80.

46 For a discussion of this passage, especially of Tacitus' depiction of Nero creating a foreign setting in Rome, see Anthony Woodman's *Tacitus Reviewed*, 168–89.

47 For a thorough discussion of the marriage and fire, see Ash, *Book XV*, 174–93.

48 As Miller has noted, "what is clear, is Roman outrage at the distortion of the ancient ceremony" Norma Miller, *Cornelii Taciti Annalium Liber XV* (New York: Macmillan Education, 1973), 87. I would mention that there are other scholarly opinions concerning this scene, including that the event was either a Hellenic-style celebration of the Floralia, or potentially a form of sham initiation rite. See, respectively, Walter Allen et al., "Nero's Eccentricities before the Fire (Tac. *Ann.* 15.37)," *Numen* 9 (1962): 99–109; and Edward Champlin, *Nero* (Cambridge: Harvard University Press, 2003), 165–67.

49 Additionally, he suggests that the Roman populace held Nero responsible. See Elizabeth Keitel's "The Art of Losing: Tacitus and the Disaster Narrative," in *Ancient Historiography and Its Contexts: Studies in Honour of A.J. Woodman*, Christina Kraus, John Marincola, and Christopher Pelling, eds., 331–52 (Oxford: Oxford University Press, 2010), 342.

50 Both Koestermann and Syme have commented on the dramatic speed of the juxtaposition between these two actually unrelated scenes. See Koestermann vol. 4, 234, and Syme, *Tacitus*, 310.

51 O'Gorman, *Irony*, 171 states that: "The fire at Rome is represented almost as a consequence of the myriad transgressions depicted, opening with the words 'a disaster ensued.'" See also Ash, *Tacitus*, 93 and Paul Murgatroyd, "Tacitus on the Great Fire of Rome." *Eranos* 103 (2005), 49.

52 Tacitus also uses the attractive cut at 6.29.1 and 16.2.1.

53 For more on the implications of this cut, see Murray Pomerance, *The Horse Who Drank the Sky: Film Experience beyond Narrative and Theory* (New Brunswick: Rutgers University Press, 2008), 141–42.

54 For discussions of this cut in *Lawrence*, see Ken Dancyger, *The Technique of Film and Video Editing* (Boston: Focal, 1993), 95, and Paul Monaco's *American Cinema: The Sixties 1960–1969* (Berkeley: University of California Press, 2001), 97–98.

55 For more concerning the visuality of this scene, see Brilliant, *Visual Narratives*, 99.

56 E.g., Syme dismisses this episode as "brief, isolated, and meaningless," suggesting that Tacitus added it simply to fill space. Syme, *Tacitus*, 745. Moore omits this section from his compilation of "dramatic endings" in the *Annales*, and Morford believed it "devoid of symbolic meaning." Moore, "Annalistic Method," 9; and Morford, "Tacitus' Historical Methods," 1604 n. 88.

57 See e.g., Franklin Krauss, *An Interpretation of the Omens, Portents and Prodigies Recorded by Livy, Tacitus and Suetonius* (Philadelphia: University of Philadelphia, 1930), 30–31.

58 See John Liebeschuetz, *Continuity and Change in Roman Religion* (Oxford: Oxford University Press, 1979), 193–94; and, specifically on religion in Tacitus' *Annales*, see Kelly Shannon-Henderson's *Religion and Memory in Tacitus'* Annals (Oxford: Oxford University Press, 2019), esp. 10–17, 285–350.

59 For other instances of misinterpreted omens, see 4.58.2 (Tiberius destined never to return to the city) and 14.22.1 (a comet foretells a change in kingdoms).

60 For a contrary view, see "Poetic History," by Segal, who believes the regrowth of the fig to be an ironic comment on the immorality of Nero.

61 A number of scholars have suggested that the Ruminal Fig episode exists to foretell the eventual doom of Rome, but these interpretations either omit or downplay the significance of the tree's regrowth. Wuilleumier *Livre XIII*, 104; Oliver Devillers, *L'art de la persuasion dans les Annales de Tacite* (Brussels: Latomus, 1994), 84; and Jason Davies, *Rome's Religious History: Livy, Tacitus and Ammianus on their Gods* (Cambridge: Cambridge University Press, 2004), 205, 213, and 220.

62 Harold McCulloch, Jr. "Literary Augury at the End of 'Annals' XIII." *Phoenix* 34 (1980): 238, 240–41. McCulloch suggests that Tacitus' comment that the Fig was regarded as a portent until it regrew indicates that the omen was initially misread, believing that the withering was the important aspect of the event rather than the later new growth. Shannon-Henderson suggests that the withering of the Ruminal Fig denotes the end of Nero's *quinquennium*, and is tied to the upcoming death of Agrippina. Shannon-Henderson, *Religion and Memory*, 290–92.

63 Even Syme, who believes the passage of the Ruminal Fig is devoid of structural import, has noted that all of the other books of the *Annales* end with significant passages. Syme, *Tacitus*, 269.

64 Although I do not cover this specific example in more detail in chapter 4, sections 13.57.3 and 14.1–13 illustrate Tacitus' use of foreshadowing, and are replete with verbal echoes to further emphasize the connection. See Liebeschuetz, *Continuity*, 156; McCulloch, "Literary Augury," 237–38; and Devillers, *L'art de la persuasion*, 84.

65 The mechanics of this device are known in narratology as the "embedded story." As Bal defines the technique, it "explains the primary story, or it resembles the primary story . . . in the second [case] the explanation is usually left to the reader, or merely hinted at, in the fabula." Bal, *Narratology*, 58.

66 It is commonly believed that the death of Nero occurs somewhere in the now-lost portions of the *Annales*.

67 As Tacitus himself states, his account is offered "*sine ira et studio*" ("without anger and partiality") (1.3.1). As we have seen, however, Tacitus is able to employ his literary skill, including the use of the collision cut, to leave the reader with the *impression* of Nero's guilt and wrongdoing, even where Nero could not possibly have played a role.

Works Cited

Adam, Adeline. "Agrippine l'Aînée ou le paradoxe. Les femmes de la domus Augusta et le pouvior dans les *Annales* de Tacite (livres 1 à 4)." *Pallas* 99: *Femmes et actes de mémoire: La temporalité dans les échanges 2015* (2015): 111–32.

Allen, Walter et al. 1962. "Nero's Eccentricities before the Fire (Tac. *Ann.* 15.37)." *Numen* 9 (1962): 99–109.

Ash, Rhiannon. *Tacitus*. London: Bristol Classical Press, 2006.

Ash, Rhiannon. *Tacitus Annals Book XV*. Cambridge: Cambridge University Press, 2018.

Bakewell, Geoff. "The One-Eyed Man is King: Oedipal Vision in *Minority Report*." *Arethusa* 41.1 (2008): 95–112.

Bal, Mieke. *The Mottled Screen: Reading Proust Visually*, translated by Anna-Louise Milne. Stanford: Stanford University Press, 1997.

Bal, Mieke. *Narratology: Introduction to the Theory of Narrative*. 3rd edn. Toronto: University of Toronto Press Incorporated, 2009.

Balázs, Béla. "The Close-Up." Collected in *Film Theory and Criticism: Introductory Readings*, edited by Leo Braudy and Marshall Cohen. Oxford: Oxford University Press, 2016.

Baron, James. "*9 to 5* as Aristophanic Comedy." In *Classics and Cinema*, edited by Martin Winkler, 232–50. Lewisburg: Bucknell University Press, 1991.

Barthes, Roland and Lionel Duisit. "An Introduction to the Structural Analysis of Narrative." *New Literary History* 6 (1975): 237–72.

Bartsch, Shadi. *Actors in the Audience: Theatricality and Doublespeak from Nero to Hadrian*. Cambridge: Harvard University Press, 1994.

Bartsch, Shadi. *The Mirror of the Self: Sexuality, Self-Knowledge, and the Gaze in the Early Roman Empire*. Chicago: University of Chicago Press, 2006.

Bazin, André. "The Evolutions of the Language of Cinema." In *Film Theory and Criticism*. 6th edn. edited by Leo Braudy and Marshall Cohen, 41–53. Oxford: Oxford University Press, 2004.

Beard, Mary. *The Roman Triumph*. Cambridge: Harvard University Press, 2007.

Bernstein, Michael. *Foregone Conclusions: Against Apocalyptic History*. Berkeley: University of California Press, 1994.

Bhatt, Shreyaa. "Useful Vices: Tacitus's Critique of Corruption." *Arethusa* 50 (2017): 311–33.

Billerbeck, Margarethe. "Die dramatische Kunst des Tacitus." *ANRW II* 33.4 (1991): 2752–71.

Bordwell, David. *Narration in the Fiction Film*. Madison: University of Wisconsin Press, 1985.

Bordwell, David. *Making Meaning: Inference and Rhetoric in the Interpretation of Cinema*. Cambridge: Harvard University Press, 1989.

Bordwell, David. *Poetics of Cinema*. New York: Routledge, 2008.

Bordwell, David. *Reinventing Hollywood: How 1940s Filmmakers Changed Movie Storytelling*. Chicago: University of Chicago Press, 2017.

Bordwell, David, Janet Staiger and Kristin Thompson. *The Classical Hollywood Cinema: Film Style and Mode of Production to 1960*. New York: Columbia University Press, 1985.

Bordwell, David and Kristin Thompson. *Film Art: An Introduction*. 8th edn. Boston: McGraw-Hill, 2008.

Braudy, Leo and Marshall Cohen, eds. *Film Theory and Criticism*, 6th edn. Oxford: Oxford University Press, 2004.

Brilliant, Richard. *Visual Narratives: Storytelling in Etruscan and Roman Art*. Ithaca: Cornell University Press, 1984.

British Museum, Dept. of Coins Medals, and Harold Mattingly. *Coins of the Roman Empire in the British Museum*. 5 vols. London: Trustees of the British Museum, 1923.

Champlin, Edward. *Nero*. Cambridge: Harvard University Press, 2003.

Cichorius, Conrad. *Die Reliefs der Trajanssäule*. Berlin: G. Reimer, 1896.

Coarelli, Filipo. *Rome and Environs: An Archaeological Guide*, translated by James Clauss and Daniel Harmon. Berkeley: University of California Press, 2007.

Cohn, Dorrit. "Signposts of Fictionality: A Narratological Perspective." *Poetics Today* 11.4 (1990): 775–804.

Comito, Terry. "*Touch of Evil*." *Film Comment* 7 (1971): 51–53.

Cooper, Anna. *An American Abroad: Imperialist Aesthetics in Postwar Hollywood Cinema*. New York: Bloomsbury Press, Forthcoming.

Courbaud, Edmond. *Les Procédés d'Art de Tacite dans les "Histoires."* Paris: Hachette, 1918.

Cowan, Eleanor. "Tacitus, Tiberius and Augustus," *CA* 28 (2009): 179–210.

Cyrino, Monica. *Big Screen Rome*. Oxford: Blackwell, 2005.

Cyrino, Monica, ed. *Rome, Season One: History Makes Television*. Oxford: Blackwell, 2008.

Cyrino, Monica, ed. *Rome, Season Two: Trial and Triumph*. Edinburgh: University of Edinburgh Press, 2015.

Cyrino, Monica and Antony Augoustakis, eds. *STARZ Spartacus: Reimagining an Icon on Screen*. Edinburgh, University of Edinburgh Press, 2017.

Damon, Cynthia. "The Historian's Presence, or, There and Back Again." In *Ancient Historiography and its Contexts: Studies in Honour of A.J. Woodman*. Edited by Christina Kraus, John Marincola, and Christopher Pelling, 353–63. Oxford: Oxford University Press, 2010.

Damon, Cynthia, transl. *Tacitus: Annals*. London: Penguin Books, 2012.

Dancyger, Ken. *The Technique of Film and Video Editing*. Boston: Focal, 1993.
Davies, Jason. *Rome's Religious History: Livy, Tacitus and Ammianus on their Gods*. Cambridge: Cambridge University Press, 2004.
Day, Kirsten. *Cowboy Classics: The Roots of the American Western in the Epic Tradition*. Edinburgh: University of Edinburgh Press, 2016.
Day, Kirsten, ed. *Celluloid Classics: New Perspectives on Classical Antiquity in Modern Cinema = Arethusa* 41.1 (2008).
De Jong, Irene. *A Narratological Commentary on the* Odyssey. Cambridge: Cambridge University Press, 2001.
De Jong, Irene. *Narratology and Classics: A Practical Guide*. Oxford: Oxford University Press, 2014.
De Jong, Irene, Reneé Nünlist, and Angus Bowie, eds. *Narrators, Narratees, and Narratives in Ancient Greek Literature*. Leiden: Brill, 2004.
Devillers, Olivier. *L'art de la persuasion dans les Annales de Tacite*. Brussels: Latomus, 1994.
Devillers, Olivier, ed. *Les* opera minora *et le développement de l'historiographie tacitéenne*. Bordeaux: Ausonius Scripta Antiqua, 2014.
Doane, Mary Ann. *The Desire to Desire: The Woman's Film of the 1940s*. Bloomington: Indiana University Press, 1987.
Doane, Mary Ann. "The Woman's Film: Possession and Address." In *Home is Where the Heart Is: Studies in Melodrama and the Woman's Film*, edited by Christine Gledhill, 283–98. London: British Film Institute, 1987.
Dorey, Thomas, ed. *Tacitus*. London: Routledge, 1969.
Ducos, Michèle. "La justice et les procès dans les livres I et II des *Annales* de Tacite." *Vita Latina* 187–88 (2013): 248–66.
Eisenstein, Sergei. *Film Form: Essays in Film Theory*. Edited and translated by Jay Leyda New York: Harcourt, Brace, 1949.
Elsner, Jaś. *Roman Eyes: Visuality and Subjectivity in Art and Text*. Princeton, Princeton University Press, 2007.
Elsner, Jaś, ed. *Art and Text in Roman Culture*. Cambridge: Cambridge University Press, 1996.
Fawell, John. *Hitchcock's Rear Window: The Well-Made Film*. Carbondale: Southern Illinois University Press, 2001.
Feldherr, Andrew. *Spectacle and Society in Livy's History*. Berkeley: University of California Press, 1998.
Flower, Harriet. *The Art of Forgetting: Disgrace and Oblivion in Roman Political Culture*. Chapel Hill: The University of North Carolina Press, 2006.
Fowkes, Katherine. *The Fantasy Film*. Chichester: Wiley-Blackwell, 2010.
Fowler, Don. *Roman Constructions*. Oxford: Oxford University Press, 2000.
Galtier, Fabrice. "Le motif du rivage dans l'épisode de la mort d'Agrippine (Tac., *Ann.*, 14.1–10)." In *Neronia IX: La villégiature dans le monde romain de Tibère à Hadrien*, edited by Olivier Devillers, 309–16. Paris: Bordeaux, 2014.

Gamel, Mary-Kay. "An American Tragedy: *Chinatown*." In *Classics and Cinema*, edited by Martin Winkler, 209–31. Lewisburg: Bucknell University Press, 1991.

Gates, Philippa. "The Three Sam Spades: The Shifting Model of American Masculinity in the Three Films of *The Maltese Falcon*." *Framework* 49.1 (2008): 7–26.

Gauer, Werner. *Untersuchungen zur Trajanssäule*. Berlin: Gebr. Mann Verlag, 1977.

Genette, Gérard. *Narrative Discourse*, translated by Jane Lewin. Ithaca: Cornell University Press, 1980.

Gerber, A. and A. Greef. *Lexicon Taciteum*. Hildesheim: Georg Olms Verlagsbuchhandlung, 1962.

Gil, Christopher and Timothy Wiseman, eds. *Lies and Fiction in the Ancient World*. Austin: University of Texas Press, 1993.

Gingras, Marie. "Annalistic Format, Tacitean Themes and the Obituaries of *Annals* 3." *CJ* 87 (1992): 241–56.

Goodyear, Francis. *Tacitus: Greece and Rome: New Surveys in the Classics* 4, 1970.

Goodyear, Francis. *The Annals of Tacitus, vol. 1 (Annals 1.1–54)*. Cambridge: Cambridge University Press, 1972.

Goodyear, Francis. *The Annals of Tacitus Volume II (Annals 1.55–81 and Annals 2)*. Cambridge: Cambridge University Press, 1981.

Greene, Naomi. "Family Ceremonies: or, Opera in *The Godfather Trilogy*." In *Francis Ford Coppola's* The Godfather *Trilogy*, edited by Nick Browne, 133–55. Cambridge: Cambridge University Press, 2000.

Gribble, Jim. "*The Third Man*: Graham Greene and Carol Reed." *Literature/Film Quarterly* 26 (1998): 235–39.

Griffin, Miriam. "The Lyons Tablet and Tacitean Hindsight." *CQ* 32 (1982): 404–18.

Griffin, Miriam. "Claudius in Tacitus." *CQ* 40 (1990): 482–501.

Hahn, Eleonore. *Die Exkurse in den Annalen des Tacitus*. Borna-Leipzig: Universitätsverlag von Robert Noske, 1933.

Hedrick, Charles Jr. *History and Silence: Purge and Rehabilitation of Memory in Late Antiquity*. Austin: University of Texas Press, 2000.

Heubner, Heinrich, ed. *P. Cornelius Tacitus, Tomus I, Annales*. Stuttgart: B.G. Teubner, 1983.

Holland, Richard. *Nero: The Man Behind the Myth*. Thrupp: Sutton Publishing, 2000.

Hommel, Hildebrecht. "Die Bildkunst des Tacitus." *Würzburger Studien zur Altertumswissenschaft* 9 (1936): 116–48.

Horsfall, Nicholas. "Labeo and Capito." *Historia* 23 (1974): 252–54.

Huet, Valérie. "Stories One Might Tell of Roman Art: Reading Trajan's Column and the Tiberius Cup." In *Art and Text in Roman Culture*, edited by Jaś Elsner, 8–31. Cambridge: Cambridge University Press.

Keitel, Elizabeth. "Tacitus on the Deaths of Tiberius and Claudius." *Hermes* 109 (1981): 206–14.

Keitel, Elizabeth. "The Non-Appearance of the Phoenix at Tacitus 'Annals' 6.28." *AJP* 120 (1999): 429–42.

Keitel, Elizabeth. "The Art of Losing: Tacitus and the Disaster Narrative." In *Ancient Historiography and its Contexts: Studies in Honour of A.J. Woodman*, edited by Christina Kraus, John Marincola, and Christopher Pelling, 331–52. Oxford: Oxford University Press, 2010.

Keitel, Elizabeth. "'No vivid writing, please': *Evidentia* in the *Agricola* and *Annals*." In *Les* opera minora *et le développement de l'historiographie tacitéenne*, edited by Olivier Devillers, 59–70. Bordeaux: Ausonius Scripta Antiqua, 2014.

Klingner, Friedrich. "Beobachungen über Sprache und Stil des Tacitus am Anfang des 13. Annalenbuches." *Hermes* 83 (1955): 187–200.

Koestermann, Erich. *Annalen*. 4 vol. Heidelberg: Carl Winter Universitätsverlag, 1963.

Koortbojian, Michael. *Myth, Meaning, and Memory on Roman Sarcophagi*. Berkeley: University of California Press, 1995.

Kraus, Christina, John Marincola, and Christopher Pelling, eds. *Ancient Historiography and Its Contexts: Studies in Honour of A. J. Woodman*. Oxford: Oxford University Press, 2010.

Krauss, Franklin. *An Interpretation of the Omens, Portents and Prodigies Recorded by Livy, Tacitus and Suetonius*. Philadelphia: University of Philadelphia, 1930.

Laird, Andrew. *Powers of Expression, Expressions of Power: Speech Presentation and Latin Literature*. Oxford: Oxford University Press, 1999.

Lapsky, Robert and Michael Westlake. *Film Theory: An Introduction*. Manchester, Manchester University Press, 1988.

Leigh, Matthew. *Lucan: Spectacle and Engagement*. Oxford: Oxford University Press, 1997.

Leitch, Thomas. *Crime Films*. Cambridge: Cambridge University Press, 2002.

Levene, David, ed. *Clio and the Poets*. Leiden: Brill, 2002.

Levick, Barbara. *Tiberius the Politician*. London: Thames and Hudson, 1976.

Liebeschuetz, John. *Continuity and Change in Roman Religion*. Oxford: Oxford University Press, 1979.

Liveley, Genevieve. *Narratology*. Oxford: Oxford University Press, 2019.

Luce, Torrey and Anthony Woodman, eds. *Tacitus and the Tacitean Tradition*. Princeton: Princeton University Press, 1993

Malissard, Alain. "Une nouvelle approche de la Colonne Trajanne." *ANRW II* 12.1 (1982): 579–606.

Malloch, Simon. *The Annals of Tacitus Book 11*. Cambridge: Cambridge University Press, 2013.

Maltby, Richard. *Hollywood Cinema*, 2nd edn. Oxford: Blackwell Publishing, 2003.

Marincola, John. *Authority and Tradition in Ancient Historiography*. Cambridge: Cambridge University Press, 1997.

Martin, Ronald. "Tacitus and the Death of Augustus." *CQ* 5 (1955): 123–28.

Martin, Ronald. "Tacitus and His Predecessors." In *Tacitus*, edited by Thomas Dorey. London: Routledge, 1969.

Martin, Ronald. *Tacitus*. Berkeley: University of California Press, 1981.

Martin, Ronald. "Structure and Interpretation in the *Annals* of Tacitus." *ANRW II* 33.2 (1990): 1500–581.

Martin, Ronald and Anthony Woodman, *Tacitus Annals Book IV*. Cambridge: Cambridge University Press, 1989.

McCulloch, Harold Jr. "Literary Augury at the End of 'Annals' XIII." *Phoenix* 34 (1980): 237–42.

Mellor, Ronald. *Tacitus*. London: Routledge, 1993.

Mellor, Ronald. *Tacitus' Annals*. Oxford: Oxford University Press, 2011.

Miller, Norma. *Tacitus Annals Book I*. London: Methuen, 1959.

Miller, Norma. "Style and Content in Tacitus." In *Tacitus*, edited by Thomas Dorey, 99–116. London: Routledge, 1969.

Miller, Norma. *Cornelii Taciti Annalium Liber XV*. New York: Macmillan Education, 1973.

Mitry, Jean. *The Aesthetics and Psychology of the Cinema*. C. King, (transl.) Bloomington: Indiana University Press, 1997.

Modleski, Tania. *The Women Who Knew Too Much: Hitchcock and Feminist Theory*, 3rd edn. New York: Routledge, 2016.

Moles, John. "Truth and Untruth in Herodotus and Thucydides." In *Lies and Fiction in the Ancient World*, edited by Christopher Gil and Timothy Wiseman, 88–121. Austin: University of Texas Press, 1993.

Monaco, Paul. *American Cinema: The Sixties 1960–1969*. Berkeley: University of California Press, 2001.

Moore, Frank. "Annalistic Method as Related to the Book Divisions in Tacitus." *TAPA* 54 (1923): 5–20.

Morford, Mark. "Tacitus' Historical Methods in the Neronian Books of the *Annals*." *ANRW II* 33.2 (1990): 1582–627.

Morson, Gary. *Narrative and Freedom: The Shadows of Time*. New Haven, Yale University Press, 1994.

Mulvey, Laura. "Visual Pleasure and Narrative Cinema." In *Visual and Other Pleasures*, 2nd edn. Laura Mulvey, 16–21. New York: Palgrave Macmillan, 2009.

Murgatroyd, Paul. "Tacitus on the Great Fire of Rome." *Eranos* 103 (2005): 48–54.

Naremore, James. "John Huston and *The Maltese Falcon*." *Literature/Film Quarterly* 1 (1973): 239–49.

Naremore, James. *The Magic of Orson Welles*, 3rd edn. Urbana: University of Illinois Press, 2015.

O'Gorman, Ellen. *Irony and Misreading in the Annals of Tacitus*. Cambridge: Cambridge University Press, 2000.

O'Sullivan, Jane. "Virtual Metamorphoses: Cosmetic and Cybernetic Revisions of Pygmalion's 'Living Doll.'" *Arethusa* 41.1 (2008): 133–56.

Padilla, Mark. *Classical Myth in Four Films of Alfred Hitchcock*. Lanham: Lexington Books, 2016.

Pagán, Victoria. "Beyond Teutoburg: Transgression and Transformation in Tacitus *Annales* 1.61–62." *CP* 94 (1999): 302–20.

Pagán, Victoria. "Actium and Teutoburg: Augustan Victory and Defeat in Vergil and Tacitus." In *Clio and the Poets*, edited by David Levene, 45–59. Leiden: Brill, 2002.

Pagán, Victoria. "Shadows and Assassinations: Forms of Time in Tacitus and Appian," *Arethusa* 39 (2006): 193–218.

Passman, Kristina. "The Classical Amazon in Contemporary Cinema." In *Classics and Cinema*, edited by Martin Winkler, 81–105. Lewisburg: Bucknell University Press, 1991.

Pelling, Christopher. "Tacitus and Germanicus." In *Tacitus and the Tacitean Tradition*, edited by Torrey Luce and Anthony Woodman, 59–85. Princeton: Princeton University Press, 1993.

Pelling, Christopher. "Tragical Dreamer: Some Dreams in the Roman Historians." *G&R* 44 (1997): 197–213.

Pelling, Christopher. "Tacitus' Personal Voice." In *The Cambridge Companion to Tacitus*, edited by Anthony Woodman, 147–67. Cambridge: Cambridge University Press, 2009.

Poirier, Michel. "L'organisation de l'espace dans trois textes latines célèbres, entre géométrie et découpage cinématographique (Hor., *O.*, 2.3; Liv., 5.41; Tac., *An.*, 13.16)." In *Nouveaux horizons sur l'espace antique et moderne: actes du symposium "Invitation au voyage" juin 2013, Lycée Henri IV*, edited by Marie-Ange Julia. *Scripta Receptoria* 2, 81–88. Bordeaux: Ausonius, 2015.

Pomerance, Murray. *The Horse Who Drank the Sky: Film Experience beyond Narrative and Theory*. New Brunswick: Rutgers University Press, 2008.

Potter, David and Cynthia Damon. "Senatus Consultum de Cn. Pisone Patre," *AJP* 120 (1999): 13–42.

Prince, Gerald. *Narratology: The Form and Functioning of Narrative*. Berlin: Mouton Publishing, 1982.

Prince, Gerald. *A Dictionary of Narratology*. Lincoln: University of Nebraska Press, 1987.

Rossi, Lino. *Trajan's Column and the Dacian Wars*. Translated by Jocelyn Toynbee. London: Thames & Hudson, 1971.

Ryberg, Inez. "Tacitus' Art of Innuendo." *TAPA* 73 (1942): 383–404.

Sailor, Dylan. *Writing and Empire in Tacitus*. Cambridge: Cambridge University Press, 2008.

Sallitt, Daniel. "Point of View and 'Intrarealism' in Hitchcock." *Wide Angle* 4 (1980): 38–43.

Santoro L'Hoir, Francesca. "Tacitus and Women's Usurpation of Power." *CW* 88 (1994): 5–25.

Santoro L'Hoir, Francesca. *Tragedy, Rhetoric, and the Historiography of Tacitus' Annales*. Ann Arbor: University of Michigan Press, 2006.

Schwab, Ulrike. "Authenticity and Ethics in the Film *The Third Man*." *Literature/Film Quarterly* 28 (2000): 2–6.

Seager, Robin. *Tiberius*. Berkeley: University of California Press, 1972.

Segal, Charles. "Tacitus and Poetic History: the End of *Annals XIII*." *Ramus* 11 (1973): 107–26.

Shannon-Henderson, Kelly. *Religion and Memory in Tacitus'* Annals. Oxford: Oxford University Press, 2019.

Shaw, Daniel. "The Mastery of Hannibal Lecter." In *Dark Thoughts: Philosophic Reflections on Cinematic Horror*, edited by Steven Schneider and Daniel Shaw, 10–24. Oxford: Scarecrow Press, 2003.

Small, Jocelyn. *Wax Tablets of the Mind: Cognitive Studies of Memory and Literacy in Classical Antiquity*. London: Routledge, 1997.

Smith, Susan. *Hitchcock: Suspense, Humour and Tone*. London: British Film Institute, 2000.

Solomon, Jon. *The Ancient World in the Cinema*. 2nd edn. New Haven: Yale University Press, 2008.

Sörbom, Gunnar. *Variatio Sermonis Tacitei Aliaeque Apud Eundem Quaestiones Selectae*. Upsalia: Almquist & Wiksell Soc., 1935.

Spoto, Donald. *The Art of Alfred Hitchcock: Fifty Years of His Motion Pictures*. Garden City, NY: Doubleday, 1976.

Strunk, Thomas. "Collaborators Among the Opposition?: Deconstructing the Imperial *Cursus Honorum*." *Arethusa* 48 (2015): 47–58.

Sullivan, Donald. "Innuendo and the 'Weighted Alternative' in Tacitus." *CJ* 71 (1976): 312–26.

Sutherland, Humphrey. *Coinage in Roman Imperial Policy: 31 B.C.–A.D. 68*. London: Methuen & Co., 1951.

Syme, Ronald. *Tacitus*. (2 vol.) Oxford: Oxford University Press, 1958.

Tanner, Ronald. "The Development of Thought and Style in Tacitus." *ANRW II* 33.4 (1991): 2689–751.

Telotte, J. P. "Effacement and Subjectivity: *Murder My Sweet's* Problematic Vision." *Literature/Film Quarterly* 15 (1987): 230.

Thompson, Kristin. "The Formation of the Classical Style: 1909–1928." In *The Classical Hollywood Cinema: Film Style and Mode of Production to 1960*, edited by David Bordwell, Janet Staiger, and Kristin Thompson, 155–240. New York: Columbia University Press, 1985.

Thompson, Kristin. *Storytelling in the New Hollywood: Understanding the Classical Narrative Technique*. Cambridge: Harvard University Press, 1999.

Varner, Eric. *Mutilation and Transformation: Damnatio Memoriae and Roman Imperial Portraiture*. Leiden: Brill, 2004.

Vasaly, Ann. *Representations: Images of the World in Ciceronian Oratory*. Berkeley: University of California Press, 1993.

von Fritz, Kurt. "Tacitus, Agricola, Domitian, and the Problem of the Principate." *CP* 52 (1957): 73–97.

Waddell, Philip. "Eloquent Collisions: the *Annales* of Tacitus, the Column of Trajan, and the Cinematic Quick-cut." *Arethusa* 46 (2013): 471–97.

Waldman, Diane. "At Last I Can Tell It to Someone!: Feminine Point of View and Subjectivity in the Gothic Romance Film of the 1940s." *Cinema Journal* 23.2 (1984): 29–40.

Walker, Andrew. "*Enargeia* and the Spectator in Greek Historiography." *TAPA* 123 (1993): 353–77.

Walker, Elizabeth. *The Annals of Tacitus: A Study in the Writing of History*. Manchester: Manchester University Press, 1952.

Walbank, Frank. "History and Tragedy." *Historia* 9 (1960): 216–34.

Winkler, Martin, ed. *Classics and Cinema*. Lewisburg: Bucknell University Press, 1991.

Wiseman Timothy. "Calpurnius Siculus and the Claudian Civil War." *JRS* 72 (1987): 57–67.

Wood, Robin. *Hitchcock's Films Revisited*. New York: Columbia University Press, 1989.

Wood, Robin. "*Strangers on a Train*," in *A Hitchcock Reader*, 2nd edn. Edited by Marshall Deutelbaum and Leland Poague, 172–81. Oxford: Blackwell Publishing, 2009.

Woodman, Anthony. *Rhetoric in Classical Historiography: Four Studies*. London: Croom Helm, 1988.

Woodman, Anthony. "Tacitus' Obituary of Tiberius." *CQ* 39 (1989): 197–205.

Woodman, Anthony. *Tacitus Reviewed*. Oxford: Oxford University Press, 1998.

Woodman, Anthony, transl. *Tacitus: The Annals*. Indianapolis: Hackett Publishing Company, 2004.

Woodman, Anthony. *The Annals of Tacitus Book 4*. Cambridge: Cambridge University Press, 2018.

Woodman, Anthony and Ronald Martin. *The Annals of Tacitus Book 3*. Cambridge: Cambridge University Press, 1996.

Wuilleumier, Pierre. *Tacite: Annales Livre XIII*. Paris: Presses Universitaires de France, 1964.

Wyke, Maria. *Projecting the Past: Ancient Rome, Cinema, and History*. New York: Routledge, 1997.

Zangara, Adrianna. *Voir l'histoire: Théories anciennes du récit historique*. Paris: Éd. de l'EHESS, 2007.

Zanker, Graham. "*Enargeia* in the Ancient Criticism of Poetry." *RhM* 124 (1981): 297–311.

Index Locorum

General Index